SPOKEN ENGLISH GRAMMAR BOOK

FOR
BEGINNERS AND FRESHERS

By

Mohd Ashraf Ansari

A new and modern way to learn English for students and general people because English is for all.

- *Practical and easy rules for grammar and translation.*
- *A practice book for basic learners.*
- *An English grammar book to learn English fast.*
- *Daily used words, tests and exercises for practice with answers.*

Pharos Books

NIEV EDUCATION

SPOKEN ENGLISH

Mayur Vihar Phase-1

OFFICE

32-D Prahlad Complex, Mayur Vihar Phase-1, Delhi-110091
www.nieveducation.com, www.nievision.com, www.nievisions.com

Contact us:

+918860201978 **+919313337638**

ISBN: 978-93-55461-73-5

Publisher: **Pharos Books (P) Ltd.**
Plot No.-55, Main Mother Dairy Road
Pandav Nagar, East Delhi-110092
Phone: 011-40395855
WhatsApp: +91 8368220032
E-mail: sales@pharosbooks.in
Website: www.pharosbooks.in
Edition: 2022
Printed By: Sushma Book Binding House, Okhla
Industrial Area, Phase II, New Delhi-110020

Spoken English Grammar Book
Author: Mohd Ashraf Ansari

"Spoken English Grammar Book"

(for Beginners and Freshers)

By

Mohd Ashraf Ansari

This book will help the learners in:-

- Academic Exams
- Competitive Exams
- Interviews
- Confidence Level
- Job Skills
- Educational Performance
- Expanding Vocabulary
- Using Grammar in Real Life
- Reading, Writing, Listening and Speaking

Preface

All the students who come from Indian families speak in Hindi and they are comfortable in Hindi because Hindi is their "Mother Tongue", therefore most of them have faulty pronunciation and awkward construction in English Keeping these points in mind, this book has been specially prepared to meet the needs of them.

The objective of this book is "the development of sense in English instead of translation from one language to another language to express views, thoughts, ideas or feelings. Special focus has been given on sentence formation which is very important in students' life and it will improve reading, writing, listening and speaking skills.

As we know that 'Hindi' has three ways like 'how to say', 'how to refuse' "or" 'how to ask', similarly we need to learn these ways in English, it is so simple. Actually, we do not know Hindi but we know 'Hindustani' the mixture of other languages that we learn through 'environment'. Making learners understand grammar and its uses easily, Hindi has been specially used in this book so that they can understand easily and independently.

Aim : To simplify the essential grammatical concepts for learning and understanding.

- To make this book all-in-one package of English so that one book can satisfy all the needs of both teachers and students.
- To make English easy all the chapters have been connected with real-life situations.

Need : Most of the people do not understand grammar due to its difficult rules and lack of practical approach, however this book actively guides the learners in using grammar in day-to-day life

Approach : This book has twenty units, three tests alongwith answers at the last, the rich reading material which is the heart of the book and a very powerful content for the beginners. Moreover, it has vocabulary which is based on daily life.

I am thankful to almighty 'God' for making my dream come true. Finally, I extend my gratitude to all my well-wishers and specially the teachers who taught such a "tiny one".

Contents

1 Alphabet

Alphabet with pictures:-

A for **A a**  Apple	**B** for **B b**  Ball	**C** for **C c**  Cat
D for **D d**  Dog	**E** for **E e**  Elephant	**F** for **F f**  Fan
G for **G g**  Girl	**H** for **H h**  Hen	**I** for **I i**  Ice-cream
J for **J j**  Jar	**K** for **K k**  Kite	**L** for **L l**  Lion

M for M m
Monkey

N for N n
Nest

O for O o
Ox

P for P p
Pen

Q for Q q
Queen

R for R r
Rat

S for S s
Spoon

T for T t
Telephone

U for U u
Umbrella

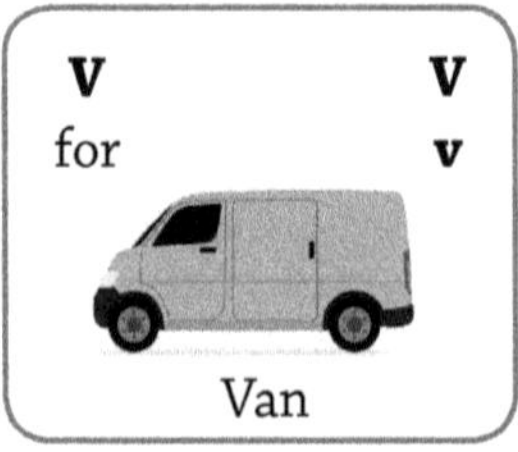
V for V v
Van

W for W w
Watch

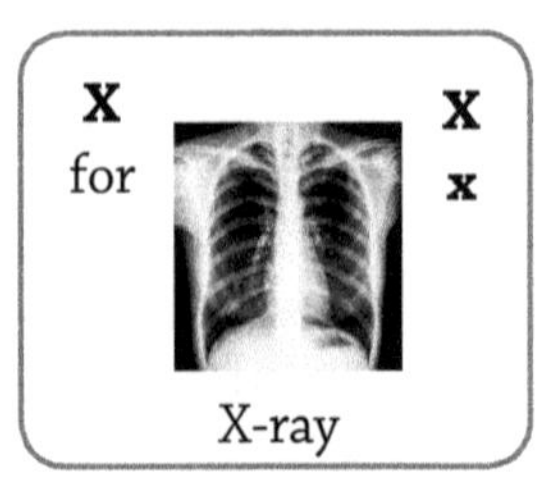
X for X x
X-ray

Y for Y y
Yak

Z for Z z
Zebra

Capital Letters:-

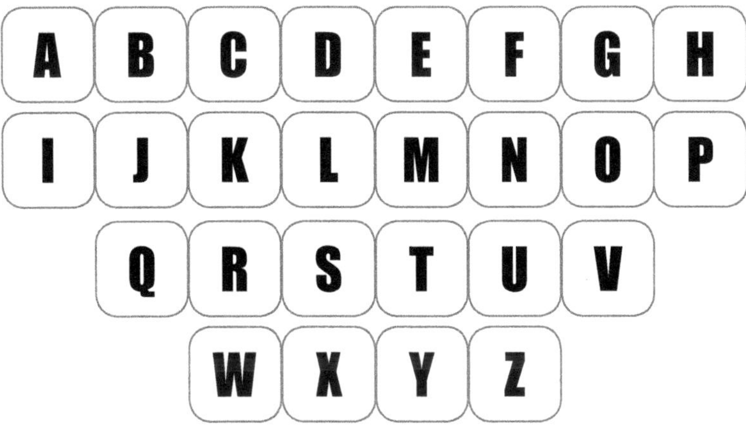

Let us help you:-

Alphabetical order: The order in which we recall all the letters of the English alphabet, is called alphabetical order.

Small Letters:-

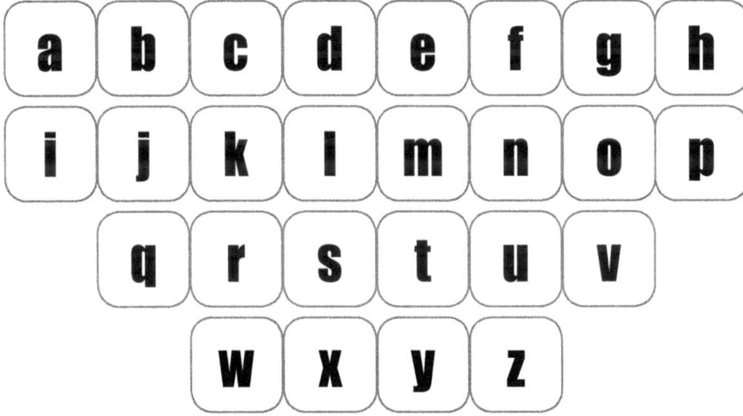

Exercise-1

Write capital letters in the boxes:-

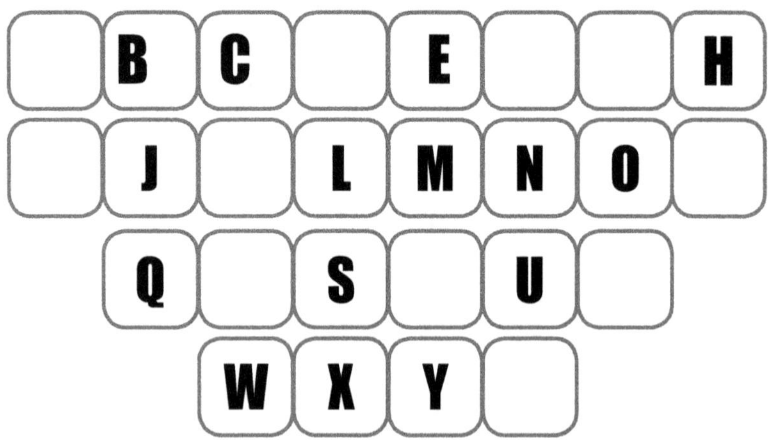

Exercise-2

Write small letters in the boxes:-

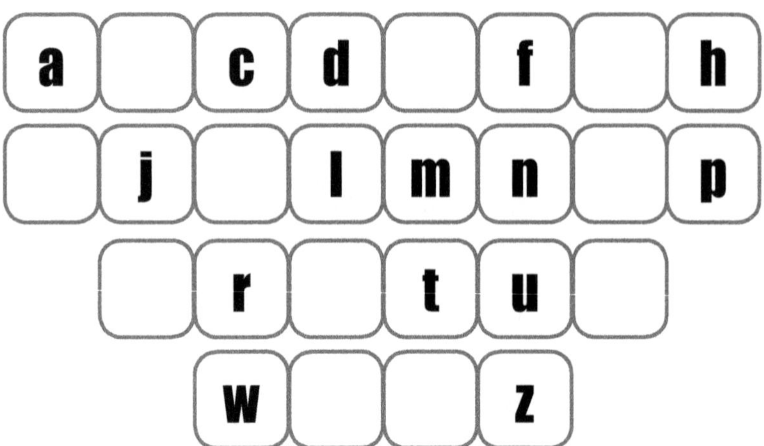

1. Capital letters in disorder. (Read loudly)

2. Small letters in disorder. (Read loudly)

Exercise-3

Look and write:-

Capital	Small

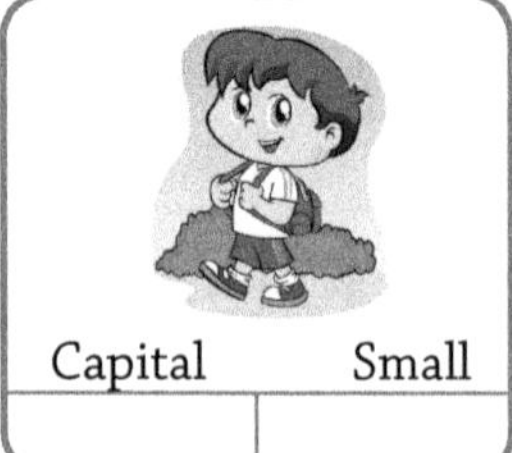

Capital	Small

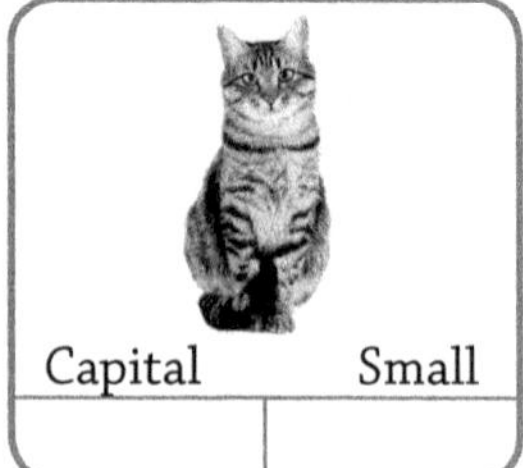

Capital	Small

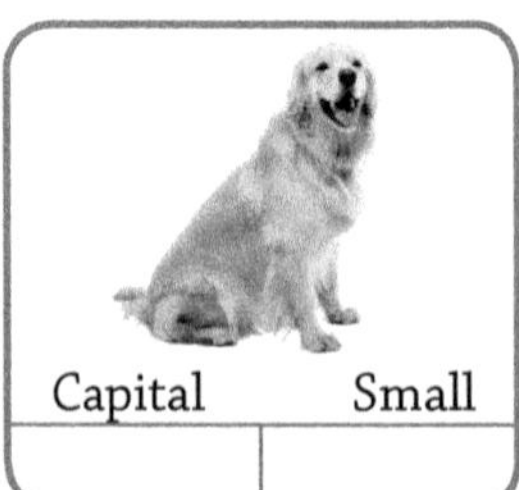

Capital	Small

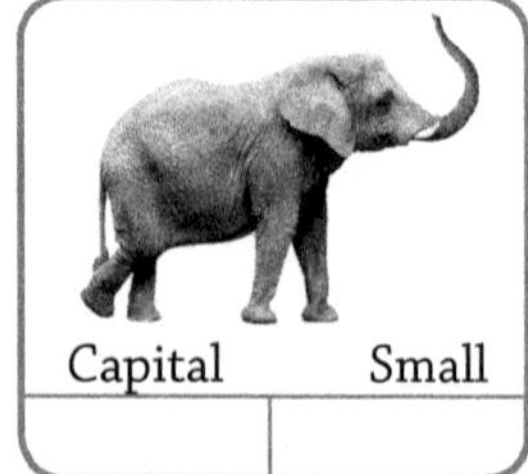

Capital	Small

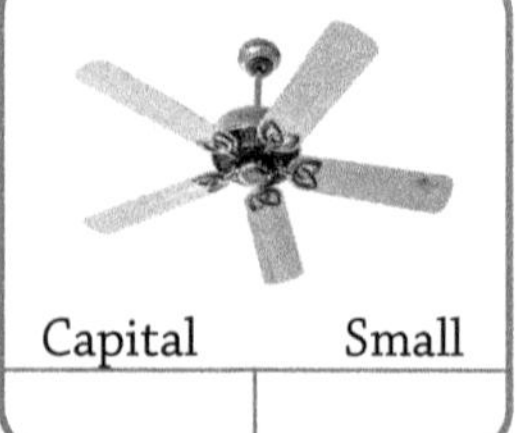

Capital	Small

Capital	Small

Capital	Small

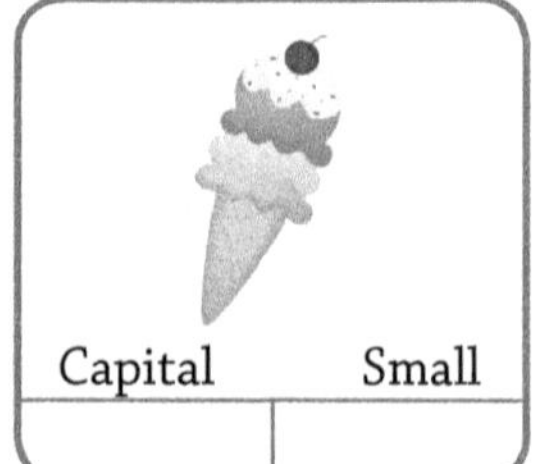

Capital	Small

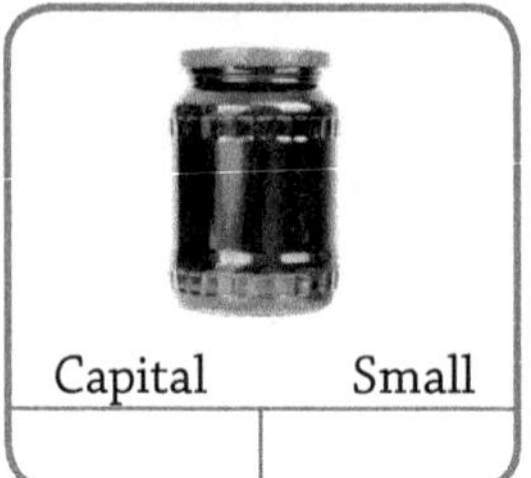

Capital	Small

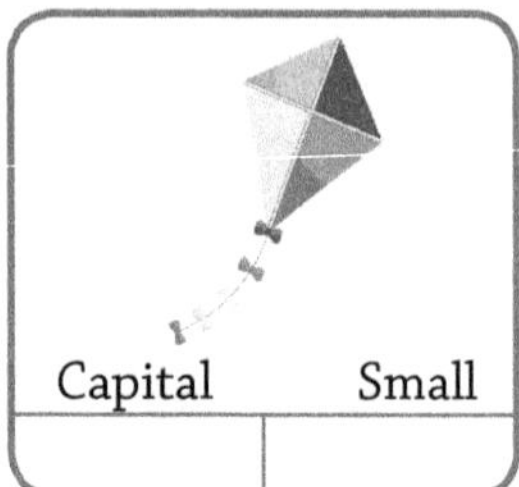

Capital	Small

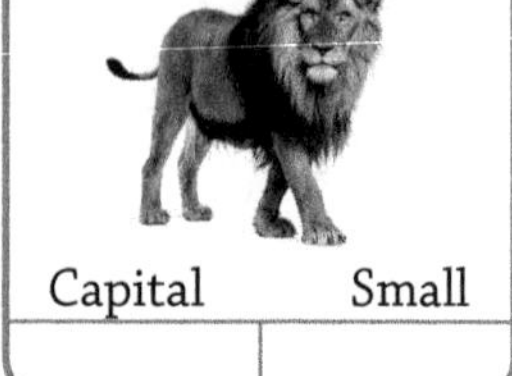

Capital	Small

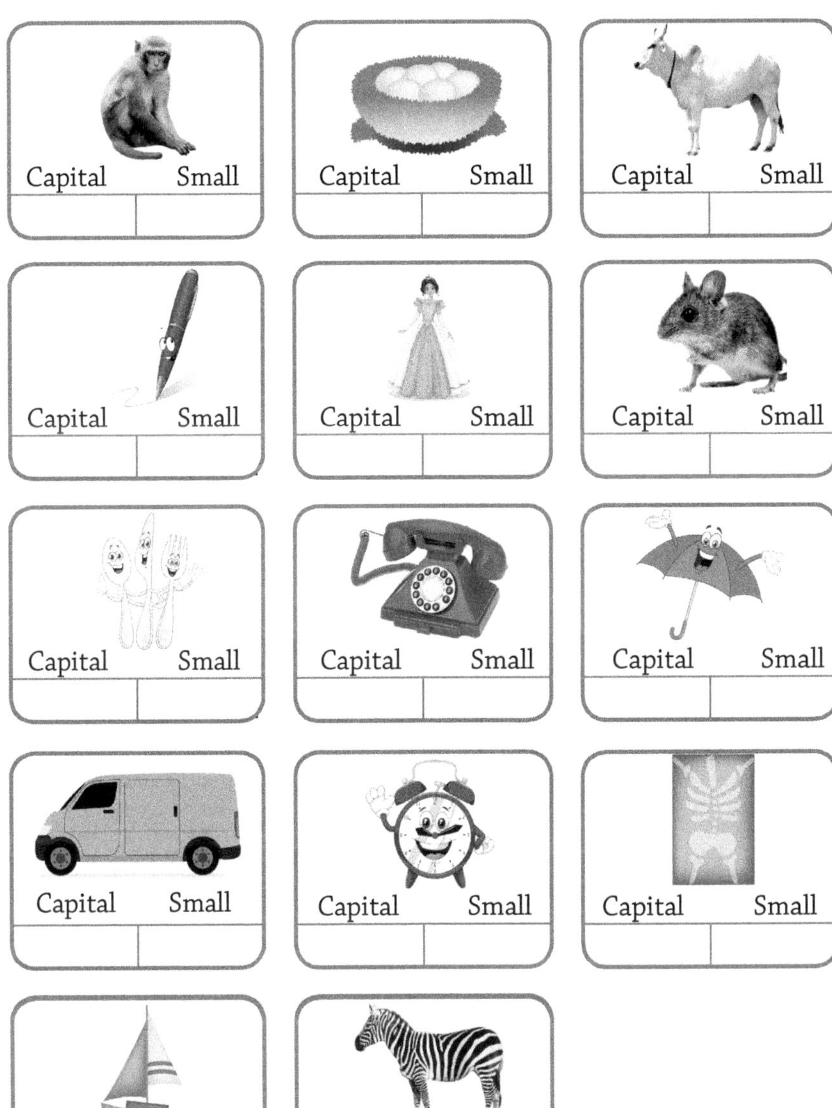
Capital
Small
Capital
Small
Capital
Small
Capital
Small
Capital
Small
Capital
Small
Capital
Small
Capital
Small
Capital
Small
Capital
Small
Capital
Small
Capital
Small
Capital
Small
Capital
Small

Look and Remember:-

There are 26 letters in the English alphabet.

How many Letters: 26

5 Vowels: a e i o u

21 Consonants:

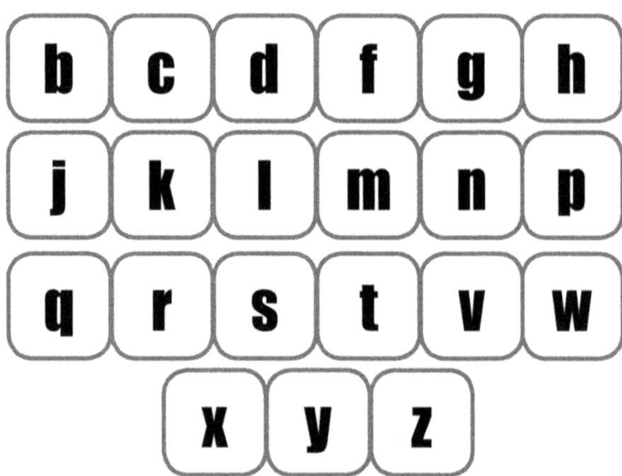

Exercise-4

Write in numbers:-

(a) Letters: ______ (b) Vowels: ______

(c) Consonants: ______

Read Loudly and Remember:-

How to spell words over the phone in daily life.			
A	Alpha	a	ए
B	Bravo	b	बी
C	Charlie	c	सी
D	Delta	d	डी
E	Echo	e	ई
F	Foxtrot	f	एफ
G	Golf	g	जी
H	Hotel	h	एच
I	India	i	आई
J	Juliett	j	जे
K	Kilo	k	के
L	Lima	l	एल
M	Mike	m	एम
N	November	n	एन
O	Oscar	o	ओ
P	Papa	p	पी
Q	Quebec	q	क्यू
R	Romeo	r	आर
S	Sierra	s	एस
T	Tango	t	टी
U	Uniform	u	यू
V	Victor	v	वी
W	Whiskey	w	डब्ल्यू
X	X-ray	x	एक्स
Y	Yankee	y	वाई
Z	Zulu	z	ज़ेड

2 Vowel Sounds

Sound of 'A'- 'a':-

BAT (बल्ला)

CAT (बिल्ली)

MAN (पुरुष)

FAN (पंखा)

MAT (चटाई)

CAR (कार)

Vocabulary :

BAR	(बार)	सलाखें	TAP	(टैप)	नल
PAN	(पैन)	कड़ाही	SAD	(सैड)	दु:खी
AT	(एट)	पर	FAT	(फैट)	मोटा
HAT	(हैट)	टोपी	MAP	(मैप)	नक्शा
AND	(एंड)	और	RAT	(रैट)	चूहा
SAW	(सोव)	आरी	NAP	(नैप)	झपकी
CAN	(कैन)	सकना/सकता	FAN	(फैन)	पंखा

Examples:-

This is a fat cat.	यह एक मोटी बिल्ली है।
This is a tap.	यह एक नल है।
This is a man.	यह एक आदमी है।
These are maps.	ये नक्शे हैं।
These are rats.	ये चूहे हैं।
These are bats.	ये बल्ले हैं।

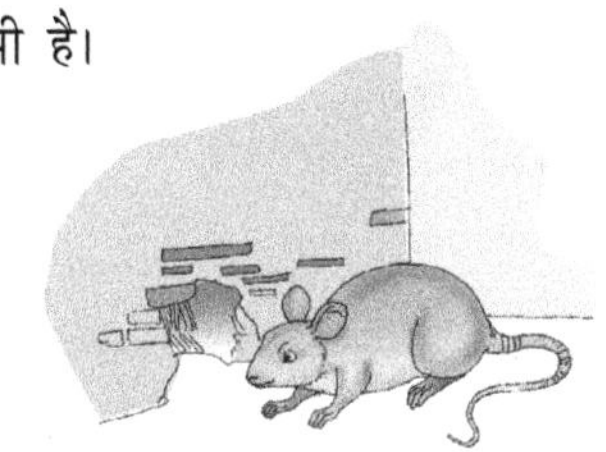

Read loudly:-

1. Cab	2. Nab	3. Had
4. Dad	5. Bad	6. Ram
7. Mad	8. Van	9. Ran
10. Man	11. Fan	12. Pan

Read the following words:-

Rat	Pan	Lad	Map
May	Cat	Fan	Dad
Gap	Lay	Mat	Ran
Mad	Tap	Day	

Let us help you:-

When we are young, we learn the sounds of our language from our parents and society, but when we learn English we need to understand and pay attention to the sounds.

Sound of 'E'- 'e':-

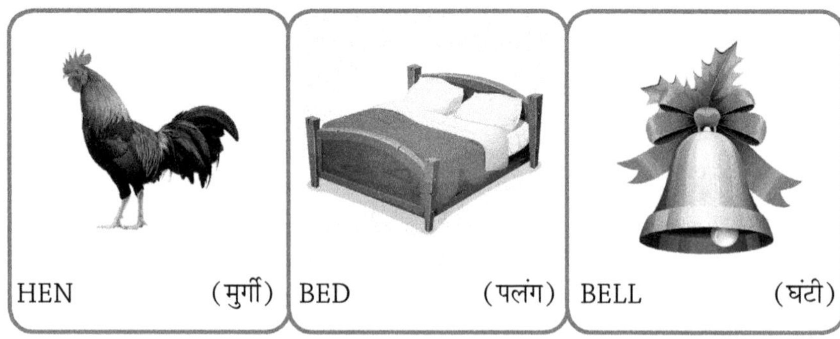

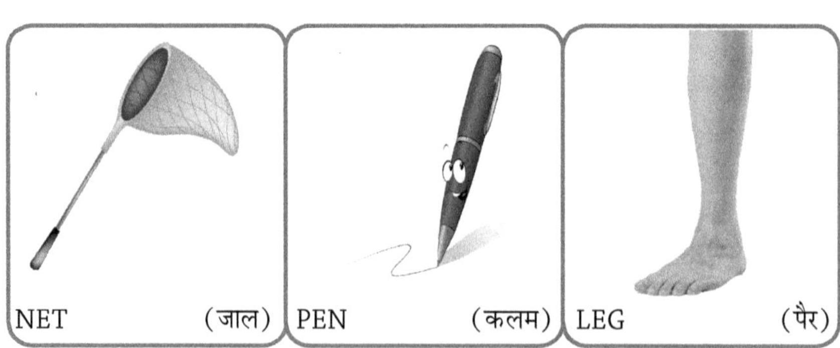

Vocabulary :

SHE	(शी)	वह स्त्री	RED	(रेड)	लाल
TELL	(टेल)	बताना	TEN	(टेन)	दस
LET	(लेट)	आज्ञा देना	YET	(येट)	फिर भी
HER	(हर)	उसका, उसकी	PET	(पेट)	पालतू
WET	(वेट)	गीला	CELL	(सेल)	बैटरी
SET	(सेट)	बैठा हुआ	JET	(जेट)	धारा
MET	(मेट)	मिला	MEN	(मेन)	आदमी

Examples:-

This is a wet pet.	यह एक गीला पशु है।
This is red colour.	यह लाल रंग है।
This is a well.	यह एक कुआँ है।
These are hens.	ये मुर्गियाँ हैं।
These are two old bells.	ये दो पुरानी घंटियाँ हैं।
These are two beds in this room.	इस कमरे में दो पलंग हैं।

Read loudly:-

1. Leg	2. Wed	3. Bed
4. Web	5. Beg	6. Peg
7. Jet	8. Get	9. Bend
10. Send	11. Rent	12. Test

Read the following words:-

Eye	Well	Den	Tea
Key	Hen	Web	Net
Jet	Men	Yet	Ten
Red	Cell	Pen	Set
Let	Tell	Her	Pet

Sound of 'I'- 'i':-

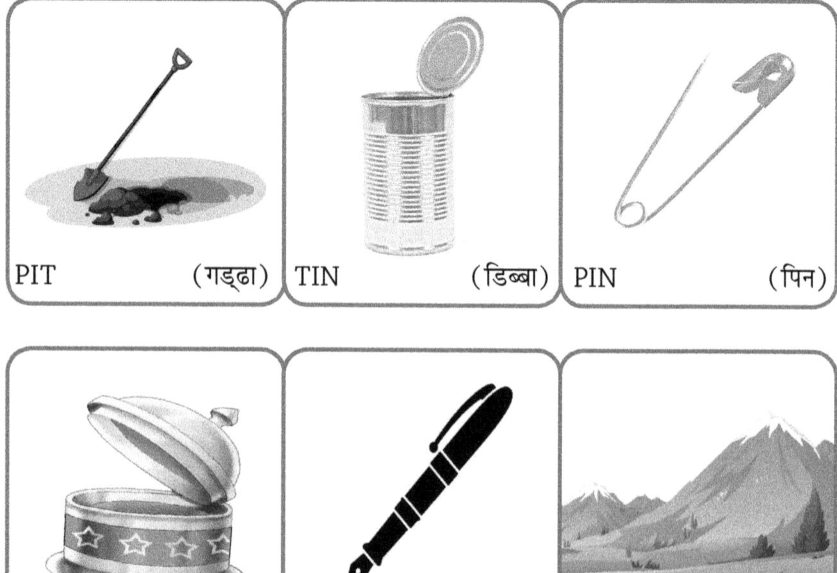

PIT (गड्ढा) | TIN (डिब्बा) | PIN (पिन)

LID (ढक्कन) | NIB (नोक) | HILL (पहाड़ी)

Vocabulary :

RIB	(रिब)	पसली	SING	(सिंग)	गाना
PINK	(पिंक)	गुलाबी	BIG	(बिग)	बड़ा
HIM	(हिम)	उसका/उसकी	KILL	(किल)	मारना
IT	(इट)	चीज़	FILL	(फिल)	भरना
IN	(इन)	अंदर	TILL	(टिल)	अबतक
IF	(इफ)	अगर	TIP	(टिप)	नोक
SIT	(सिट)	बैठना	LIP	(लिप)	ओंठ

Examples:-

That is a pit.	वह गड्ढा है।
That is a lid.	वह एक ढक्कन है।
That is a nib of pen.	वह कलम की नोक है।
Those are big hills.	वे बड़ी पहाड़ियाँ हैं।
Those are tins.	वे डिब्बे हैं।
Those are his ribs.	वे उसकी पसलियाँ हैं।

Read loudly:-

1. King	2. Sit	3. Hit
4. Kid	5. Fig	6. Fix
7. Mix	8. Him	9. His
10. Hib	11. Chin	12. Tip

Read the following words:-

Fish	King	Milk	Pin
Zip	Bin	Kite	Ring
Sing	Tip	Shine	Sit
Lip	Till	Lid	Nib
Big	Fill	Ink	Pink

Sound of 'O'- 'o':-

TOP (लट्टू)

SHOP (दुकान)

BOMB (बम)

TOY (खिलौना)

DOG (कुत्ता)

BOX (बक्सा)

Vocabulary :

GO	(गो)	जाना
ROT	(रोट)	सड़ना
DO	(डू)	करना
SO	(सो)	इसलिए
NO	(नो)	मना करना
NOT	(नाट)	नहीं
HOT	(हॉट)	गर्म
OF	(ऑफ)	का, के, की
SOW	(सो)	बीज बोना
LOG	(लोग)	लट्ठा
POT	(पॉट)	बर्तन
COT	(कोट)	चारपाई
BOY	(बॉय)	लड़का
ROSE	(रोज)	गुलाब

Examples:-

That is a top.	वह एक लट्टू है।
That is a cot.	वह एक चारपाई है।
That is a pot of water.	वह एक पानी का बर्तन है।
Those are dogs.	वे कुत्ते हैं।
Those are rotten apples.	वे सड़े हुए सेब हैं।
Those are dolls.	वे गुड़ियाँ हैं।

Read loudly:-

1. Log
2. On
3. Odd
4. Cop
5. Fog
6. Mop
7. Toss
8. Blog
9. Lot
10. Pop
11. Lock
12. Loss

Read the following words:-

Hot	Toy	Shop	Fort
Boy	Mango	Corn	Rose
Top	Cot	Doll	Toss
Log	Loss	Mop	Sow
Don	Pot	Do	Of

Sound of 'U'- 'u':-

SUN (सूरज)

BUS (बस)

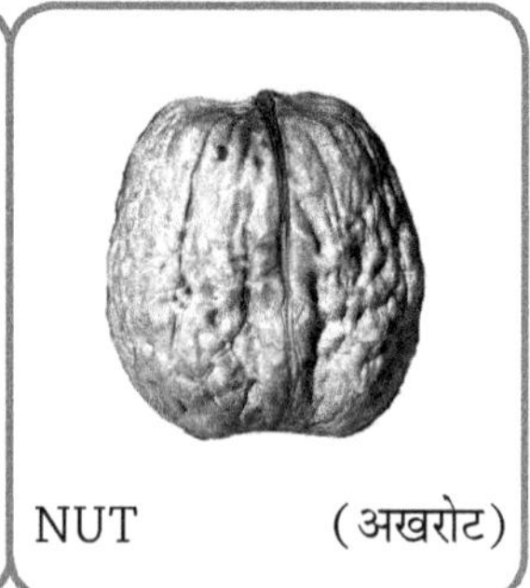
NUT (अखरोट)

CUP (कप)

GUN (बदूंक)

HUT (झोपड़ी)

Vocabulary :

TUB	(टब)	टब	PUT	(पुट)	रखना
CURD	(कर्ड)	दही	CUT	(कट)	काटना
UNDER	(अन्डर)	नीचे	BUT	(बट)	पर
US	(अस)	हम लोग	SHUT	(शट)	बंद करना
BUZZ	(बज़)	मक्खी की आवाज़	UP	(अप)	ऊपर
RUN	(रन)	दौड़ना	HUT	(हट)	झोपड़ी
PUPPY	(पप्पी)	कुत्ते का बच्चा	SUN	(सन)	सूरज

Examples:-

This is a jug.	यह एक जग है।
That is a bus.	वह एक बस है।
That is the sun.	वह सूरज है।
These are guns.	ये बंदूके हैं।
Those are nuts.	वे अखरोट हैं।
Those are huts of poor.	वे ग़रीबों की झोपड़ियाँ हैं।

Read loudly:-

1.	Mud	2.	Jug	3.	Plum
4.	Thumb	5.	Drum	6.	Sum
7.	Fuss	8.	Tuck	9.	Luck
10.	Duck	11.	Gum	12.	Fun

Read the following words:-

Utensil	Cup	Thumb	Bus
Up	U-turn	Umbrella	Hut
Mug	Bug	Unicorn	Run
Lunch	Drum	Gum	Jug
Butter	Duck	Uncle	Cub

Sound of 'A'- 'a':-

Exercise-1

Fill in the blanks to complete the following words.

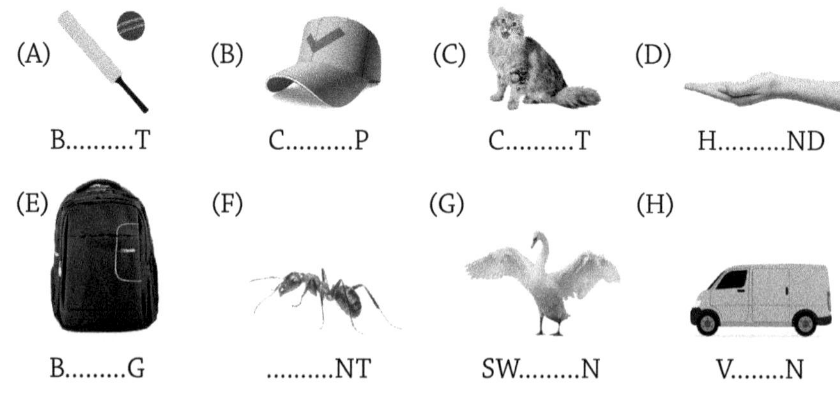

(A) B..........T
(B) C..........P
(C) C..........T
(D) H..........ND
(E) B.........G
(F) ....NT
(G) SW.........N
(H) V........N

Sound of 'E'- 'e':-

Exercise-2

Fill in the blanks to complete the following words.

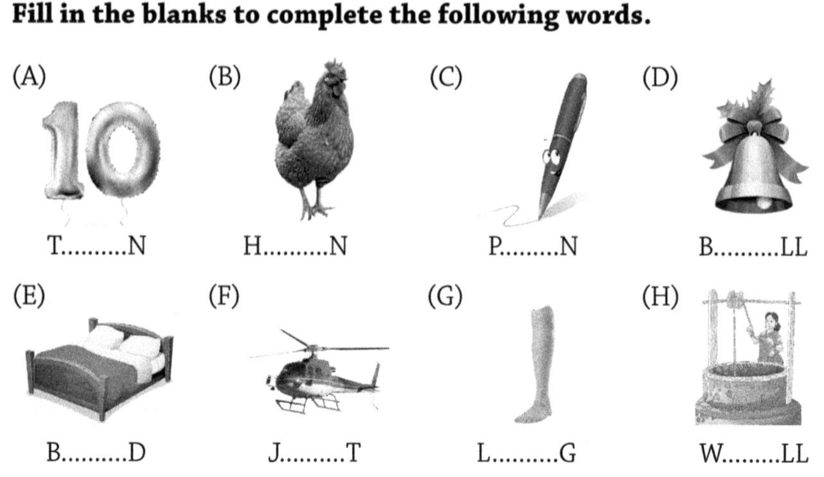

(A) T..........N
(B) H..........N
(C) P.........N
(D) B..........LL
(E) B..........D
(F) J.........T
(G) L..........G
(H) W.........LL

Sound of 'I'- 'i':-

Exercise-3

Fill in the blanks to complete the following words.

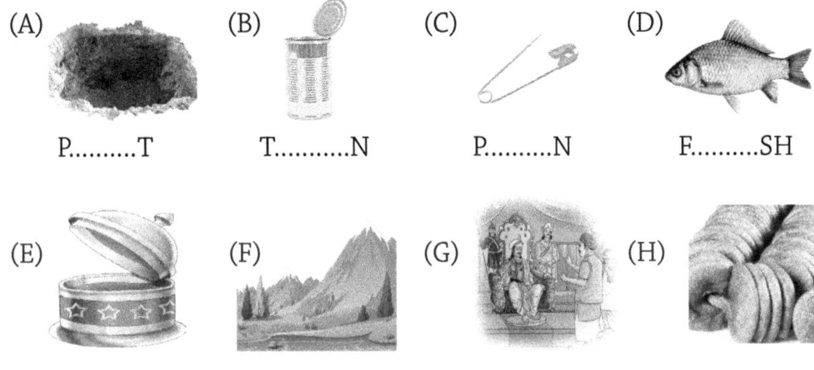

(A) P..........T (B) T...........N (C) P..........N (D) F..........SH

(E) L..........D (F) H........LL (G) K.........NG (H) F..........G

Sound of 'O'- 'o':-

Exercise-4

Fill in the blanks to complete the following words.

(A) F..........X (B) D..........G (C) B..........Y (D) P..........T

(E) B..........X (F) L........CK (G) M..........P (H) FR........G

Sound of 'U'- 'u':-

Exercise-5

1. Fill in the blanks to complete the following words.

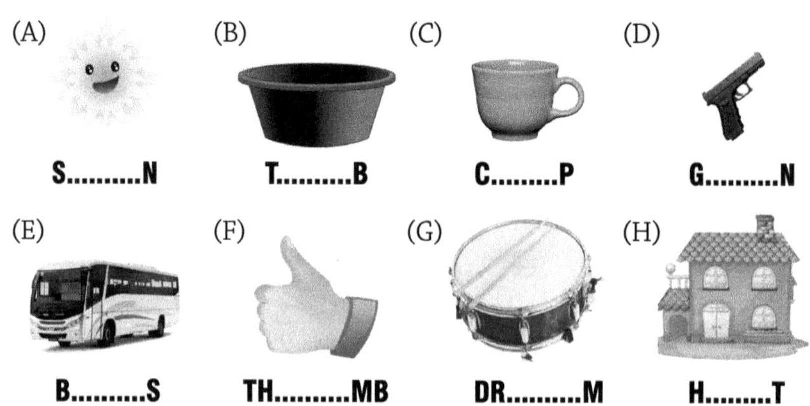

2. Complete the picture by drawing the number line.

3 Sentences

Look at the picture and read the group of words:

(a) A book

(b) A book on the table, (does not make complete sense but)

(c) A book is on the table makes a complete sense Hence, it is called a sentence.

A sentence is a group of words that makes a complete sense. It begins with a capital letter and ends with a full stop, question mark and exclamation mark. A sentence contains a subject and a verb.

शब्दों का ऐसा समूह जिनका भाव पूरा समझ आए या पूर्ण हो Sentence कहलाता है।

Let us read some examples to understand what a sentence is.

1. Mohan goes to school. मोहन स्कूल जाता है।

2. They are reading a book. वे लोग किताब पढ़ रहे हैं।

3. Sonu is ill. सोनू बीमार है।

Exercise-1

(A) Put (✓) in front of sentences and put (✗) if the group of words are not sentences.

1. Ram is a cute boy. ☐
2. In the morning. ☐
3. The moon shines in the night. ☐
4. Mohan is an intelligent boy. ☐
5. On the table book. ☐
6. He two balls. ☐

(B) Fill in the blanks with suitable words to complete the sentences.

runs, reads, plays, has, am

1. Mohan ____________ two books in his bag.
2. I ______________ a teacher.
3. The boy ______________ the newspaper.
4. The horse ____________ very fast.
5. The girl __________ with a football in the park.

(C) Match the following group of words to make a complete sentence.

1. It rained	(a) interested in business.
2. The class	(b) marry priya.
3. Mohan is	(c) the award in 2010.
4. Rohit wants to	(d) throughout the day.
5. I won	(e) started at 7:30 a.m.

Exercise-2

Rearrange the following words to make meaningful sentences:-

1. Doctor he a became. ______________________
2. Beautifully sang she. ______________________
3. Reading the children were. ______________________
4. Questions difficult very are these. ______________________
5. Has father bike sold his. ______________________
6. An story told he interesting me. ______________________
7. Crying is baby the. ______________________
8. To go asked him we. ______________________

Let us help you:-

- A sentence always has a verb.
- It starts with a capital letter.
- It ends with a full stop (.) question mark (?) exclamation mark (!)
- It makes a complete sense.

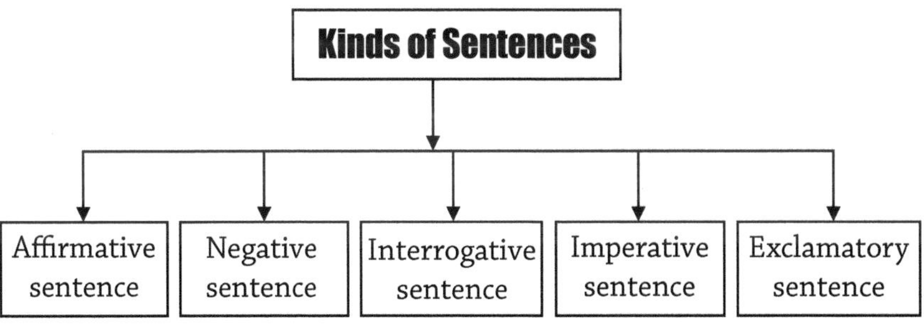

Affirmative Sentence:-

We say or tell something or we make a positive statement, is called an affirmative sentence. It starts with a capital letter and ends with a full stop. जिस वाक्य में कुछ बताया या कहा जाता है, उसे affirmative sentence कहते हैं।

Read these sentences:-

(a)	This is a ball.	यह एक गेंद है।
(b)	Mohan is a teacher.	मोहन एक शिक्षक है।
(c)	Rani and Ram are good friends.	रानी और राम अच्छे दोस्त हैं।

Note: Affirmative sentence is also known as declarative or assertive sentence.

Negative Sentence:-

The sentence in which we deny or refuse something, is called a negative sentence. It starts with a capital letter and ends with a full stop.
जिस वाक्य में किसी चीज़ के लिए या कुछ करने के लिए मना किया जाता है, उसे negative sentence कहते हैं।

Read these sentences:-

(a)	There is no water in the tank.	टंकी में पानी नहीं है।
(b)	He is not in the class.	वह कक्षा में नहीं है।
(c)	No one is here.	यहाँ कोई नहीं है।

Note: Deny or refuse means न कहना या मना करना।

Interrogative Sentence:-

The sentence in which we ask a question is called an interrogative sentence. It starts with a capital letter and ends with a question mark.

जिस वाक्य में कुछ पूछा जाता है, उसे interrogative sentence कहते हैं।

Read these sentences:-

(a) Who is there? — वहाँ कौन है?

(b) Are you my friend? — क्या आप मेरे दोस्त हैं?

(c) Is Mohan an intelligent boy? — क्या मोहन एक होशियार लड़का है?

Imperative Sentence:-

The sentence in which we give a command, an order or make a request is called an imperative sentence. It starts with a capital letter and ends with a full stop or a mark of exclamation.

जिस वाक्य में आदेश (command) आज्ञा (order) या निवेदन (request) हो, उसे imperative sentence कहते हैं।

Read these sentences:-

(a) Please, come here. — कृपया, यहाँ आएँ।

(b) Stand up! — खड़े हो जाओ।

(c) Get out! — बाहर निकल जाओ।

Exclamatory Sentence:-

The sentence in which we show some sudden feeling of happiness, sadness and surprise is called an exclamatory sentence. It starts with a capital letter and ends with an exclamation mark.

जिस वाक्य में सुख, दुःख या आश्चर्य भाव होता है, उसे exclamatory sentence कहते हैं।

Read these sentences:-

(a) Aah! I have failed. — आह! मैं असफल हो गया।

(b) Hurrah! We have won. — वाह! हम जीत गए।

(c) How beautiful it is! — यह कितना सुन्दर है!

Exercise-3

(A) Identify the different types of sentences and write their names in the blanks.

1. What are they teaching? ________________
2. Go there and sit down. ________________
3. The moon is shining in the sky. ________________
4. Please, do it. ________________
5. Don't walk fast. ________________
6. How nice you are! ________________
7. They don't go there. ________________
8. They are intelligent. ________________
9. Is she your friend? ________________
10. Are you my friend? ________________
11. Sit silently, please. ________________
12. How cold it is! ________________
13. What a beautiful building! ________________

(B) Tick (✓) the correct options to identify the given sentences.

1. How do you do this work?
   (Declarative, Negative, Interrogative, Imperative, Exclamatory)
2. Sachin is a great player.
   (Declarative, Negative, Interrogative, Imperative, Exclamatory)

3. What are you doing?
   (Declarative, Negative, Interrogative, Imperative, Exclamatory)
4. I can't believe him to be the murderer.
   (Declarative, Negative, Interrogative, Imperative, Exclamatory)
5. Do you want to leave English?
   (Declarative, Negative, Interrogative, Imperative, Exclamatory)
6. He catches the bus for his office.
   (Declarative, Negative, Interrogative, Imperative, Exclamatory)
7. Elephants have good memory.
   (Declarative, Negative, Interrogative, Imperative, Exclamatory)

8. What a beautiful view of the sun!
   (Declarative, Negative, Interrogative, Imperative, Exclamatory)
9. Go there and sit down.
   (Declarative, Negative, Interrogative, Imperative, Exclamatory)

10. How nice the world is!
    (Declarative, Negative, Interrogative, Imperative, Exclamatory)
11. Please, come to me.
    (Declarative, Negative, Interrogative, Imperative, Exclamatory)
12. Children don't lie.
    (Declarative, Negative, Interrogative, Imperative, Exclamatory)

Let us help you:-

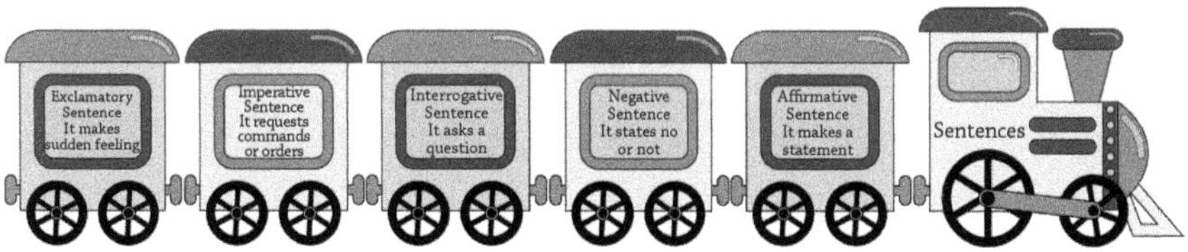

Subject and Predicate

Look at the picture and read the following sentences.

(a) I am a doctor.

(b) Rohan is reading his book.

(c) The boy swims in the swimming pool.

- I, Rohan, the boy are subjects.
- am a doctor, is reading his book, swims in the swimming pool are predicates.

The part which tells about the person or thing we speak about is called subject.
In other words, a person or a thing that is doing an action in a sentence is called the subject.

वाक्य में जिसके बारे में कोई बात हो रही हो या वाक्य में जो कार्य करता है उसे Subject (कर्ता) कहते हैं।

Predicate: It is the part which tells us what the subject is doing.

वाक्य में Subject के बारे में जो बात हो रही है, उसे Predicate कहते हैं।

How to identify subject?

Step 1:- First, we should find the verb in the sentence.

Step 2:- Then make question by placing who or what before the verb.

Example 1:- Mohan and his sister study for two hours.

First: verb-Study.

Second: Who-study!

Third: Subject = Mohan and his sister.

Example 2:- The left leg of a white elephant broke.

First: Verb - Broke.

Second: What broke?

Third: Subject = The left leg of a white elephant.

Let us read some more sentences to understand subject and predicate:-

Subject	Predicate
(i) Animals	live in the forest.
(ii) The birds	fly in the sky.
(iii) Children	are playing games.

Exercise-1

(A) Circle the subjects and underline the predicates in the following sentences.

1. Shambhu wrote a letter.
2. Students are in the school.
3. They will come tomorrow.
4. Mohan is teaching well.
5. Children are playing in the park.

(B) Match the subjects with the predicates to make sentences.

1. It	(a) is in August.
2. I	(b) was upset with her result.
3. My favourite food	(c) am going to Punjab for an interview.
4. My anniversary	(d) is raining heavily.
5. Renu	(e) is Chinese.

Exercise-2

(A) Identify the subjects and the predicates in the following sentences and write in the box below:

1. The boy stood on the wall.
2. What a horrible sight it was!
3. Has Mohan been watering the plants?
4. Get out of the room.
5. How shocking it is!
6. Shall we go to the park tomorrow?
7. The child was weeping.
8. May I help you?
9. Rahul has been doing his work.
10. The children are swimming in the pond.

Subject	Predicate
1.	
2.	
3.	
4.	
5.	
6.	
7.	
8.	
9.	
10.	

(B) Underline the subjects in the following sentences:

1. The paths of glory lead but to the grave.
2. The days of our youth are over now.
3. All the five boys took part in the debate.
4. Some very beautiful girls presented the show.
5. Karan, my neighbour wants to be an engineer.
6. Those who live in glass houses should not throw stones at others.
7. The boy with the blue trousers is my class fellow.
8. The rumour that he has passed, is not true.
9. The man who wrote this book got a prize.
10. Some boys and girls were swimming in the pool.

Let us help you:-

- A sentence has two parts- subject and predicate.
- The subject may have one or more than one word.
- In an imperative sentence, the subject is 'you' which is not mentioned in the sentence.

Examples:-

Open the door.

Don't touch it.

In both the sentences 'you' is hidden but it is not mentioned however, it is understood.

5 Naming words or Nouns

The name of a person, place, animal, bird and thing is called noun.

Look at these pictures:-

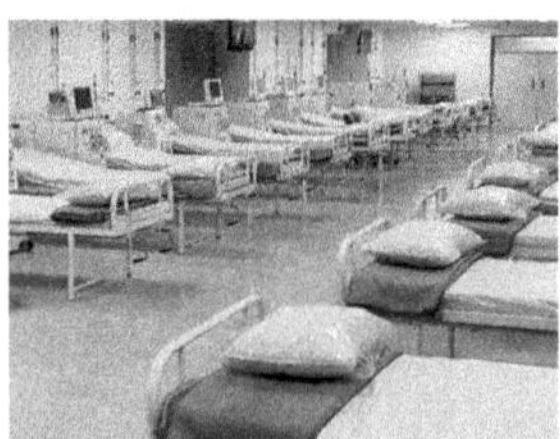

Hospital

Dr. Mohan

Cat

T.V.

Here, hospital is the name of a place, Dr. Mohan is the name of a person, cat is the name of an animal and T.V. is the name of a thing. All these names are called nouns. They are also called naming words.

> **Note:** Name of anything is called noun.
> किसी व्यक्ति, स्थान या वस्तु के नाम को noun कहते हैं।

Name of persons	lawyer, woman, teacher
Name of places	classroom, park, college
Name of animals and birds	parrot, hen, elephant
Name of things	book, sky, tree.

Exercise-1

Write the names of the things shown in the pictures which are given in the box below.

1. ________ 2. ________ 3. ________ 4. ________

5. ________ 6. ________ 7. ________ 8. ________

Exercise-2

Match the pictures of persons with their names.

1.	Cobbler	(a)	
2.	King	(b)	
3.	Carpenter	(c)	

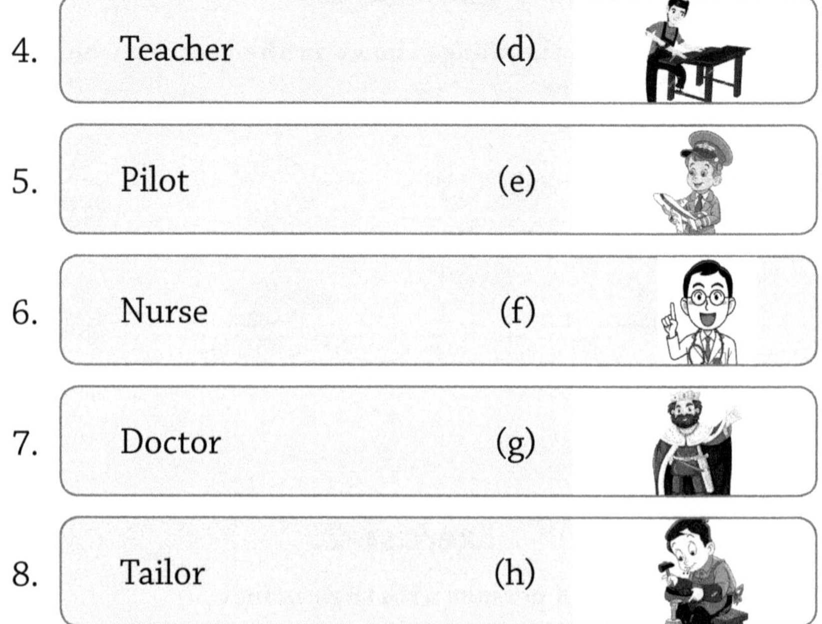

Exercise-3

Pick out the names of persons, places, animals and things from the list of words given below.

America, Truck, Computer, Child, Garden, Book, Lion, Ox, Woman, Air, Elephant, Red Fort, School, Ant, Boy, Pilot

Places	Animals	Persons	Things
________	________	________	________
________	________	________	________
________	________	________	________
________	________	________	________

Exercise-4

(A) Write the names of four places:

1. .... 2. ....
3. .... 4. ....

(B) Write the names of two animals and two birds:

1. .... 2. ....
3. .... 4. ....

(C) Write the names of four persons:

1. .... 2. ....
3. .... 4. ....

(D) Write the names of four things:

1. .... 2. ....
3. .... 4. ....

Kinds of Nouns

Common Noun	Proper Noun	Collective Noun	Material Noun	Abstract Noun

1. **Common Noun:-** Common noun is a noun that does not refer to any particular person, place or thing, it gives a common name to a person, an animal or a thing of the same class.

यह किसी व्यक्ति विशेष या विशेष स्थान का नाम नहीं होता बल्कि जाति सभी प्राणियों या वस्तुओं के नाम का बोध कराता है। उसे Common Noun कहते हैं।

Examples:- Girl, Glass, Boy, Clock, Pencil, Village.

2. **Proper Noun:-** A proper noun is the name of particular person, place or thing.

   यह किसी विशेष व्यक्ति, स्थान या वस्तु का नाम बोध कराता है। उसे Proper Noun कहते हैं।

   Examples:- Kapil Dev, Delhi, Japan, Pacific Ocean, Sunday.

3. **Collective Noun:-** A collective noun is a noun that names a group or a class of similar things or persons taken as one whole or unit is called Collective Noun.

   यह किसी एक ही तरह के व्यक्तियों के समूह के नाम का बोध कराता है, उसे Collective Noun कहते हैं।

   Examples:- Police, Army, Crowd, People, Fleet.

4. **Material Noun:-** A material noun is a noun that refers to a substance from which things are made such as silver, gold, iron, cotton, diamond and plastic.

   यह किसी वस्तु को बनानें में जो चीज़ प्रयोग होती है या नापी, तोली, जाने वाली वस्तु का नाम होता हैं।

   Examples:- Water, Milk, Cotton, Gold, Wood.

5. **Abstract Noun:-** An abstract noun is a noun which refers to an idea, concept, quality, feeling or some thing which cannot be touched or seen is called Abstract Noun.

   यह किसी विचार अथवा अवस्था (State) के नाम का बोध कराता है। उसे Abstract Noun कहते हैं, ना इसे हम छू सकते और ना ही देख सकते हैं।

   Examples:- Hope, Bravery, Freedom, Health.

Exercise-5

(A) Underline the Common Nouns and Proper Nouns in the given sentences and write their types in the blanks.

1. That is a dog. ____________________
2. Pooja is in hospital. ____________________
3. Mohan is a fat boy. ____________________
4. They are from Rajasthan. ____________________
5. May I see your pen? ____________________

(B) Underline the Material Nouns and Collective Nouns in the given sentences and write their types in the blanks.

1. The police arrested them. ____________________
2. She purchased rice. ____________________
3. Gold is a costly thing. ____________________
4. Our class is not happy. ____________________
5. The bottle is made of plastic. ____________________

(C) Underline the Abstract Nouns in the given sentences.

1. The labourers are on strike.
2. They were awarded for boldness.
3. The freshness of fruits is very attracting.
4. Health is wealth.
5. Bravery is a virtue.

Let us help you:-

1. A proper noun starts with a capital letter.
2. The names which are common to place, person, thing or animal are called common nouns.
   Examples:- Girl, Dog, Pen.
3. Countable Nouns are those nouns which can be counted.
   Examples:- A pen, an elephant, many trees.
4. Uncountable nouns are those nouns which cannot be counted.
   Examples: Water, Honey, Milk.

6 Singular and Plural Nouns

Read carefully:-

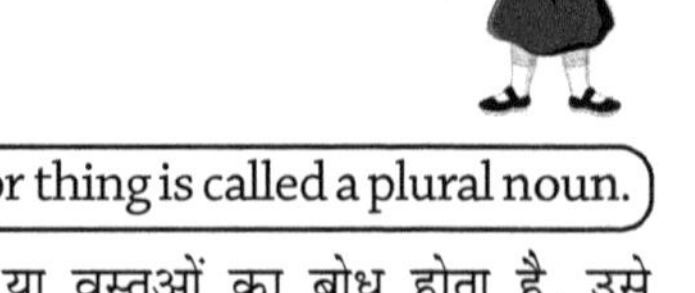

A noun which refers to one person or thing is called a singular noun.

संज्ञा का ऐसा रूप जिसमें एक व्यक्ति, या वस्तु का बोध हो, उसे singular noun कहते हैं।

Examples:- Boy, Girl, Child, Photo, Pen

A noun which refers to more than one person or thing is called a plural noun.

संज्ञा का ऐसा रूप जिसमें एक से अधिक व्यक्तियों या वस्तुओं का बोध होता है, उसे plural noun कहते हैं।

Examples:- Boys, Girls, Children, Photos, Pens.

(i) When we change a singular noun to a plural noun, we usually add 's' or 'es' to the noun.

- **We add 's' as suffix to the nouns.**

Examples:-

Singular	Plural
Pen	Pens
Book	Books
Person	Persons
Tree	Trees

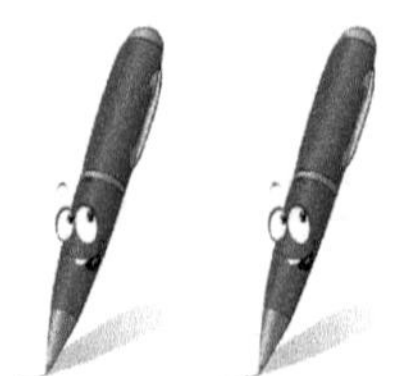

Pens

- **We add 'es' as suffix to the nouns.**

Examples:-

Singular	Plural
Match	Matches
Glass	Glasses
Bench	Benches
Box	Boxes

Boxes

Note:- If the noun ends at (s, ss, sh, ch, o, x or z) then we add 'es' to make plural.

Singular	Plural
One watch	Two watches
One mango	Two mangoes
One dish	Two dishes
One box	Two boxes

Exercise-1

Fill in the blanks with the plurals of the following.

1. Stool ____________ 2. Site ____________ 3. Bucket ____________
4. Moon ____________ 5. Tree ____________

Exercise-2

Look at the pictures and tick (✓) the correct option.

1. (a) Book ☐ (b) Books ☐
2. (a) Cup ☐ (b) Cups ☐

3. (a) Plate ☐  (b) Plates ☐

4. (a) Dog ☐  (b) Dogs ☐

5. (a) Boy ☐  (b) Boys ☐

6. (a) Brush ☐  (b) Brushes ☐

Exercise-3

Fill in the blanks with the plurals of the following.

1.  One box Two box ______ 
2.  One tomato Two tomato ______ 
3.  One watch Three watch ______ 
4.  One brush Four brush ______ 
5.  One glass Two glass ______

(ii) When the nouns end with 'y' we add 'ies' to make plural.

Singular	**Plural**	**Singular**	**Plural**
One lady	Two ladies	One baby	Two babies

Here are some more examples:-

Singular	**Plural**
Body	Bodies
Story	Stories
Reply	Replies
Family	Families
Country	Countries
Fairy	Fairies
Diary	Diaries

However, if the nouns end with 'y' but vowels come before y, then we add 's' to make plural.

Singular	**Plural**	**Singular**	**Plural**
One key	Two keys	One toy	Two toys

Here are some more examples:-

Singular	Plural
Storey	Storeys
Ray	Rays
Donkey	Donkeys
Valley	Valleys

Exercise-4

(A) Fill in the blanks with the plurals of the following.

1. One lady two ____________
2. One candy two ____________
3. One cherry two ____________
4. One butterfly two ____________
5. One baby many ____________
6. One berry three ____________

(B) Fill in the blanks with the plurals of the following.

1. One toy two ____________
2. One ray two ____________
3. One boy two ____________
4. One day three ____________
5. One donkey four ____________
6. One key many ____________

(iii) When the nouns end with 'f' or 'fe' we add 'ves' to make plural.

Singular	Plural	Singular	Plural
One leaf	Two leaves	One knife	Two knives

Exercise-5

Fill in the blanks with the plurals of the following.

1. One life Many ____________
2. One knife Two ____________
3. One wolf Many ____________
4. One wife Two ____________
5. One leaf Many ____________
6. One thief Three ____________

(iv) However, some nouns do not change.
They have same plural and singular forms.

Examples:-

Singular	Plural
Aircraft	Aircraft
Sheep	Sheep
Deer	Deer
Fish	Fish

Here are some more examples:

furniture, scenery, information, advice

(v) Some nouns are always in plural forms.

Examples:-

Singular	Plural
Scissors	Scissors
Trousers	Trousers
Jeans	Jeans
Clothes	Clothes
Spectacles	Spectacles
Socks	Socks
Politics	Politics
Mathematics	Mathematics

Note: We should use plural verbs.

Examples:-

(a) Where are the spectacles?
(b) Here, the scissors are in almirah.

(vi) But some nouns are always in singular forms like, news, furniture, information, dozen.

Examples:-

(a) The sheep is in the garden.
(b) The hunter has killed many sheep.
(c) I bought six dozen eggs.

Note: There is no plural form of Abstract Nouns and Material Nouns.
Examples:- Love, Anger, Beauty, Gold, Paper, Stone.

(vii) When the nouns end with 'is' then we add 'es' to make plural.

Singular	**Plural**
Basis	Bases
Diagnosis	Diagnoses

(viii) When the nouns end with 'on' then we add 'a' to make Plural.

Singular	**Plural**
Phenomenon	Phenomena
Criterion	Criteria

Some exceptional cases are:

Singular	**Plural**
Cactus	Cacti
Antenna	Antennae
Stimulus	Stimuli

Exercise-6

Write the plural forms of the following singular forms.

S. No.	Singular	Plural	S. No.	Singular	Plural
1.	Photo		7.	Shelf	
2.	Child		8.	Calf	
3.	Roof		9.	Tooth	
4.	Ox		10.	Wish	
5.	Mouse		11.	Sheep	
6.	Family		12.	Deer	

There is a list of irregular plural forms of nouns which is very important to remember.

S. N.	Singular	Plural
1.	Aircraft (वायुयान)	Aircraft
2.	Analysis (जाँच)	Analyses
3.	Apex (सर्वोच्च)	Apexes
4.	Army (सेना)	Armies
5.	Baby (बच्चा)	Babies
6.	Bacterium (जीवाणु)	Bacteria
7.	Beach (समुद्र तट)	Beaches
8.	Bee (मधुमक्खी)	Bees
9.	Bench (बेंच)	Benches
10.	Bird (पक्षी)	Birds
11.	Bison (जंगली साँड)	Bison
12.	Boat (नाव)	Boats
13.	Bottle (बोतल)	Bottles
14.	Box (डिब्बा)	Boxes
15.	Boy (लड़का)	Boys

16.	Broom (झाड़ू)	Brooms
17.	Brush (ब्रश, झाड़ी)	Brushes
18.	Buffalo (भैंस)	Buffaloes
19.	Bus (बस)	Buses
20.	Cactus (नागफनी)	Cacti
21.	Call (पुकारना)	Calls
22.	Calf (गाय का बच्चा)	Calves
23.	Cargo (माल, भार/जहाज में लदा माल)	Cargoes
24.	Car (कार)	Cars
25.	Cat (बिल्ली)	Cats
26.	Chair (कुर्सी)	Chairs
27.	Cherry (चेरी)	Cherries
28.	Chief (मुख्य)	Chiefs
29.	Child (बच्चा)	Children
30.	City (शहर)	Cities
31.	Cod (कॉड, फली)	Cod
32.	Copy (नकल)	Copies
33.	Corpus (राशि, समूह)	Corpora
34.	Country (देश)	Countries
35.	Cow (गाय)	Cows
36.	Crisis (संकट का समय)	Crises
37.	Criterion (मापदंड)	Criteria
38.	Cup (कप)	Cups
39.	Curriculum (पाठ्यक्रम)	Curriculums
40.	Daisy (गुलबहार)	Daisies
41.	Datum (आँकड़ा)	Data
42.	Day (दिन)	Days

43.	Deer (हिरण)	Deer
44.	Desk (मेज़)	Desks
45.	Diagnosis (अंदाजा)	Diagnoses
46.	Die (पासा)	Dice
47.	Dish (थाली)	Dishes
48.	Dog (कुत्ता)	Dogs
49.	Doll (गुड़िया)	Dolls
50.	Dress (पोशाक)	Dresses
51.	Duty (कर्तव्य)	Duties
52.	Echo (गूंज)	Echoes
53.	Egg (अंडा)	Eggs
54.	Elf (बौना)	Elves
55.	Essay (निबंध)	Essays
56.	Eye (आँख)	Eyes
57.	Family (परिवार)	Families
58.	Foot (पैर)	Feet
59.	Fish (मछली)	Fish
60.	Fly (मक्खी)	Flies
61.	Flower (फूल)	Flowers
62.	Flush (प्रफुल्लता, लाली)	Flushes
63.	Focus (केंद्र)	Foci
64.	Fox (लोमड़ी)	Foxes
65.	Fork (काँटा)	Forks
66.	Fungus (फफूंद)	Fungi
67.	Gallery (गैलरी, बालकनी)	Galleries
68.	Game (खेल)	Games
69.	Gas (गैस)	Gases

70.	Goose (बत्तख)	Geese
71.	Girl (लड़की)	Girls
72.	Glass (गिलास)	Glasses
73.	Gulf (खाई)	Gulfs
74.	Half (आधा)	Halves
75.	Hero (नायक)	Heroes
76.	Hoof (खुर)	Hoofs
77.	House (घर)	Houses
78.	Kidney (गुर्दा)	Kidneys
79.	Kiss (चुम्मा)	Kisses
80.	Knife (चाकू)	Knives
81.	Lady (महिला)	Ladies
82.	Lamb (भेड़ का बच्चा)	Lambs
83.	Leaf (पत्ती)	Leaves
84.	Louse (जूं)	Lice
85.	Life (ज़िंदगी)	Lives
86.	Loaf (पाव रोटी)	Loaves
87.	Maid-servant (नौकरानी)	Maid-servants
88.	Mango (आम)	Mangoes
89.	Memo (नोट)	Memos
90.	Man (आदमी)	Men
91.	Mess (गड़बड़)	Messes
92.	Mouse (चूहा)	Mice
93.	Moose (एक प्रकार का हिरण)	Moose
94.	Mosquito (मच्छर)	Mosquitoes
95.	Moss (काई)	Mosses
96.	Mother (माता)	Mothers

97.	Motto (सिद्धांत)	Mottoes
98.	Mug (मग, लोटा)	Mugs
99.	Nanny (आया)	Nannies
100.	Nest (घोंसला)	Nests
101.	Nucleus (केंद्र)	Nuclei
102.	Octopus (ओक्टपस)	Octopi
103.	Offspring (वंशज)	Offspring
104.	Ox (बैल)	Oxen
105.	Party (पार्टी)	Parties
106.	Passer-by (राही)	Passers-by
107.	Pass (सफलता)	Passes
108.	Pencil (पेंसिल)	Pencils
109.	Penny (पैसे)	Pennies
110.	Pen (कलम)	Pens
111.	Person (व्यक्ति)	People
112.	Phenomenon (घटना)	Phenomena
113.	Photo (चित्र)	Photos
114.	Pitch (ऊँचाई)	Pitches
115.	Plant (पौधा)	Plants
116.	Plate (प्लेट, रकाबी)	Plates
117.	Policeman (सिपाही)	Policemen
118.	Pony (टट्टू)	Ponies
119.	Poppy (खसखस)	Poppies
120.	Potato (आलू)	Potatoes
121.	Proof (सबूत)	Proofs
122.	Quiz (परीक्षा)	Quizzes
123.	Ray (किरण)	Rays

124.	Reflex (छाया)	Reflexes
125.	Reply (उत्तर)	Replies
126.	River (नदी)	Rivers
127.	Roof (छत)	Roofs
128.	Rose (गुलाब)	Roses
129.	Runner-up (दौड़ने वाला)	Runners-up
130.	Scarf (दुपट्टा)	Scarves
131.	School (स्कूल)	Schools
132.	Series (श्रेणी)	Series
133.	Sheaf (गुच्छा)	Sheaves
134.	Sheep (भेड़)	Sheep
135.	Shelf (ताक)	Shelves
136.	Shirt (शर्ट)	Shirts
137.	Shop (दुकान)	Shops
138.	Sister (बहन)	Sisters
139.	Snake (साँप)	Snakes
140.	Son-in-law (जमाई)	Sons-in-law
141.	Species (जाति)	Species
142.	Spy (जासूस)	Spies
143.	Splash (छप-छप)	Splashes
144.	Step-son (सौतेला बेटा)	Step-sons
145.	Stereo (स्टोरियो सिस्टम/तख्ती)	Stereos
146.	Sticker (चिप्पी)	Stickers
147.	Stitch (टांका, सिलाई)	Stitches
148.	Story (कहानी)	Stories
149.	Syllabus (सारांश)	Syllabuses/Syllabi
150.	Tax (कर)	Taxes

151.	Tooth (दाँत)	Teeth
152.	Thesis (वचन)	Theses
153.	Thief (चोर)	Thieves
154.	Tomato (टमाटर)	Tomatoes
155.	Tornado (आँधी)	Tornadoes
156.	Toy (खिलौना)	Toys
157.	Tray (ट्रे, थाली)	Trays
158.	Tree (पेड़)	Trees
159.	Try (कोशिश)	Tries
160.	Valley (घाटी)	Valleys
161.	Volcano (ज्वालामुखी)	Volcanoes
162.	Waltz (एक प्रकार का नाच)	Waltzes
163.	Washer-man (धोबी)	Washer-men
164.	Wash (धुलाई)	Washes
165.	Watch (घड़ी)	Watches
166.	Way (मार्ग)	Ways
167.	Wharf (घाट)	Wharves
168.	Window (खिड़की)	Windows
169.	Wish (प्रार्थना)	Wishes
170.	Wife (पत्नी)	Wives
171.	Wolf (भेड़िया)	Wolves
172.	Woman (औरत)	Women
173.	Year (वर्ष)	Years

English बोलने और लिखने के लिए Singular and Plural याद करना बहुत ज़रुरी है।

Let us help you:-

1. Some nouns seem to be singular but are always used as plural.

   Examples:- Cattle, people, pants

   The cattle are in the field.

   we always use 'are'

2. Some nouns seem to be plural but are always used as singular.

   Examples:- Politics, mathematics, news, innings

   we always use 'is'

3. Some nouns which do not change.

   Examples:- Child Children

   Woman Women

4. Some nouns are always plural.

   Examples:- Trousers, pants.

5. Some nouns are always singular.

   Examples:- News, Politics

English Develops Personality.

Personality Creates Status.

Status Gives Respect in the Society.

7 Gender

The word that indicates whether a noun or pronoun is masculine, feminine, common or neuter is called gender.
जिस संज्ञा शब्द से किसी व्यक्ति के लिंग का पता चलता हैं, उसे Gender कहते हैं। इससे यह पता चलता है, कि वह पुरूष लिंग है या स्त्री लिंग है।

Examples:-

Mohan is my brother.
He is a nice boy.

Poonam is my sister.
She is a nice girl.

Let us read some more examples to understand gender of noun or pronoun clearly.

Male	**Female**
Father	Mother
Lion	Lioness
Uncle	Aunt
Horse	Mare
Boy	Girl

Exercise-1

(A) Write the words in the correct headings:

Bride, Sister, Daughter, Aunt, Groom, Brother, Son, Horse, Uncle, Mare

Male:

________ ________ ________ ________ ________

Female:

________ ________ ________ ________ ________

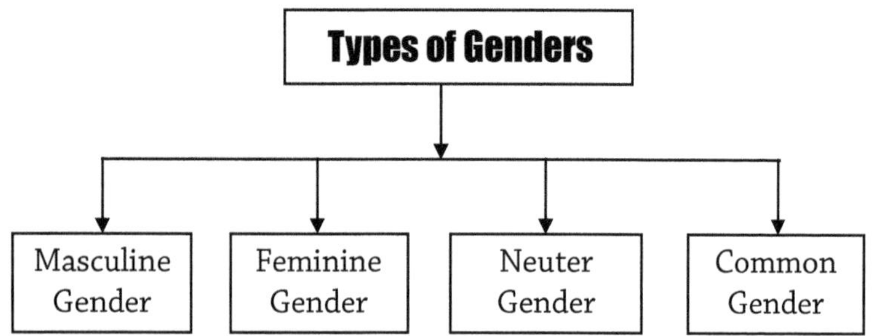

1. **Masculine Gender:** Nouns and pronouns that stand for male are called masculine gender.

   संज्ञा जो पुरूष जाति के बारे में जानकारी देती है, उसे Masculine Gender कहते हैं।

   Examples:- Boy, Father, Tiger, Peacock

2. **Feminine Gender:** Nouns and pronouns that stand for female are called feminine gender.

   संज्ञा जो स्त्री जाति के बारे में जानकारी देती है, उसे Feminine Gender कहते हैं।

   Examples:- Girl, Mother, Tigress, Peahen

3. **Neuter Gender:** Nouns and pronouns that are not masculine or feminine is called neuter gender.

   वे संज्ञा जो न ही स्त्री जाति और न ही पुरूष जाति का बोध कराती है, उसे Neuter Gender कहते हैं।

   Examples:- Pen, Table, Tree, Ball

4. **Common Gender:** Nouns and pronouns that stand for both male or female is called common gender.

   वे संज्ञा जो दोनों Gender का बोध कराए, उसे Common Gender कहते हैं।

   Examples:- Doctor, Teacher, Lawyer, Friend

Remember the Masculine and Feminine forms.

Masculine	Meaning	Feminine	Meaning
Man	पुरूष	Woman	स्त्री
Father	पिता	Mother	माता
Husband	पति	Wife	पत्नी
Son	बेटा	Daughter	बेटी
Brother	भाई	Sister	बहन
Dog	कुत्ता	Bitch	कुतिया
Cock	मुर्गा	Hen	मुर्गी
Horse	घोड़ा	Mare	घोड़ी
Bull	बैल	Cow	गाय
King	राजा	Queen	रानी
Peacock	मोर	Peahen	मोरनी
Uncle	चाचा	Aunt	चाची
Nephew	भतीजा	Niece	भतीजी
Grandfather	दादा, नाना	Grandmother	दादी, नानी
Hero	नायक	Heroine	नायिका
Lion	शेर	Lioness	शेरनी
Actor	अभिनेता	Actress	अभिनेत्री
Author	लेखक	Authorous	लेखिका
God	देवता	Goddess	देवी
Prince	राजकुमार	Princess	राजकुमारी
Boy	लड़का	Girl	लड़की
He	वह (पुरूष)	She	वह (स्त्री)
Him	उसे (पुरूष)	Her	उसे (स्त्री)
His	उसका (पुरूष)	Her	उसका (स्त्री)
Manservant	(पुरूष) नौकर	Maidservant	नौकरानी

(B) Match the following masculine with their feminine:-

	Masculine	Feminine
1.	Father	Vixen
2.	Daughter	Cow
3.	Bull	Mother
4.	Fox	Peahen
5.	Peacock	Son

(C) Fill in the blanks

	Masculine	Feminine
1.	King	____________
2.	____________	Spinster
3.	Man	____________
4.	Monk	____________
5.	____________	Madam
6.	Lord	____________

(D) Pick the right genders and write them in the correct columns.

Mobile	Lioness	Teacher	Person	Hero
Parent	Fox	Banker	Carrot	Queen
Lion	Truck	Waitress	Drone	Stag
Bird	Stewardess	Car	Bull	Table

S. N.	Masculine	Feminine	Neuter	Common
1.				
2.				
3.				
4.				
5.				

Let us help you:-

1. There are four types of gender:

   (a) Masculine Gender (b) Feminine Gender
   (c) Common Gender (d) Neuter Gender

2. It is important to remember the gender of the nouns, because it determines the article you are going to use.
3. In case of confusion in gender whether male or female, use the words 'male' or 'he' for masculine and 'female', or 'she' for feminine.

Examples:-

(a) Hippopotamus is male but what about female, then we can use cow hippopotamus or female hippopotamus.

(b) Male ant, Female ant

(c) He goat (बकरा) goat (बकरी)

For bulky female animal we can use cow or female.

Here is a list of gender.

S. N.	Masculine	Feminine
1.	Duke (नवाब)	Duchess (रानी)
2.	Man (आदमी)	Woman (औरत)
3.	Father (पिता)	Mother (माता)
4.	Actor (अभिनेता)	Actress (अभिनेत्री)
5.	Author (लेखक)	Authoress (लेखिका)
6.	Bachelor (कुँवारा)	Spinster (कुँवारी)
7.	Boy (लड़का)	Girl (लड़की)
8.	Bridegroom (दुल्हा)	Bride (दुल्हन)
9.	Brother (भाई)	Sister (बहन)
10.	Conductor (मार्गदर्शक)	Conductress (महिला मार्गदर्शक)
11.	Czar (रूस सम्राट)	Czarina (रूस की साम्राज्ञी)

12.	Father-in-law (ससुर)	Mother-in-law (सास)
13.	Mr. (श्रीमान)	Mrs. (श्रीमती)
14.	Son (बेटा)	Daughter (बेटी)
15.	Son-in-law (दामाद)	Daughter-in-law (बहू)
16.	Step-Father (सौतेला पिता)	Step- Mother (सौतेली माँ)
17.	Man-Servant (नौकर)	Maid-Servant (नौकरानी)
18.	Milkman (दूधवाला)	Milkmaid (दूधवाली)
19.	Sir (श्रीमान, जनाब)	Madam (श्रीमती, सहिबा)
20.	Shepherd (चरवाहा)	Shepherdess (चरवाहा स्त्री)
21.	Master (अध्यापक)	Mistress (अध्यापिका)
22.	Monk (संन्यासी)	Nun (मठवासिनी)
23.	Nephew (भतीजा)	Niece (भतीजी)
24.	Papa (पिता)	Mama (माता)
25.	Poet (कवि)	Poetess (कवयित्री)
26.	Postman (डाकिया)	Postwoman (स्त्री डाकिया)
27.	Priest (पुजारी)	Priestess (पुजारिन)
28.	Prince (राजकुमार)	Princess (राजकुमारी)
29.	Prophet (पैगंबर)	Prophetess (स्त्री पैगंबर)
30.	Step-Son (सौतेला बेटा)	Step-Daughter (सौतेली बेटी)
31.	Sultan (सुल्तान)	Sultana (सुल्ताना)
32.	Tailor (दर्जी)	Tailoress (दर्जन)
33.	Uncle (चाचा)	Aunt (चाची)
34.	Waiter (परोसनेवाला)	Waitress (परोसनेवाली)
35.	Washerman (धोबी)	Washerwoman (धोबिन)
36.	Widower (मृत पत्नीक)	Widow (विधवा)
37.	Wizard (जादूगर)	Witch (जादूगरनी)
38.	Lion (शेर)	Lioness (शेरनी)

39.	Tiger (बाघ)	Tigress (स्त्री बाघ)
40.	Fox (लोमड़ी)	Vixen(स्त्री लोमड़ी)
41.	Drake (नर बत्तख)	Duck (बत्तख)
42.	Rooster (मुर्गा)	Hen(मुर्गी)
43.	Sheep (भेड़)	Ewe (भेड़ी)
44.	Stallion (नर घोड़ा)	Mare (घोड़ी)
45.	God (देवता)	Goddess (देवी)
46.	Emperor (सम्राट)	Empress (महारानी)
47.	Peacock (मोर)	Peahen (मोरनी)
48.	Hero (नायक)	Heroine (नायिका)
49.	King (राजा)	Queen (रानी)
50.	Dog (कुत्ता)	Bitch (कुतिया)
51.	Husband (पति)	Wife (पत्नी)
52.	Policeman (पुलिसवाला)	Policewoman (पुलिसवाली)
53.	Host (मेहमानदारी करने वाला)	Hostess (मेहमानदारिन)
54.	Heir (वारिस)	Heiress (उत्तराधिकारिणी)
55.	Tom (बिल्ला)	Pussy/Tabby (बिल्ली)
56.	Old Man (बुढ़ा आदमी)	Old Women (बूढ़ी औरत)
57.	Male (नर, मर्द)	Female (नारी, औरत)
58.	Elephant (हाथी)	Cow-elephant (हथनी)
59.	Hunter (शिकारी)	Huntress (शिकारिका)
60.	Songster (गायक)	Songstress (गायिका)
61.	Drone (नर मक्खी)	Bee (मक्खी)
62.	Landlord (जमींदार)	Landlady (जमींदारिन)
63.	Gaint (राक्षस)	Giantess (राक्षसी)
64.	Cock-sparrow (गौरैया)	Hen-sparrow (गौरैया)

65.	Peer (पुरूष साथी)	Peeress (स्त्री साथी)
66.	Baron (पुरूष तालुकदार)	Baroness (स्त्री तालुकदार)
67.	Hart (हिरन)	Roe (हिरनी)
68.	Stag (बारहसिंगा)	Hind (बारहासिंगा)
69.	Patron (रक्षक)	Patroness (रक्षिका)
70.	Tempter (बहकाने वाला)	Temptress (बहकाने वाली)
71.	Abbot (महंत)	Abbess (महन्तिन)
72.	Doctor (चिकित्सक)	Lady Doctor (स्त्री चिकित्सक)
73.	Traitor (गद्दार)	Traitress (स्त्री गद्दार)
74.	Benefactor (दानदेनेवाला)	Benefactress (दानदेनेवाली)
75.	Salesman (विक्रेता)	Salesgirl (विक्रेती)
76.	Steward (प्रबंधक)	Stewardess (भंडारिन)
77.	Dad (पिता)	Mom (माता)
78.	Fiance (मंगेतर)	Fiancee (स्त्री मंगेतर)
79.	Lover (प्रेमी)	Beloved (प्रेमिका)
80.	Jew (यहूदी)	Jewess (यहूदी महिला)
81.	Executor (प्रंबधक)	Executrix (प्रंबधिका)
82.	He Bear (भालू)	She Bear (स्त्री भालू)
83.	Maternal-Uncle (मामा)	Maternal-Aunt (मामी)
84.	Maternal-grand-father (नाना)	Maternal-grand-mother (नानी)
85.	Bullock (बैल)	Heifer (बछिया)
86.	Swain (नौजवान)	Nymph (अप्सरा)
87.	He-Buffalo (पुरूष भैंस)	She-Buffalo (भैंस)
88.	He-Viceroy (सूबेदार)	She-Vicereine (स्त्री सूबेदार)
89.	He-ape (पुरूष बंदर)	She-ape (स्त्री बंदर)
90.	Fisher-man (मछुआरा)	Fisher-woman (मछुआरिन)

91.	He-Camel (ऊँट)	She-Camel (ऊँटनी)
92.	He-Kangaroo (पुरूष कंगारू)	She-Kangaroo (स्त्री कंगारू)
93.	He-Mule (पुरूष खच्चर)	She-Mule (स्त्री खच्चर)
94.	He-Hare (पुरूष खरगोश)	She-Hare (स्त्री खरगोश)
95.	He-Squirrel (पुरूष गिलहरी)	She-Squirerl (स्त्री गिलहरी)
96.	He-Rhinoceros (पुरूष गैंडा)	She-Rhinoceros (स्त्री गैंडा)
97.	He-Mouse (चूहा)	She-Mouse (चूहिया)
98.	He-Mole (पुरूष छछुंदर)	She-Mole (स्त्री छछुंदर)
99.	He-Zebra (पुरूष ज़ेबरा)	She-Zebra (स्त्री ज़ेबरा)
100.	Leopard (चीता)	Leopardess (स्त्री चीता)
101.	He-Mongoose (पुरूष नेवला)	She-Mongoose (स्त्री नेवला)
102.	He-Chimpanzee (पुरूष चिंपाजी)	She-Chimpanzee (स्त्री चिंपाजी)
103.	He-Sheep (पुरूष भेड़)	She-Sheep (स्त्री भेड़)
104.	He-Hyena (पुरूष लकड़बग्घा)	She-Hyena (स्त्री लकड़बग्घा)
105.	He Hound (पुरूष शिकारी कुत्ता)	She-Hound (स्त्री शिकारी कुत्ता)
106.	He-Jackal (पुरूष सियार)	She-Jackal (स्त्री सियार)
107.	He-Porcupine (साही)	She-Porcupine (स्त्री साही)
108.	Oil Man (तेल वाला)	Oil Woman (तेल वाली)
109.	Tutor (अनुशिक्षक)	Governess (अध्यपिका)
110.	Grand-Son (पोता)	Grand-Daughter (पोती)
111.	Steward (प्रंबधक)	Stewardess (प्रंबधिका)
112.	Lad (बालक)	Lass (बालिका)
113.	Millionaire (करोड़पति)	Millionaires (स्त्री करोड़पति)
114.	Murderer (खूनी)	Murderess (स्त्री खूनी)
115.	Negro (हबशी)	Negress (स्त्री हबशी)
116.	Protector (रक्षक)	Protectress (रक्षिका)

Let us help you:-

1. Masculine के लिए, he, male use करते हैं।

Examples:-

(a) He goat or Male goat (बकरा)
(b) He fox or Male fox (नर लोमड़ी)

2. Feminine के लिए she, female use करते हैं।

Examples:-

(a) She Pigeon or Female Pigeon (कबूतरी)
(b) She Monkey or Female Monkey (बंदरिया)

3. Bulky Animals के लिए cow, she, female use करते हैं।

Examples:-

(a) Cow Elephant, She Elephant or Female Elephant (हथनी)
(b) Cow Rhino, She Rhino or Female Rhino (मादा गैंडा)

Elephant (हाथी)

Cow Elephant (हथनी)

Bulky female animal के साथ 'Cow' लगाकर feminine बनाते हैं।

8 Apostrophe

Read the following sentences:-

This is Mohan.
Mohan's book is in his hand.
Mohan's book is thick.

The crow has a long beak.
The crow's beak is long.
The crow's colour is black.

We use 's to show the relation of someone or something with noun.

वाक्यों में जब हम का, के, की का प्रयोग करते हैं जैसे:-

Santosh's bike – संतोष की बाइक

Mohan's house – मोहन का घर

वैसे तो English में 's (Apostrophe 's') और 'of' लगाकर हम Noun का Possessive case बनाते हैं।

Remember some rules of 'S

Rule 1:- We should use 'S with living beings at the end of singular noun. (living beings) singular noun के अंत में 'S जोड़कर Possessive case बनाते है।

Examples:-

1. Mohan's book मोहन की पुस्तक।
2. The girl's dog लड़की का कुत्ता।
3. The boy's toy बच्चे का खिलौना।

'is called apostrophe.

Rule 2: When a plural noun ends with s then we do not use 's but ' only.
अगर plural noun के अंत में S हो, तब हम उसमें सिर्फ Apostrophe (') जोड़ते हैं।

Examples:-

1. It is hostel of girls.
   It is girls' hostel.
2. These are toys of boys.
   These are boys' toys.

Rule 3: When a plural noun does not end at 's' then we use 's.
जब plural noun के अंत में S न हो, तब हम 's लगाते हैं।

Examples:-

1. It is the school of children.
   It is children's school.
2. The clothes of men.
   Men's clothes.

Rule 4:- When a singular noun ends with 'S' then we use ' जब singular noun के अंत में S हो, तब हम (') लगाते हैं।

Example:-

This is the bike of Vikas.
This is Vikas' bike.

Rule 5:- We do not use 's with non-living things.
(non-living things) के साथ 'S का प्रयोग नहीं होता।

Examples:-

1. The smell of rose is nice. गुलाब की खुशबू अच्छी होती है।
2. The burger of Delhi is tasty. दिल्ली का बर्गर स्वादिष्ट होता है।

Rule 6:- We use both 'of' and 's with living beings to make possessive case of noun. (living beings) noun के साथ दोनों ही यानी 'of' या 's लगा कर possessive case बना सकते हैं।

1. The father of Ram = Ram's father. राम के पिता।
2. The hand of leader = The leader's hand. नेता का हाथ।
3. The tail of dog = The dog's tail. कुत्ते की पूँछ।

Read Carefully: (We use 'the' before noun if 'of' comes after noun.)

- This is Mohan.
  Mohan's house is very big.
- That is Mohan's mother.
  She is a teacher.

Exercise-1

Write the following sentences using 'S or '

1. The house of Mohan. ____________
2. The heater of Rita is in her room. ____________
3. The car belongs to Peter. ____________
4. The tail of the dog waves. ____________
5. The pen of Vishvas is red. ____________

Exercise-2

(A) Fill 'S or ' in the blanks:-

1. ____________ father is a businessman. (Mohan)
2. That is ____________ pen. (Sunita)
3. ____________ clothes are expensive. (women)
4. ____________ car is red. (Vikas)
5. Five ____________ lives are at risk. (persons)

(B) Tick the correct ('s) or (') in the following sentences.

1. My brother wants to purchase Bisvas ('s or ') car.
2. It is my parents ('s or ') decision.
3. Purple is girls ('s or ') favourite colour.
4. It is the doctors ('s or ') responsibility.
5. Mohan ('s or ') house is very big.

Let us help you:-

1. With non-living things we use 'of' but we also use 'the' before the noun whereas we use 'S or ' with living things.

Exercise-3

1. किसानों की समस्याएँ।

____

2. भारत का इतिहास।

____

3. फूलों के पौधे।

____

4. दिल्ली का लाल किला।

____

5. मोहन का मोबाइल।

____

6. इस किताब की कीमत एक सौ पचास रूपये है।

____

7. ये घोड़े सुनील के हैं।

____

8. उस ग्लास का पानी गंदा था।

____

9. मेरे पिता के भाई डॉक्टर है।

10. कुतुब मिनार की ऊचाई अस्सी फीट है।

11. चीन के लोग मेहनती होते हैं।

12. इस कुएँ का पानी मीठा है।

13. यह जगमोहन की गाय नहीं है।

14. इस गली के लड़के पढ़े-लिखे नहीं हैं।

15. इस पुस्तक की कीमत सौ रूपय नहीं है।

16. क्या दिल्ली भारत की राजधानी नहीं है।

17. क्या उसके घर की दिवार टूटी हुई है।

18. मेरे घर के लोग आलसी नहीं हैं।

19. क्या लड़की का नाम कलावती नहीं था।

20. क्या उसकी दादी का स्वास्थ्य अच्छा नहीं होगा।

21. यह लड़कियों का कॉलेज है।

22. वे लोग राजा के दोस्त हैं।

Let us help you:-

1. (') is called an apostrophe.
2. When singular and plural nouns end with S, then we use (') after S. Example:- Girls' rooms.
3. When singular and plural nouns do not have S, then we use 'S. Examples:- Pooja's pen, people's rights.

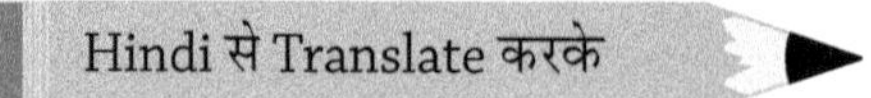

No Environment
No English

English नहीं सीखी जा सकती,

लेकिन इस Book में Hindi को

माहौल बनाओ
English **बोलो।**

सिर्फ Concept Clear करने के लिए use किया गया है।

Use of Surnames Mr., Mrs., Ms. and Miss, [Titles]

We should use titles (Mr., Mrs., Ms., and Miss) before surnames or full names as a sign of respect.

When we know the person or people

Mister (Mr.): We use Mr. for all men above 18-years-old whether they are married or not, before their surnames or full names.

Mr. का प्रयोग 18 वर्ष से अधिक उम्र वाले पुरूषों के लिए किया जाता है चाहे वे married या unmarried हों।

Examples:-

(a) Mr. Khan (b) Mr. Rakesh Sharma

(c) Mr. Rohan

Note: We should use Mr. before fullname or surname of a man in English, therefore example C Mr. Rohan is wrong.

See more examples:

- Mr. Rohan
- Mr. Dalbir
- Mr. Anees these are wrong examples according to rule of English.

Hello, Mr. Ravi Verma (right)	Hello, Mr. Ravi (wrong)	Hello, Mr. Verma (right)

Let us help you:-

- Singular: Short form of Mister is Mr.
  Example:- Mr. Kumar.
- Plural: Short Form of Messers is M/s.
  Example:- M/s. Khan and sons. M/s. Ram Kumar and Sons.
- Never use Mr. with first name of a man. Example, Mr. Rohan is wrong (×)
- It is not important to use (.) We can use or we cannot use.

According to British, Master is used for a young boy under 16-years-old.
Example: Master Rohan

According to American- Master is used for a 12-years-old boy.
Example: Master Vikram.
There is no hard and fast rule to use first name or surname with master.

Mrs. (Missus): We use Mrs. for all married women before their surnames of full names.

Mrs. का प्रयोग married women के surname या full name से पहले क्या जाता है।

Examples:-

(a) Mrs. Arora (b) Mrs. Alka Arora (c) Mrs. Alka

Note: We should use Mrs. before surname or full name of a married woman, therefore example (C) is wrong.

See more examples:

Mrs. Nisha (×) Mrs. Monika (×) Mrs. Pooja Aggarwal (✓)

Miss: We should use Miss before a surname or full name of an unmarried girl or a young girl.

Examples:-

(a) Miss Nisha Arora (✓) (b) Miss Arora (✓) (c) Miss Nisha (×)

Let us help you:-

- In case of a young girl, use full name or only surname of family.

Ms. (Miz.): We use Ms. for those whose marital status we do not know. Ms. (miz) is very professional to be used. It is used with surname or full name.

(a) Ms. Santosh Malhotra

(b) Ms. Malhotra

(c) Ms. Santosh

Note: We should use Ms. before surname or full name of a woman, therefore example C is wrong.

Ms.: It is important to understand the pronunciation of Ms. is (miz). It is used mostly used in the corporate world or in business. Ms. stands for all women, like, widow, divorcee, married, unmarried who is older or above 24 or 25-years-old.

Let us help you:-

In case of no surname for a stranger, we should use Sir or Mister for male whereas Ma'am or Miss for female.

Male : Use 'Sir' for older, elder.
Use 'mister' for a young man.

Female: Use 'ma'am' for older, elder.
Use 'miss' for a young girl.

English Practice से आती है।

No Environment No English

10 Adjectives

Read the following sentences:

This boy is **intelligent**.
That house is **big**.

My father is **fat**.
This book is **thick**.

I have **two** dolls.
This is **black** cat.

A word that describes or gives information about a noun or pronoun is called an adjective.

Noun or Pronoun की विशेषता बताने वाले शब्दों को adjective कहते हैं।

Adjective को Describing words भी कहा जाता है।

Let us help you:-

An adjective can be placed before or after a noun to describe them. Examples- This is a big ball. or This ball is big.

Adjective word को noun से पहले या बाद में लगा सकते हैं।

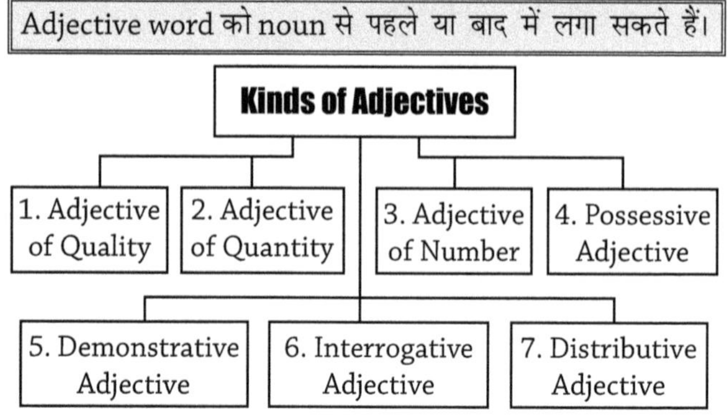

1. **Adjective of Quality: The words that tell us about the shape, size, colour, quality and disquality of a noun or a pronoun is called Adjective of Quality.**

   (जिस शब्द से Noun या Pronoun के रूप, रंग, आकार या अन्य किसी गुण, दोष का बोध हो, उसे Adjective of Quality कहते हैं।)

Examples:-

1. Mohan is a tall boy.
2. It is a big college.
3. I have a blue pen.
4. He is a useless doctor.

2. **Adjective of Quantity: The words that tell us about the quantity of a noun or a pronoun is called Adjective of Quantity.**

   (जिस शब्द से Noun या Pronoun की मात्रा का बोध हो, उसे Adjective of Quantity कहते हैं।)

Examples:-

1. There is much sugar in the milk.
2. There is little water in the tank.
3. Could you give me some money?

3. **Adjective of Number: The words that tell us about the number of a noun or a pronoun is called Adjective of Number.**

   (जिस शब्द से Noun या Pronoun की संख्या का बोध हो उसे Adjective of Number कहते हैं।)

Examples:-

1. Five boys are in the class.
2. There are ten chairs in the class.
3. All boys are here.

4. **Possessive Adjective: The words that tell us about ownership or relation of a noun or a pronoun is called Possessive Adjective.**

(जिस शब्द से Noun या Pronoun के अधिकार या सबंध का बोध हो, उसे Possessive Adjective कहते हैं।)

Examples:-

1. This is my pen.
2. It is their car.
3. Your shirt is in the almirah.

5. **Demonstrative Adjective: The words that point out about a noun or a pronoun is called Demonstrative Adjective.**

(जिस शब्द से किसी Noun या Pronoun की ओर संकेत का बोध होता है उसे Demonstrative Adjective कहते हैं।)

Examples:-

1. This pen is mine.
2. That shirt is yours.
3. These men are theives.

6. **InterrogativeAdjective:Thewordsthattellusaboutinterrogation of a noun or a pronoun is called Interrogative Adjective.**

(जिस शब्द को प्रश्न पूछने के लिए किसी Noun या Pronoun के साथ प्रयोग किया जाता है, उसे Interrogative Adjective कहते हैं।)

Examples:-

1. Whose house is this?
2. Which pen is yours?
3. What colour is water?

7. **Distributive Adjective: When we use the words each, every, either, before a noun or a pronoun it is called Distributive Adjective.**

(जिस शब्दों को Noun या Pronoun से पहले प्रयोग किया जाता है (जैसे each, every, either) ऐसे शब्द को Distributive Adjective कहते हैं।)

Examples:-

1. Each boy is in the class.
2. Trees are on either side of the road.
3. Neither answer was correct.

Look at the pictures and read the following sentences.

Is Mohan tall?
No, Mohan is not tall.
Mohan is thin.

Is this cold tea?
No, this is not cold tea.
This is hot tea.

Is that a green pen?
No, that is not a green pen.
This is a blue pen.

Are these two dolls?
Yes, these are two dolls.

Is this a big house?
Yes, this is a big house.

Is there less sugar in the milk?
No, there is not less sugar in the milk.
There is much sugar in the milk.

From the above examples, we have learnt different types of adjectives.

The words tell us about quality.

Examples: Hot tea, tall, cold tea, thin, big house, green pen, blue pen, etc.
These words tell us about the shape, size and colour.

Examples: Two dolls, less sugar, much sugar, etc.
These words tell us about quantity or numbers.

Exercise-1

old, blind, two, big, small

Choose the suitable words and fill in the blanks:

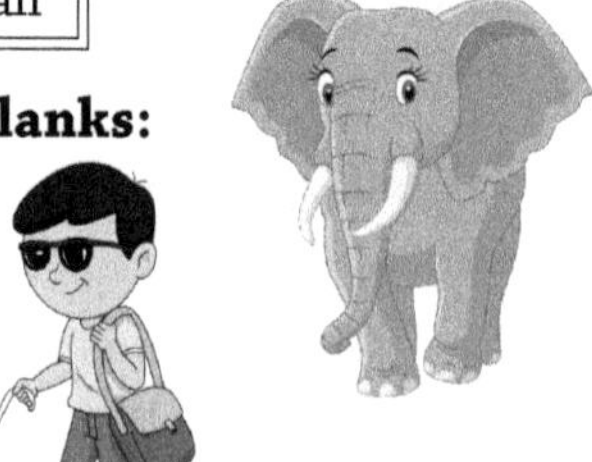

1. This is a ___________ elephant.
2. That is a ___________ ball.
3. Mohan is a ___________ boy.
4. Rita has ___________ dolls.
5. Grandfather is an ___________ man.

Exercise-2

Underline the naming words and describing words from the sentences and write them.

1. Mother is angry.
2. Mohan has two balloons.
3. Giraffe is a tall animal.
4. Tea is hot.

Naming words	Describing words

Note: Naming words are also called nouns.

Exercise-3

Underline the describing words in the following sentences and write their types in the box.

1. It is my house. ☐
2. I have a red doll. ☐
3. There are two cups on the table. ☐
4. These books are yours. ☐
5. Each boy is here. ☐
6. There is some honey in the jar. ☐
7. How much water is in the bottle? ☐

Exercise-4

Match the adjectives in column A to the right pairs in column B.

A-Column	B-Column
1. Sun	(a) Green
2. Knife	(b) Clever
3. Blanket	(c) Hot
4. Man	(d) Beautiful
5. Fox	(e) Rich
6. Girl	(f) Soft
7. Grapes	(g) Sharp

Exercise-5

Fill in the blanks with the correct describing words.

sweet, cold, interesting, three, big, warm, hot

In the winter, it was very (a) ________ . Pushpa and Sunil were in their (b) ________ quilts. Father gave them (c) ________ tea. Pushpa wanted to read an (d) ________ book. Sunil wanted to go out for walking. He went out and sat under a (e) ________ tree. It was an orange tree. He plucked (f) ________ oranges. The oranges were very (g) ___________ .

Exercise-6

(A) Read the story of naughty Toto and circle the adjectives.

Toto is a naughty monkey. He loves to snatch ripe fruits from the people living in the village. One day, while Toto is eating a yellow banana. A bear comes and snatches the banana from his hand. Toto is sad. He becomes a good monkey after that.

(B) Choose the words from the box and fill in the blanks:

red, four, two, four, big

It is a (a) ________ car. The colour of this car is (b) ________ . It has (c) ________ wheels and (d) ________ doors. It has (e) ________ head lights.

Position of Adjectives

Adjectives are usually placed before nouns:

Examples:-

Mohan is a laborious man.
She is a fat lady.
It is a thick book.

Some adjectives can be placed after nouns:

Examples:-

Father is angry.
They are lazy.
The woman is fat.

Use of much, many

Much and many usually give the same idea. However, Much is an adjective of quantity, so we use Much with uncountable things whereas Many is an adjective of number, therefore we use Many with countable things.

Much का प्रयोग उन वस्तुओं के साथ होता है जिन्हें गिना न जा सके लेकिन Many का उपयोग गिनी जाने वाली वस्तुओं के साथ होता है।

Examples:-

1. There is much water in the tank.
2. There is much sugar in the milk.
3. There are many students in the school.
4. She has many cosmetic items.

Few, A few, little, A little.

Few and Little usually give the same idea. However, 'Few' is an adjective of number So, we use few with countable things whereas the word 'Little' is an adjective of quality, therefore we use Little with uncountable things.

Few का प्रयोग उन वस्तुओं के साथ किया जाता हैं, जिन को गिना जा सके, जबकि Little शब्द गिनी न जाने वाली वस्तुओं के साथ प्रयोग होता है।

Examples:-

1. There were few students in the class. (almost no student)
2. There were a few students in the class. (some students)
3. I have little time for you. (almost no time)
4. I have a little time for you. (some time)

Countable सख्या में few ना के बराबर a few सख्या में कम है लेकिन है।

The few: सख्या में कम है लेकिन वह definite है।

Uncountable मात्रा में little ना के बराबर a little मात्रा में कम है लेकिन है।

The Litttle: सख्या में कम है लेकिन वह definite है।

Exercise-7

Fill in the blanks using few/little, A few/A little, the few/ the little.

1. The doctor adviced her to rest for ________ days.
2. ________ knowledge is a dangerous thing.
3. The show was cancelled as ________ people turned up to see it.
4. ________ water I kept for you has been finished by him.
5. I cannot prepare tea for you. There is ________ milk in the pan.

Let us help you:-

Note: We should not use the words 'Little' and 'few' when quantity and number are given in a sentence.

Examples:-

Little quantity of food is left. (×)
Small quantity of food is left. (✓)

Look at the pictures:-

Degrees of Comparison

Big

Bigger

Biggest

Read the following sentences:

1. The boy is <u>taller</u> than the girl.
2. A tree is <u>bigger</u> than a plant.
3. The book is <u>thicker</u> than the diary.
4. Father is <u>older</u> than uncle.
5. Roopa is <u>more</u> beautiful than Heena.

Let us help you:-

We use comparative adjectives to compare two persons, animals, things, places, etc:

There are three degrees of comparison.

Degress of Comparison		
Positive Degree	Comparative Degree	Superlative Degree

Positive Degree: When there is no comparison, we use positive degree of an adjective.

Examples:-

1. Mohan is handsome.
2. It is a beautiful picture.

Note: When we talk about one person, a thing or an animal only then we use positive degree.

जब हम किसी एक व्यक्ति, वस्तु या जानवर की बात करते हैं, तो Positive Degree प्रयोग करते हैं।

Comparative Degree: When we compare two persons or things, then we use comparative degree of an adjective.

Examples:-

1. Mohan is better than Sohan.
2. This house is bigger than that house.

Note: When we talk about comparison of two persons, two things or two animals, then we use Comparative Degree.

जब हम दो व्यक्ति, दो वस्तुओं या दो जानवरों के बीच में तुलना करते हैं, तब हम Comparative Degree का प्रयोग करते हैं।

Superlative Degree: When we talk about more than two persons, things or animals, we use the superlative degree of an adjective.

Examples:-

1. It is the best book in the library.
2. He is the tallest student in the school.

Note: When we talk about the comparison of more than two persons, things or animals then we use superlative degree.

जब दो से ज़्यादा व्यक्ति, वस्तुओं या जानवरों के बीच की तुलना करें तो **Superlative Degree** प्रयोग होती है।

Formation of Comparative and Superlative degree.

1. We add '-er' and '-est' to the positive degree.

Positive	Comparative	Superlative
Thick	Thicker	Thickest
Bold	Bolder	Boldest
Rich	Richer	Richest
Young	Younger	Youngest

2. We add '-r' and ''-st' to the positive degree ending at 'E'.

Positive	Comparative	Superlative
Fine	Finer	Finest
Brave	Braver	Bravest
Wise	Wiser	Wisest
Noble	Nobler	Noblest

3. We add 'ier' and 'est' to the positive degree that ends at 'Y' and has a consonant before 'Y'.

Positive	Comparative	Superlative
Pretty	Prettier	Prettiest
Heavy	Heavier	Heaviest
Lazy	Lazier	Laziest

4. We add '-er' and 'est' to the positive degree when it ends at 'Y' and has a vowel before 'Y'.

Positive	Comparative	Superlative
Grey	Greyer	Greyest
Gay	Gayer	Gayest

5. We add 'more' and 'most' before the positive degree.

Positive	Comparative	Superlative
Beautiful	More beautiful	Most beautiful
Suitable	More suitable	Most suitable
Difficult	More difficult	Most difficult

Comparison of Adjectives

Some adjectives do not follow any rules. They are irregular adjective degrees. Here are the different forms of adjectives.

S. N.	Positive	Comparative	Superlative
1	Accurate (शुद्ध)	More accurate	Most accurate
2	Active (फुर्तीला)	More active	Most active
3	Anger (गुस्सा)	Angrier	Angriest
4	Attractive (मोह लेने वाला)	More attractive	Most attractive
5	Bad (खराब)	Worse	Worst
6	Beautiful (सुंदर)	More beautiful	Most beautiful
7	Big (बड़ा)	Bigger	Biggest
8	Bitter (कड़वा)	Bitterer	Bitterest
9	Black (काला)	Blacker	Blackest
10	Bland (बेस्वाद)	Blander	Blandest
11	Bloody (कठोर)	Bloodier	Bloodiest
12	Blue (नीला)	Bluer	Bluest

13	Bold (साहसिक)	Bolder	Boldest
14	Bossy (धौंस देने वाला)	Bossier	Bossiest
15	Brave (बहादुर)	Braver	Bravest
16	Brief (मुख्तसर)	Briefer	Briefest
17	Bright (चमकदार)	Brighter	Brightest
18	Brilliant (बहुत बढ़िया)	More brilliant	Most brilliant
19	Broad (व्यापक)	Broader	Broadest
20	Busy (व्यस्त)	Busier	Busiest
21	Calm (शांत)	Calmer	Calmest
22	Careful (चिंतित)	More careful	Most careful
23	Cheap (सस्ता)	Cheaper	Cheapest
24	Chewy (अधिक चबाने वाला)	Chewier	Chewiest
25	Chubby (गोलमोल)	Chubbier	Chubbiest
26	Classy (ऊंचे दर्जे का)	Classier	Classiest
27	Clean (स्वच्छ)	Cleaner	Cleanest
28	Clear (साफ़)	Clearer	Clearest
29	Clever (चतुर)	Cleverer	Cleverest
30	Cloudy (बादल से घिरा हुआ)	Cloudier	Cloudiest
31	Clumsy (अनाड़ी, भद्दा)	Clumsier	Clumsiest
32	Coarse (खुरखुरा)	Coarser	Coarsest
33	Cold (सर्दी)	Colder	Coldest
34	Common (सामान्य)	Commoner	Commonest
35	Cool (ठंडा)	Cooler	Coolest
36	Costly (महँगा)	Costlier	Costliest
37	Courageous (बहादुर)	More courageous	Most courageous
38	Crazy (पागल)	Crazier	Craziest
39	Creamy (मलाईदार)	Creamier	Creamiest
40	Creepy (रेगंने वाला)	Creepier	Creepiest
41	Crispy (खस्ता)	Crispier	Crispiest
42	Cruel (निर्दयी)	Crueler	Cruelest

43	Crunchy (कुरकुरे)	Crunchier	Crunchiest
44	Cunning (चालाक)	More cunning	Most cunning
45	Curly (घुंघराले)	Curlier	Curliest
46	Curvy (घुमावदार)	Curvier	Curviest
47	Cute (प्यारा)	Cuter	Cutest
48	Damp (गीला)	Damper	Dampest
49	Dark (अंधेरा)	Darker	Darkest
50	Deadly (घातक)	Deadlier	Deadliest
51	Deep (गहरा)	Deeper	Deepest
52	Dense (घना)	Denser	Densest
53	Difficult (कठिन)	More difficult	Most difficult
54	Dim (धुंधला)	Dimmer	Dimmest
55	Dirty (गंदा)	Dirtier	Dirtiest
56	Dry (सूखा)	Drier	Driest
57	Dull (फीका)	Duller	Dullest
58	Dumb (गूंगा)	Dumber	Dumbest
59	Dusty (गंदा)	Dustier	Dustiest
60	Early (जल्दी)	Earlier	Earliest
61	Easy (आसान)	Easier	Easiest
62	Evil (बुरा)	Worse	Worst
63	Faint (बेहोश)	Fainter	Faintest
64	Fair (गोरा)	Fairer	Fairest
65	Faithful (ईमानदार)	More faithful	Most faithful
66	Famous (मशहूर)	More famous	Most famous
67	Fancy (पसंद)	Fancier	Fanciest
68	Far (दूर)	Farther	Farthest
69	Fat (मोटी)	Fatter	Fattest
70	Few (थोड़ा)	Fewer	Fewest
71	Fierce (क्रोधी)	Fiercer	Fiercest

72	Filthy (गंदा)	Filthier	Filthiest
73	Fine (ठीक)	Finer	Finest
74	Fit (स्वस्थ)	Fitter	Fittest
75	Flaky (परतदार)	Flakier	Flakiest
76	Flat (समतल)	Flatter	Flattest
77	Fresh (ताज़ा)	Fresher	Freshest
78	Friendly (दयालु)	Friendlier	Friendliest
79	Full (पूरा)	Fuller	Fullest
80	Funny (मज़ेदार)	Funnier	Funniest
81	Gentle (कोमल)	Gentler	Gentlest
82	Gloomy (उदास)	Gloomier	Gloomiest
83	Good (अच्छा)	Better	Best
84	Grand (बड़ा)	Grander	Grandest
85	Grave (गंभीर)	Graver	Gravest
86	Greasy (चिकना)	Greasier	Greasiest
87	Great (महान)	Greater	Greatest
88	Greedy (लालची)	Greedier	Greediest
89	Grey (धूसर)	Greyer	Greyest
90	Gross (कुल)	Grosser	Grossest
91	Guilty (दोषी)	Guilter	Guiltiest
92	Hairy (बालदार)	Hairier	Hairiest
93	Happy (खुशी)	Happier	Happiest
94	Hard (कठिन)	Harder	Hardest
95	Harsh (कड़ा)	Harsher	Harshest
96	Heavy (भारी)	Heavier	Heaviest
97	High (ऊँचा)	Higher	Highest
98	Hip (कमर)	Hipper	Hippest
99	Horrible (भयंकर)	More horrible	Most horrible
100	Hot (गरम)	Hotter	Hottest

101	Humble (सादा)	Humbler	Humblest
102	Hungry (भूखा)	Hungrier	Hungriest
103	Icy (ठंडा)	Icier	Iciest
104	Ill (बीमार)	Worse	Worst
105	Important (ज़रूरी)	More important	Most important
106	Itchy (खुजली होना)	Itchier	Itchiest
107	Juicy (रसदार)	Juicier	Juiciest
108	Kind (मेहरबान)	Kinder	Kindest
109	Large (विशाल)	Larger	Largest
110	Late (देर से)	Later	Latest
111	Lazy (आलसी)	Lazier	Laziest
112	Light (रोशनी)	Lighter	Lightest
113	Likely (उपयुक्त)	Likelier	Likeliest
114	Little (थोड़ा)	Less	Least
115	Lively (जीवित)	Livelier	Liveliest
116	Lonely (तनहा, शांत)	Lonlier	Loneliest
117	Long (लंबा)	Longer	Longest
118	Loud (ज़ोरदार)	Louder	Loudest
119	Lovely (सुंदर)	Lovlier	Lovliest
120	Low (हल्का)	Lower	Lowest
121	Mad (पागल)	Madder	Maddest
122	Many (अनेक)	More	Most
123	Mean (घटिया)	Meaner	Meanest
124	Messy (गंदा)	Messier	Messiest
125	Mild (नरम)	Milder	Mildest
126	Moist (नमी)	Moister	Moistest
127	Much (बहुत)	More	Most
128	Narrow (संकीर्ण)	Narrower	Narrowest
129	Nasty (बुरा)	Nastier	Nastiest
130	Naughty (शरारती)	Naughtier	Naughtiest

131	Near (पास में)	Nearer	Nearest
132	Neat (स्वच्छ)	Neater	Neatest
133	Needy (जरुरतमंद)	Needier	Neediest
134	New (नया)	Newer	Newest
135	Nice (अच्छा)	Nicer	Nicest
136	Odd (अजीब)	Odder	Oddest
137	Oily (तेल का)	Oilier	Oiliest
138	Old (पुराना)	Older	Oldest
139	Plain (सादा)	Plainer	Plainest
140	Pleasant (सुहाना)	Pleasanter	Pleasantest
141	Polite (नर्म)	Politer	Politest
142	Poor (घटिया, गरीब)	Poorer	Poorest
143	Popular (प्रमुख)	More popular	Most popular
144	Pretty (सुंदर)	Prettier	Prettiest
145	Proper (असली)	More proper	Most proper
146	Proud (अंहकारी)	Prouder	Proudest
147	Pure (असली)	Purer	Purest
148	Quick (शीघ्र)	Quicker	Quickest
149	Quiet (शांत)	Quieter	Quietest
150	Rare (गिनाचुना)	Rarer	Rarest
151	Raw (कच्चा)	Rawer	Rawest
152	Rich (धनी)	Richer	Richest
153	Risky (खतरनाक)	Riskier	Riskiest
154	Roomy (विशाल)	Roomier	Roomiest
155	Rough (रूखा)	Rougher	Roughest
156	Rude (अक्खड़)	Ruder	Rudest
157	Rusty (जंग लगा)	Rustier	Rustiest
158	Sad (उदास)	Sadder	Saddest
159	Safe (महफूज)	Safer	Safest

160	Salty (नमकीन)	Saltier	Saltiest
161	Sane (समझदार)	Saner	Sanest
162	Scary (भयानक)	Scarier	Scariest
163	Shallow (उथला)	Shallower	Shallowest
164	Shiny (चमकीला)	Shinier	Shiniest
165	Short (छोटा)	Shorter	Shortest
166	Shy (शर्मीला)	Shyer	Shyest
167	Silly (मूर्ख)	Sillier	Silliest
168	Simple (सरल)	Simpler	Simplest
169	Sincere (ईमानदार)	Sincerer	Sincerest
170	Skinny (चमड़ादार)	Skinnier	Skinniest
171	Sleepy (सुस्त, शांत)	Sleepier	Sleepiest
172	Slim (पतला)	Slimmer	Slimmest
173	Slow (हल्का)	Slower	Slowest
174	Small (छोटा)	Smaller	Smallest
175	Smart (होशियार)	Smarter	Smartest
176	Smelly (बदबूदार)	Smellier	Smelliest
177	Smooth (चिकना)	Smoother	Smoothest
178	Soft (मुलायम/कोमल)	Softer	Softest
179	Soon (जल्द ही)	Sooner	Soonest
180	Sore (नाराज़)	Sorer	Sorest
181	Sorry (शर्मिन्दा)	Sorrier	Sorriest
182	Sour (खट्टा)	Sourer	Sourest
183	Spicy (मसालेदार)	Spicier	Spiciest
184	Splendid (शानदार)	More splendid	Most splendid
185	Steep (तीव्र ढलान वाला)	Steeper	Steepest
186	Stingy (कंजूस)	Stingier	Stingiest
187	Strange (अजनबी)	Stranger	Strangest
188	Strict (सख़्त)	Stricter	Strictest

189	Stupid (बेवकूफ)	Stupider	Stupidest
190	Subtle (सूक्ष्म)	Subtler	Subtlest
191	Suitable (योग्य)	More suitable	Most suitable
192	Sunny (धूप)	Sunnier	Sunniest
193	Sure (जरूर)	Surer	Surrest
194	Sweaty (पसीने से तर)	Sweatier	Sweatiest
195	Sweet (मीठा)	Sweeter	Sweetest
196	Tall (लंबा)	Taller	Tallest
197	Tan (धूप से झूलस पाना)	Tanner	Tannest
198	Tasty (मज़ेदार)	Tastier	Tastiest
199	Thick (मोटा)	Thicker	Thickest
200	Thin (पतला)	Thinner	Thinnest
201	Thirsty (प्यासा)	Thirstier	Thirstiest
202	Tiny (नन्हा)	Tinier	Tiniest
203	Tough (कठोर)	Tougher	Toughest
204	True (सच)	Truer	Truest
205	Ugly (बुरा)	Uglier	Ugliest
206	Warm (गर्म)	Warmer	Warmest
207	Weak (कमजोर)	Weaker	Weakest
208	Wealthy (धनी)	Wealthier	Wealthiest
209	Weird (अजीब)	Weirder	Weirdest
210	Well (ठीक)	Better	Best
211	Wet (गीला)	Wetter	Wettest
212	Wild (जंगली)	Wilder	Wildest
213	Windy (तुफानी)	Windier	Windiest
214	Wise (समझदार)	Wiser	Wisest
215	Worldly (संसारिक)	Worldlier	Worldliest
216	Worthy (योग्य, लायक)	Worthier	Worthiest
217	Young (जवान)	Younger	Youngest

Remember Some Rules of Adjectives

Rule1: Double Comparatives and Superlatives cannot be used in a sentence.

दो Comparative और दो Superlative Degree का प्रयोग एक साथ नहीं होता है।

Examples:-

1. This is more better than that. (×)
   This is better than that. (✓)
2. He is the most cleverest of all the students. (×)
   He is the cleverest of all the students. (✓)

Rule 2: Superlative Degree के पहले article 'the' का प्रयोग होता है।

Example:-

1. He is the best student of the class.

Rule 3: 'Ior' में खत्म होने वाले Adjectives के बाद 'than' नहीं आता बल्कि 'to' का उपयोग होता है।

like: Superior, inferior, senior, junior, prior, anterior, posterior

Example:

He is senior than me. (×)
He is senior to me. (✓)

Rule 4: Adjective 'preferable' का प्रयोग सिर्फ Comparative Degree में होता है, इसके साथ न तो 'than' का प्रयोग होता है और न ही 'more' केवल 'to' आता है।

Examples:-

1. This is more preferable than that. (×)
   This is preferable to that. (✓)
2. I prefer tea to coffee. (✓)

Note:- Prefer के साथ to के स्थान पर rather than का भी प्रयोग हो सकता है।

Example: I prefer tea rather than coffee.

Exercise-8

Tick (✓) the correct words in the brackets.

1. Black dog is (bigger, smaller) than white cat.

2. Book is (thicker, thinner) than diary.

3. This doll is (more beautiful, beautiful) than that toy.

4. An elephant is (heavier, lighter) than cow.

Exercise-9

Fill in the blanks with suitable adjectives.

1. Bhangra is _________ (easy) than break dance.
2. Burj Khalifa is _________ (tall) than Qutub Minar.
3. Butterfly is _________ (big) than bee.
4. This road is _________ (risky) than that road.

Exercise-10

Fill in the blanks with the correct adjectives.

1. Papaya is _________ (bigger, biggest) than apple.
2. Anil is _________ (taller, tallest) than his father.
3. Mohan is _________ (stronger, strongest) than Rohan.

Exercise-11

Underline the correct adjectives.

1. Train is fast, faster than bus.
2. Aeroplane is the faster, fastest mode of transport.
3. Taj Mahal is the more beautiful, most beautiful building in India.

Using the Degrees of Adjectives

1. For equal comparison between two persons or two things. For suggesting equality we use as ____ as.

(a) Mohit is as strong as a Lion.
(b) My house is as big as Red Fort.
(c) Mohan is as tall as Rohan.
(d) Rohan is not so tall as Mohan. (not so...as in negative sentence)

2. Use of Older, Oldest, Elder, Eldest.

We use elder and eldest only with persons/members of the same family.

We cannot use with animals or things. (ये शब्द elder and eldest का अर्थ है, खून के रिश्ते में बड़ा)

Examples:-

(a) My elder brother is lazy.
(b) His eldest sister is a doctor.

Note: If we use the word Than in a sentence, we use older and not elder.

Example: I am older than my sister.

older and oldest (use for both persons and things)

Examples:-

(a) Rohan is the oldest boy in our class.
(b) It is the oldest building in this area.

3. **When we compare two things and one is related directly to the other, then we use 'the' ________.**

'the' जब दो वस्तुओं की तुलना में एक वस्तु सीधे-सीधे दूसरी वस्तु को प्रभावित करती है, तब हम ____ 'The' प्रयोग करके Comparison को दर्शा सकते हैं।

Examples:-

(a) The more I eat the more I feel hungry.

(b) The slower you write the better your writing will be.

4. **Late-Later-Latest: (These words refer to time.)**

Late समय को दर्शाता है।

Examples:-

(a) She was late.
(b) She came later than I.
(c) This is the lastest movie of the month.

Late - Latter - Last (These words refer to position)

Examples:-

(a) The latter part of the movie was nice.
(b) She was the last person in the class.

Far, Farther/Further both are used to show distance (दूरी).

Example:- She lives at the farther/further end of the lane.

Further का अर्थ है 'और' (Additional)

Example:- I did not receive any further information.

Let us help you:-

Positive	Comparative	Superlative
Late	Later, Latter	Latest, Last
Old	Older, Elder	Oldest, Eldest
Far	Farther, Further	Farthest, Furthest
Many, Much	More	Most
Little	Less	Least
Near	Nearer	Nearest/Next

The difference between nearest and next.

The word, nearest (shortest distance सबसे नज़दीक) The word, next (अगला).

Examples:-

(a) Which is the nearest hospital?
(b) The school is in the next building.

Later - बाद में।

Latter - बाद वाला।

Latter का opposite word 'former' होता है।

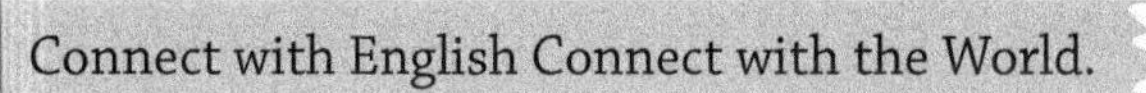

Connect with English Connect with the World.

No Environment No English.

11 Articles

अंग्रेज़ी में 26 अक्षर **[Letters]** हैं। इनमें 21 **consonants** (व्यंजन) और **5 vowels** (स्वर) हैं। **consonants** से शुरू होने वाले **noun** के साथ **'A'** का प्रयोग होता है और **vowels** से शुरू होने वाले **noun** के साथ **'An'** का प्रयोग होता है।

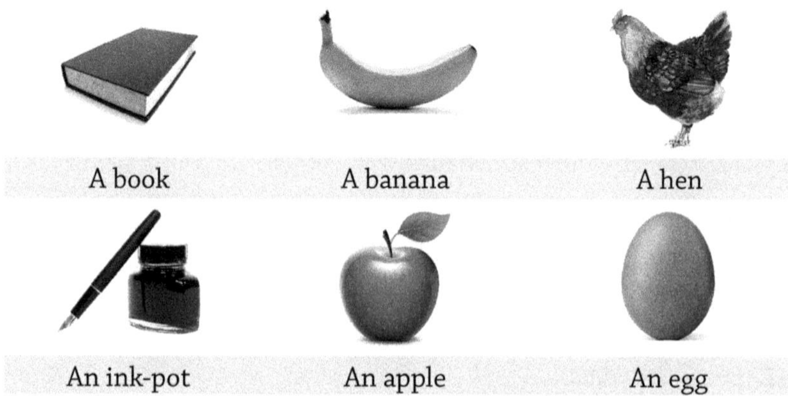

A, An, The are articles and they are used before nouns.

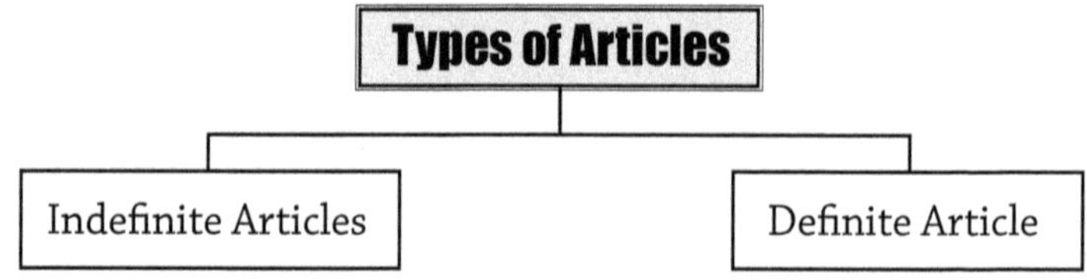

Indefinite Articles: 'A' and 'An' are called indefinite articles because we do not use them for a particular person, a place or a thing.

Examples:-

1. Mohan lives in <u>a</u> city.
2. This is <u>a</u> cat.
3. Give me <u>an</u> orange.

Definite Article: We use 'the' when we talk about a particular person, a place or a thing.

Examples:-

1. The pen you gave me is very nice.
2. I knew the person who stole your purse.
3. The water of that jar is dirty.

Articles: A, An

The meaning of A, An is one, and A, An are used before countable noun in a singular number.

Examples:- A girl, a bat, an orange, an ink-pot. Uses of 'A': we use 'A' before the word which begins with a consonant sound.

'A' का प्रयोग (Singular Countable Noun जो Consonant sound से पहले होता है।)

Examples:-

1. This is a pen.	यह एक कलम है।
2. Mohan is a student.	मोहन विद्यार्थी है।
3. This is a dog.	यह कुत्ता है।

Use of 'An': We use 'an' before the word which begins with a vowel sound.

'An' का प्रयोग (Singular Countable Noun जो Vowel sound से पहले होता है।)

Examples:-

1. This is an apple.	यह एक सेब है।
2. He is an actor.	वह अभिनेता है।
3. I saw an eagle.	मैंने एक चील देखी थी।

Where not to put 'A' - 'An': We do not put 'a' or 'an' before uncountable noun, proper noun and plural noun.

हम uncountable noun, proper noun और plural noun से पहले A/An का प्रयोग नहीं करते हैं।

Examples:-

1. Mohan has an intelligence. (×)
2. This is a Rahul. (×)
3. Give me a water. (×)

Use of 'A' 'An' as per Sounds

(i) 'A' is used before a singular countable noun that begins with a consonant sound. जो vowels (A, E, I, O and U) से शुरु होते हैं परन्तु उनका उच्चारण consonants की तरह होता है। उसके पहले 'A' का प्रयोग होता है।

Examples:-

1. A man, a boy
2. A European, a university, a utensil
3. A one-eyed dog, a one-sided game

यदि noun के पहले Adjective हो, तो A/An का प्रयोग Adjective से पहले होता है।

(ii) 'An' is used before a singular countable noun which begins with a vowel sound.

'An' सिर्फ 'A' के double sound को delete करने के लिए प्रयोग होता है:

Examples:- He is <u>an</u> M.L.A.
An honorable man.

words जो consonants से शुरु होते हैं, परन्तु उनका उच्चारण vowels की तरह होता है। उसके पहले 'An' का प्रयोग होता है।

We use 'An' to delete doubling sound of 'A'

Examples:-

1. An orange, An Apple, An American
2. An hour, An honorable man, An N.G.O.
3. An M.P, An M.L.A

Remember Some Important Points

1. To show a certain quantity.

Examples:-

(a) There is a dozen bananas.
(b) I add a spoon of sugar in one cup of tea.

2. To show profession, rank, caste, religion of a person or community.

Examples:-

(a) He is an O.B.C.
(b) He is a Sikh.
(c) He is a doctor.

3. It is very important to use 'A/An' before singular countable noun.

Examples:-

(a) I am teacher. (×)
(b) I am a teacher. (✓)

Exercise-1

(A) Fill in the blanks using 'a'/'an'.

1. Mohan is ________ (a/an) teacher.
2. This is ________ (a/an) book on the table.
3. She works in ________ (a/an) N.G.O.
4. I met ________ (a/an) M.L.A yesterday.
5. Mohan ate ________ (a/an) egg.
6. I study in ________ (a/an) university.

(B) Write 'a' or 'an' before the following nouns.

1.________ scientist 2.________ aeroplane 3.________ cow 4.________ papaya 5. ________ engineer 6. ________ song 7. ________ owl 8. ________ umbrella 9. ________ ice-cream 10. ________ book

Exercise-2

Translate into English:

1. मुकेश एक डॉक्टर है।
2. मोहन एक बहुत अच्छा लड़का है।
3. यह लोमड़ी है।
4. यह पुराना N.G.O है।
5. यह पानी है।
6. यह अशोक है।
7. ये बच्चे हैं।
8. यह साधारण व्यक्ति नहीं है।
9. मेरे पिता जी बेईमान आदमी नहीं हैं।
10. यह ऐतिहासिक घटना नहीं है।
11. वह चावल नहीं हैं।
12. वह पानी नहीं होगा।
13. क्या यह स्कूल है?
14. क्या वह एम. एल. ए. से मिला था?
15. क्या मोहन ईमानदार है?

16. क्या मक्खन लाभदायक है?

17. क्या मधुबाला मशहूर अभिनेत्री थी?

18. क्या मक्खन लाभदायक नहीं होता?

19. क्या कविता तेज़ छात्रा नहीं है?

20. क्या आप ज़िम्मेदार व्यक्ति नहीं थे?

21. क्या वह पेड़ नहीं था?

22. क्या वह छाता नहीं था?

23. क्या वह तेल नहीं है?

24. क्या वह कांना (one-eyed man) आदमी नहीं था?

25. ओबामा अमेरिका के राष्ट्रपति थे?

26. यह एक राष्ट्रीय खेल है।

27. मैं आई. ए. एस. बनूँगा।

28. मोहन आदर्श नागरिक नहीं है।

29. क्या यह एम. एल. ए. है?

30. क्या मोहन तेज़ छात्र बनेगा?

31. क्या मेरे पास नौकरी नहीं होगी?

32. क्या आपके पिता एन. सी. सी. अफ़सर नहीं हैं?

Definite Article (The)

'The' is used before:

(A) When we make someone or something particular.

Examples:-

1. Give me the book which I gave yesterday.
2. We won the game against Australia.
3. The lion which we saw was very strong.

(B) A common noun to represent a whole class.

The का प्रयोग singular common noun से पहले किया जाता है, जिससे पूरी जाति का बोध होता है।

Examples:-

1. The cow is useful.
2. The lion lives on flesh.
3. The dog is faithful.
4. The fox is a cunning animal.
5. The tiger is a cruel animal.

But, we do not put 'the' before plural common noun to represent a whole class. पूरी जाति का बोध कराने के लिए plural common noun से पहले 'The' का प्रयोग नहीं होता है।

Examples:-

1. The dogs are faithful. (×)
   Dogs are faithful. (✓)

2. The cows are useful. (×)
   Cows are useful. (✓)

(C) An adjective is used when it represents a class as a noun.

जब Adjective का प्रयोग Noun के रूप में किया जाता है।

Examples:-

1. The rich should help the poor.
2. The rich are miser.
3. The poor are honest.
4. The brave fight till the last breath.

Note: In this case we use only plural verb.

(D) The words like first, last, next, only, the fifth. The का प्रयोग **(orginal number)** से पहले होता है।

Examples:-

1. It is the first house in which hand pump was there
2. The last boy won prize.
3. The next question will be difficult.

(E) Before superlative degrees

Examples:-

1. Tanu is the best student of the class.
2. 'Baazigar' was the best movie of mine.
3. Kavita was the most intelligent girl.

(F) Before the names of:

(a) The name of rivers:
Example:- The Ganga

(b) The name of mountains:
Example:- The Himalayas

(c) The name of seas-oceans:
Example:- The Indian Ocean

(d) The name of deserts:
Example:- The Sahara Desert

(e) The name of seasons:
Example:- The Winter Season

(f) The name of epics:
Example:- The Bible

(g) The name of trains, aeroplanes, ships:
Example:- The Titanic

(h) The name of newspapers:
Example:- The Times of India

(i) The name of heavy things of the world:
Examples:- The Moon, The Sun

(j) The name of religious communities:
Examples:- The Muslims, the Hindus, the Chinese

(k) The name of political parties and government organisations and industries:

Examples:- The Congress, The Bhartiya Janta Party, The Reserve Bank of India, The Men's Club, The Reliance

(l) The name of titles or posts:
Examples:- The principal, the chairman

Exercise-3

(A) Fill in the blanks with a, an or the.

1. I wrote ________ book.
2. ________ owl was on the tree.
3. ________ books written by Kabirdas are very interesting.
4. ________ car on the road was burnt.
5. I got ________ one-rupee coin from my father.

(B) Fill in the blanks with a, an or the.

(i) 1. _______ farmer purchased 2. _______ horse from the market, he found 3. _______ horse was 4. _______ useful animal.

(ii) Seema wore 1. _______ blue dress. 2. _______ dress was very nice.

(iii) 1. ______ elephant and 2. ______ monkey were good friends. 3. ______ elephant and 4. ______ monkey ate bananas together.

(iv) I purchased 1. ______ orange. 2. ______ orange was tasty.

(v) Aarti got admission to 1. ______ new college. 2. ______ college was very far from her house.

Exercise-4

Translate into English:

1. घोड़ा उपयोगी होता है।

______

2. कुरान एक धार्मिक ग्रंथ है।

______

3. 15 अगस्त यादगार दिवस है।

______

4. बंदर सुस्त नहीं होते हैं।

______

5. हिंदू कट्टर नहीं होते हैं।

______

6. दुनिया बहुत सुंदर है।

______

7. क्या टाइम्स ऑफ इंडिया एक अंग्रेज़ी अख़बार है?

______

8. क्या ताजमहल भारत का ताज है?

______

9. क्या पंजाब के किसान अमीर हैं?

______

10. क्या पंजाब मेल अच्छी ट्रेन नहीं है?

______

11. क्या सर्दियों में पानी ठंडा नहीं रहता है?

____

12. क्या भारतीय बहादुर नहीं हैं?

____

13. क्या बिल्लियाँ शाकाहारी होती हैं?

____

14. क्या पानी स्वच्छ है?

____

15. क्या उस जार का पानी स्वच्छ है?

____

Omission of Articles

1. Articles are not used before Proper Noun, Material Noun and Abstract Noun.

Examples:-

(a) Ashok Singh is a good boy.
(b) Honesty is the best policy.
(c) Gold is yellow.
(d) Water is very useful.

2. Plural Noun: when such nouns denote a class.

Examples:-

(a) Birds eat worms.
(b) Children love ice-cream.

3. Names of games, meals, diseases, days, months.

Examples:-

(a) Children love cricket but chess is my favourite game.
(b) I take lunch at 1. pm.
(c) Malaria is a very dangerous disease.
(d) Sunday is a funny day.

Let us help you:-

1. Article is of two types (a) Indefinite articles (b) Definite article.
2. Indefinite articles:- 'a' and 'an'.
3. Definite article:- 'the'
4. 'A', 'An'-comes before singular common nouns and do not point at any particular person, a place or a thing.
5. But "the" comes before singular and plural nouns and point at a particular person, a place or a thing.
6. We do not use definite article with abstract nouns like, gold, love but, when the abstract noun particularises any person, a place or a thing then we use 'the'.

Examples:-

(a) The water which was given was dirty.
(b) The love of Juliet cannot be forgotten.
(c) Mohan is the Virat Kohli of our team.

7. Articles cannot be used before Abstract Noun, Material Noun or Proper Noun.

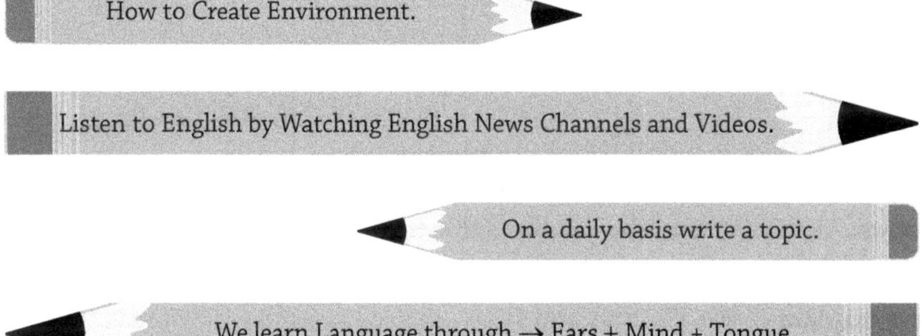

12 Pronouns

A pronoun is a word that is used in place of a noun.

जो शब्द संज्ञा के स्थान पर उपयोग होते हैं उन्हें Pronoun कहा जाता है।

Examples:- I, He, She, It, You, They, We

Read the following sentences.

(a) Kavita is an intelligent girl. She completes her work everyday.
In the above sentences, Kavita is a noun and the word "She" has been used in place of Kavita (noun) hence, the word "She" is a pronoun.

(b) Rani is a teacher.

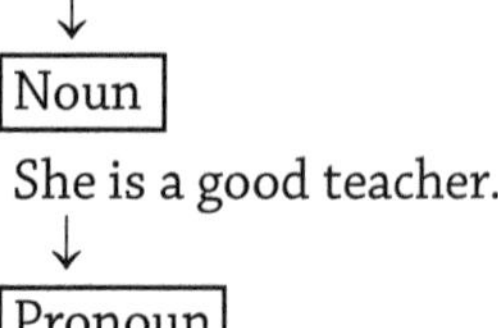

Rani is a noun but **'She'** which is used in place of noun is called **pronoun**.

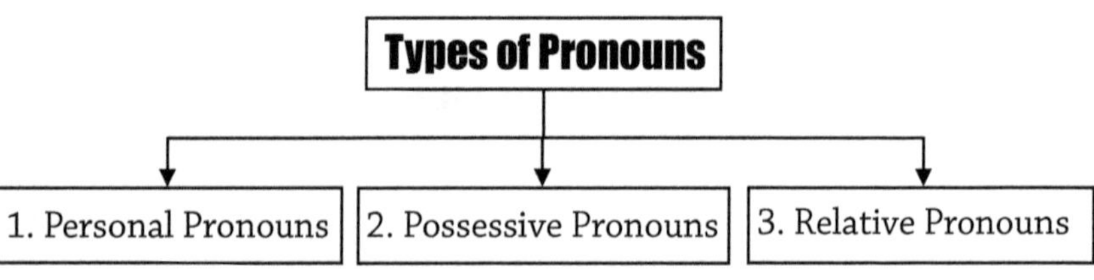

Personal Pronouns: Personal Pronouns are those pronouns which replace noun. They may function as the subject or the object in a sentence. जो शब्द सीधे किसी व्यक्ति या वस्तु को दर्शाता है उसे **Personal Pronoun** कहते हैं।

Examples:- I, We, He, She, and They, are used as a subject whereas Me, Us, Him, Her, and Them, are used as a object.

Personal Pronouns stand for three persons:

(1) The speaker of the sentence:
First person-I, We

(2) The person spoken to:
Second person- You

(3) The person that the speaker is talking about:
Third person he, she, it, they.

वे Pronouns जो तीनों pronouns जैसे First person, Second person तथा Third person में प्रयुक्त होते हैं personal pronouns कहलाते हैं।

Personal pronouns are of two types.

(1) Subjective Personal Pronouns:
(2) Objective Personal pronouns:

1. Subjective personal pronouns: When personal pronouns act as the subject of a sentence it is called subjective personal pronoun. Examples I, You, He, She, It, We and They.

Examples:-

(1) I eat an ice-cream.

(2) He runs very fast.

2. Objective personal pronouns: When personal pronouns act as the object of a sentence it is called objective personal pronoun. Examples Me, You, Him, Her, It, Us and Them.

Examples:-

(1) Please don't sit beside me.

(2) Don't look at them.

(3) We play with them.

We ↓ **Subjective**   them ↓ **Objective**

How to make object pronoun:

I becomes me | You stays at you | They becomes them

We becomes you

He becomes him | She becomes her | It stays it

Note:- Some important points are:

The word 'it' can be a normal subject pronoun as well as an objective pronoun.

Examples:-

(a) It is my favourite book.

(b) I like to read it.

In the first sentence, 'it' functions as a subject pronoun, in the second sentence 'it' functions as an object pronoun. Remember two rules to make objective case.

अगर pronoun का प्रयोग verb के बाद हो तो, objective case का प्रयोग होता है।

Example:- I teach him → object pronoun

अगर pronoun का प्रयोग let, like, between, but, except और किसी भी prepositions के बाद हो, तब Objective case का प्रयोग होता है।

Examples:-

1. There is no problem between her and me.
2. Let me do this.
3. He laughs at me.
4. Everyone ate except me.

Pronouns (Singular) I, You, He, She, It

I am a doctor.
(Pronoun)

He is Mohan.
(Pronoun)

It is a fan.
(Pronoun)

She is Monika.
(Pronoun)

You are an intelligent boy.
(Pronoun)

Let us help you:-

I	We	He	She	It	They	You
Me	Us	Him	Her	–	Them	–

Pronoun (Plural) You, They, We

We are friends.
(Pronoun)

Are you all labourers.
(Pronoun)

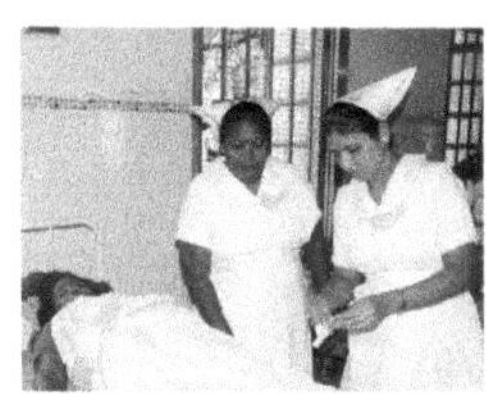

They are nurses.
(Pronoun)

Exercise-1

(A) Underline the correct pronouns in the following sentences.

(a) There is an elephant in the forest. It/He has a long trunk.
(b) Mohan is a doctor. He/I is in hospital.
(c) Monika has a book. She/It is very thick.
(d) This is Manoj. She/He is a man.

(B) Fill in the blanks with a suitable pronoun instead of underlined nouns.

(a) Sanjana is my friend. ________ is a doctor.
(b) Mr. Rohit works in the airport. ________ is a pilot.
(c) The men are constructing buildings. ________ are labourers.
(d) Mohan, Sanjana and I work in school. ________ are teachers.

(C) Fill in the blanks with 'I', She, He, It, You.

1. ________ am a scientist.
2. ________ is a singer.
3. ________ is a doctor.
4. Are ________ blind.

Let us help you:-

Labour मज़दूर	Thick मोटा	Construct इमारत बनाना
Nurse नर्स	Trunk हाथी की सूँड़	Blind अंधा

(D) I am in school.

1. My friends and I are in school ________ are students.	

2. Mohan and Rohit are in the park. ___________ are very good friends.	
3. Who is Mohan? I am Mohan. Are ___________ a teacher? Yes, I am a teacher.	

(E) Fill in the blanks with We, You, They:

1. I am Santosh. He is Ravi.
   ___________ are friends.
2. Mohan, Jennifer and Lata are in school.
   ___________ are students.
3. You are a doctor. Your wife is a teacher.
   ___________ both are working.
4. I cooked food for ___________.
   ___________ can eat it.

Let us help you:-

We	-	used for more than one person.
You	-	used for one person or more than one person.
They	-	used for more than one person or things.

- Some words like all, some, most, none, any can be used as a singular or a plural.
- When two nouns are connected by 'and' then we use 'they'.

Example:- Mohan and Ram are coming here, they are hungry.

Exercise-2

(A) Fill in the blanks using 'I' or 'Me'.

1. ________ am a teacher.
2. You can teach ________.
3. ________ run very fast.
4. Hema will see ________ tomorrow.
5. Give ________ your pen.
6. Will you tell ________ a story?

(B) Tick (✓) the correct words in the brackets.

1. (a) I have a cow. ( )
   (b) Me have a cow. ( )
2. (a) Teacher teaches I mathematics. ( )
   (b) Teacher teaches me mathematics. ( )
3. (a) I am a boy. ( )
   (b) Me am a boy. ( )

'me'
comes after the verb.

Exercise-3

(A) Fill in the blanks using 'us or we'.

1. Father told ____________ many times.
2. ____________ are good friends.
3. Our elders give ____________ knowledge.
4. ____________ went to market.
5. They like ____________.

'us'
comes after the verb.

(B) Tick (✓) the correct words in the brackets.

1. (a) We see movies. ( )
   (b) Us see movies. ( )
2. (a) Us are in Delhi. ( )
   (b) We are in Delhi. ( )
3. (a) We worship the God. ( )
   (b) Us worship the God. ( )

Exercise-4

(A) Fill in the blanks using 'They' or 'Them'.

1. ________ are at home.
2. I am with ________ .
3. Look at ________ .
4. ________ are very nice friends.

(B) Tick (✓) the correct words in the brackets.

1. (a) We see they. ( )
   (b) We see them. ( )
2. (a) Give they books. ( )
   (b) Give them books. ( )
3. (a) They are at home. ( )
   (b) Them are at home. ( )

'them'
comes after the verb.

Exercise-5

(A) Fill in the blanks using the correct words.

1. ________ (He, Him) is in my office.
2. I saw ________ (him, he) yesterday.
3. ________ (she, her) works in the hospital.
4. I like ________ (she, her) too much.

(B) Tick (✓) the correct words in the brackets.

1. (a) I like he. ( )
   (b) I like him. ( )
2. (a) Mohan is her friend. ( )
   (b) Mohan is she friend. ( )
3. (a) Her is a student. ( )
   (b) She is a student. ( )

- **Possessive Pronouns:** A pronoun that shows ownership is called possessive pronoun.

जो शब्द, जिसमें स्वयं के भाव का बोध हो उसे Possessive Pronoun कहते हैं।

	Personal pronouns	Possessive pronouns	
First Person Second Person Third Person	I, We You He, She, It, They	Mine, Ours Yours His, Hers, Theirs	It का possessive pronoun नहीं होता है।

Read the sentences given below:

1. This bike is mine.

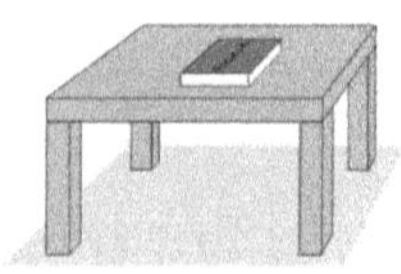

2. That book on the table is yours.

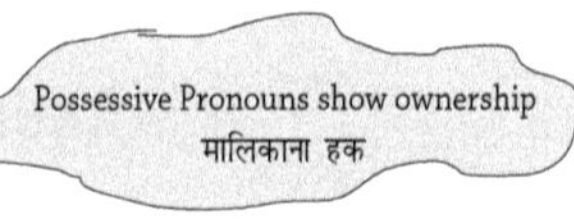

3. This laptop is theirs.

4. This school is ours.

5. That car is his.

6. The mobile on the desk is hers.

Possessive Pronoun stands alone, it comes after noun at the last in the sentences.

Exercise-6

(A) Circle the correct word in the brackets.

(a) This cat is (my, mine).
(b) These bags are (their, theirs).
(c) We have books, these are (ours, theirs).
(d) These pens are (her, hers).
(e) The mobile is (his, their).

(B) Fill in the blanks with suitable possessive pronouns. Mine, Yours, Ours, His, Hers, Theirs.

1. I bought it, therefore, it is _______.
2. I complete my work on time, do you complete _______ ?
3. Show me your gifts, we will show _______ .
4. They like cars, these cars are _______ .
5. I have my book, does she have _______ ?
6. Don't talk about my bike, has your brother brought _______ ?

Difference between Possessive Pronouns and Possessive Adjectives

We often get confused between possessive pronouns and possessive adjectives.

Read the following examples:

(a) This pen is Mohan's.
This pen is his.

(b) This book is Pooja's.
This book is hers.

The pronouns 'His', 'Hers' are the possessive pronouns. Here, we should remember that a possessive pronoun is always used in place of a noun. Moreover, it comes at the last of the sentence.

Now, read the following examples:

(a) This is his pen.
(b) This is her pen.

The pronouns 'his', 'her' are possessive adjectives because a possessive adjective is used before a noun. Possessive adjectives are my, his, her, our, your, their and its.

The words my, his, her, our, your, their and its are possessive adjectives, they come before a noun to show something belongs to someone.

Example: The mobile is new. It's screen is very smooth.
Here, 'Its' is the possessive adjective because 'Its' is used before the noun (screen). We can never use 'its' in place of noun. So it is never used as a possessive pronoun.

Here are more examples of possessive pronouns and possessive adjectives.

Possessive Pronouns	Possessive Adjectives
(a) All the books are his.	(a) This is his mobile.
(b) This purse is hers.	(b) The girl gave her application to the teacher.
(c) These buildings are theirs.	(c) The players have their balls.

 **Let us help you:-**

Possessive Pronouns	mine, ours, yours, his, hers, theirs
Possessive Adjectives	my, our, your, his, her, their, its
His	It is used for both as a possessive pronoun and as a possessive adjective.
Examples:	This is his medal. (Possessive adjective) The medal is his. (Possessive pronoun)

Read the following sentences given below:

1. This is my bike.

2. That is your book on the table.

3. This is their laptop.

4. This is our school.

5. That is his car.

6. Her mobile is on the desk.

7. Dog waves its tail.

Possessive Adjective comes before noun.

Exercise-7

(A) Circle the correct word in the brackets.

(a) This is (my, mine) cat.
(b) These are (their, theirs) bags.
(c) We have books, those are (our, their) books.
(d) These are (her, hers) pens.
(e) Dog waves (its, it's) tail.

(B) Fill in the blanks with suitable possessive adjectives.

my, our, your, his, its, her, their

1. Mohan drives ________ car.
2. I wash ________ clothes on every sunday.
3. ________ world is beautiful.
4. We have a parrot. ________ beak is red.
5. Are you ready? ________ time starts.
6. Monika is doing ________ home work.
7. They have books in ________ bags.

Let us help you:-

Possessive adjective की पहचान यह है कि यह Noun से पहले आता है।

Note:- We use 'own' with possessive adjetives like my, our, his to show forceful expression.

Examples:-

1.	This is my watch.	यह मेरी घड़ी है।
	This is my own watch.	यह मेरी अपनी घड़ी है।
2.	This is my father's car.	यह मेरे पिता की कार है।
	This is my father's own car.	यह मेरे पिता की अपनी कार है।
3.	That is his village.	वह उसका गाँव है।
	That is his own village.	वह उसका अपना गाँव है।

Remember

'Own' का प्रयोग हम ज़ोर डालने के लिए और यह केवल possessive adjectives के साथ ही प्रयोग होगा।

Exercise-8

Translate into English:

1. यह मेरा घर है।

2. यह आपकी गलती है।

3. यह उन लोगों की ज़िम्मेदारी है।

4. यह हमारी गली है।

5. यह उसकी (स्त्री) साईकिल है।

6. यह उसका (पुरूष) मोबाईल है।

7. हम लोग डॉक्टर हैं और यह हॉस्पिटल हमारा है।

8. यह कुर्सी है और उसकी एक टाँग टूटी हुई है।

9. ये उसकी गलतियाँ हैं।

10. ये पेड़ हमारे हैं।

11. मोहन मेरा बेटा है।

12. राज कुमार जी हमारे पड़ोसी हैं।

13. मैं उन लोगों का नेता बनूँगा।

14. पाकिस्तान का दुश्मन हमारा दोस्त है।

15. उसके दोस्त आलसी हैं।

16. मोहन और पूजा और उनके दोस्त खेत में हैं।

17. उसका दोस्त मेरा दोस्त नहीं है।

18. मैं आप का अच्छा साथी बनूँगा।

19. मैं अपने देश में हूँ।

20. हम लोग अपनी कक्षा में हैं।

21. चोर उन लोगों के घर में है।

22. कविता अपने गाँव में है।

23. बच्चे अपने घरों में हैं।

24. लोग अपनी गाड़ियों में हैं।

25. यह मेरी अपनी गलती है।

26. यह हम लोगों की अपनी पुस्तक है।

27. उन लोगों के दोस्त चोर नहीं थे।

28. क्या वह उसका अपना फैसला था?

29. क्या आप लोगों के दिमाग़ तेज़ नहीं हैं?

30. यह गाय मेरी है।

31. यह देश हमारा है।

32. ये मोबाईल उन लोगों के हैं।

33. यह गलती तुम लोगों की है।

34. क्या यह तुम्हारी कलम है और वह पुस्तक उन लोगो की?

35. क्या उसकी पुस्तक हाथ में थी और हमारी पुस्तकें थैले में थीं?

PRONOUN CHART				
Singular	**Subject Pronouns**	**Object Pronouns**	**Possessive Adjectives**	**Possessive Pronouns**
1st Person	I (मैं)	Me (मुझे)	My (मेरा)	Mine (मेरा) वाक्य के अंत में आता है।
2nd Person	You (आप)	You (आप)	Your (आपका)	Yours (आपका) वाक्य के अंत में आता है।
3rd Person	He (वह) पुरूष के लिए She (वह) स्त्री के लिए	Him (उसका) Her (उसकी)	His (उसका) Her (उसकी)	His (उसका) Hers (उसकी) वाक्य के अंत में आता है।
Neutral	It (यह)	It (यह)	Its (इसका)	(Not used)
Plural	**Subject Pronouns**	**Object Pronouns**	**Possessive Adjectives**	**Possessive Pronouns**
1st Person	We (हम)	Us (हमें)	Our (हमारा)	Ours (हमारा) वाक्य के अंत में आता है।
2nd Person	You (आप लोग)	You (आप लोग)	Your (आप लोगों का)	Yours (आपका) वाक्य के अंत में आता है।
3rd Person	They (ये)	Them (उनको)	Their (उनका)	Theirs (उनका) वाक्य के अंत में आता है।

 **Let us help you:-**

1st Person	The first person is the person who speaks. (बात करने वाला)
2nd Person	The second person is the person who listens to. (बात सुनने वाला)
3rd Person	The third person is the person whom we speak about. (जिसकी बात हो)
Possessive Adjectives or Possessive Pronouns	दोनों की Hindi meaning में कोई फर्क नहीं लेकिन possessive adjectives noun से पहले आता है और Possessive Pronouns अंत में आते हैं।
Its or It's	Its: का मतलब Possessive adjective It's: का मतलब It is or It has होता है।

Relative Pronouns

A relative pronoun is used to join one phrase or clause to another phrase or clause. Some of the relative pronouns are, who, whom, whose, that, which, etc.

जब किसी शब्द का प्रयोग किसी Sentence में दो phrases या clauses को जोड़ने के लिए प्रयोग होता है, तो उसे relative pronoun कहते हैं।

Note: Relative Pronoun का प्रयोग sentence में noun/pronoun के बदले होता है ताकि noun/pronoun की (Repeatation) से बचा जा सके और उस noun/pronoun का संबंध अपने से आगे वाले शब्द समूह से जोड़ता है, इसलिए इसे relative pronoun कहते हैं।

Examples:-

1. The boy <u>who</u> is wearing a white shirt is my brother. — वह लड़का जिसने सफेद कमीज़ पहनी है मेरा भाई है।
2. The girl <u>whom</u> you met is my sister. — वह लड़की जिससे आप मिले थे मेरी बहन है।
3. This is the book <u>which</u>/<u>that</u> I bought. — यह किताब है, जो मैंने ख़रीदी थी।
4. This is the mobile <u>which</u> I like the most. — यह वही मोबाईल है, जो मुझे बहुत पसंद है।
5. This is the boy <u>whose</u> friend helped us. — यही वह लड़का है, जिसके दोस्त ने हमारी मदद की।

USE OF WHO, WHOSE, WHOM, THAT, WHOM.

We use the relative pronoun, 'who' to refer to the subject of a sentence whereas whom is used as object of a verb.

Relative Pronouns	**Use**	**Examples**
Who, Whom, जो कौन, किसने, जिसने, Whom, जिसको, जिनको।	These are used for persons. (मनुष्य के लिए)	• We need girls who can clean houses. • The police caught that boy whom I was searching.
Whose, जिसका, जिनका	• It is used for both living things and non-living things in possessive cases. • Whose का प्रयोग जानदार और बेजान दोनों के लिए होता है।	• This is the boy whose father is a very big boxer. • This is the chair whose one leg is broken.

What जो	It is used for things in case of no antecedent. (पूर्वपद)	• I know what you are eating. • I have seen what no one has seen.
Which जो, जिसने/कौन/किसने	• It is used for animals and non-living things. • It is used as relative pronoun in this case preposition comes first. Like, on which, of which. Which का प्रयोग वस्तु या जानवरों के लिए होता है।	• The pen which you gave is very nice. • The cow which I bought from Mohan has died. • I know the day on which guests will come. • The mobile of which screen was broken, has been changed.
That जो, जिसने, जिसे	It is used for both living things and non-living things. सभी के लिए प्रयोग होता है। (जब antecedent (पूर्वपद) आता है। तब हम That का प्रयोग करते हैं।)	• I have seen an expensive mobile that I will purchase in next month. • I have some pens that I bought yesterday.

The relative pronouns are:

Subject	Object	Possessive
Who	Who/Whom	Whose
Which	Which	Whose
That	That	–

Defining Relative Clauses: Defining relative clause gives essential information about someone or something. In other words the part of the sentence that gives information about the person or thing is a defining relative clause. A defining relative clause comes immediately after the noun it describes.

Note: Relative Pronouns (who, whom, whose, which, what, that) to introduce a defining relative clause.

Examples:-

(a) These are interested people who want to purchase our factories.

(b) Mohan helped the girl who wanted to write a book.

(c) The mobile which you gave me on my birthday is very nice.

(d) The pen which is in your hand is mine.

(e) Here, some houses that have been affected.

In Spoken English: Indefiningrelativeclausesweoftenuse 'that' in place of 'who' or 'which'.

Examples:-

(a) These are interested people that want to purchase our factories.

(b) Mohan helped the girl that wanted to write a book.

(c) The mobile that you gave me on my birthday is very nice.

(d) The pen that is in your hand is mine.

Those sentences which are underlined are called relative clauses.

Note: Defining relative clause is also called restrictive sentence where essential information is not required any comma after subject therefore, which and that can be used.

Example:- The book which I purchased yesterday is interesting.

ऊपर दिये गये examples से यह पता चलता है कि who, which के बदले that का भी प्रयोग किया जा सकता है।

Non Defining Relative Clauses: Non defining relative clause gives extra information about someone or something. It is not necessary information about the person or thing.

We use relative pronouns (who, whose, whom, which) to introduce a non-defining relative clauses.

Examples:-

(a) Mohan, who is my friend is working with Salman Khan.

(b) Renu, who has worked in America and Britian is going to start English Speaking Course.

(c) I ate pulses and rice, which I eat daily.

(d) My father met Pooja in the village, which was a really coincidence.

Note: We do not use 'that' to introduce a non-defining clause.

Example:- Amit Gupta, who got three main of the matches in the first series, was the only player to perform well.

Note: Non-defining clause is also called non-restrictive sentence where non-essential information which is not required is given with a comma after the subject therefore, that cannot be used.

Examples:-

(a) The books are very important from the exam point of view, which are boring and thick. (✓)

(b) My father, who is 62, has retired. ऊपर दिये गये examples से यह पता चलता है कि who, which के बदले 'that' का प्रयोग नहीं किया जा सकता है।

The books are very important from the exam point of view, that are boring and thick. (×)

Note: With this kind of relative clause, we use comma.

Important Note: In case of a human being, there is no need to worry about which or that, we should use 'who' always.

Example:- The man who is dancing on the stage is my brother.

Rule 1: Relative Pronouns (who/which/that) का प्रयोग subordinate clause के subject के रूप में होता है।

Examples:-

1. The boy who came is my friend.	जो लड़का आया था, वह मेरा दोस्त है।
2. Mohan was the boy who wanted to help the farmers.	मोहन वह लड़का था, जो किसानों की मदद करना चाहता था।
3. He who works hard succeeds.	जो मेहनत करता है, वह सफल होता है।
4. This is the man who has helped me.	यही आदमी है जिसने मेरी मदद की है।
5. These are the books that I bought yesterday.	यही किताबें हैं, जो मैंने कल खरीदी थी।
6. This is the mobile which Pooja likes.	यही मोबाईल है, जो पूजा पसंद करती है।
7. The thing that is nice sells well.	जो चीज़ अच्छी होती है वह खूब बिकती है।
8. The dogs which are sharp bark at thieves.	जो कुत्तें समझदार होते हैं, चोरों पर भौंकते हैं।
9. Man is the only animal that can talk.	आदमी ही ऐसा जानवर है, जो बात कर सकता है।
10. The bread which you ate was stale.	जो ब्रेड आपने खाई, वो बासी थी।

But, sometimes when Noun or Pronoun is missing in the sentence then we should use 'one who' for singular whereas 'those who' in the case of plural.

Examples:-

1. One who is singing is my friend.	जो गा रहा है, वह मेरा दोस्त है।
2. One who is weeping is hungry.	जो रो रहा है वह भूखा है।
3. Those who are dancing are my friends.	जो नाच रहे हैं, वे मेरे दोस्त हैं।
4. One who reads this book becomes intelligent.	जो वह किताब पढ़ता है वह समझदार हो जाता है।

5. One who works hard gets success. जो मेहनत करता है, वह सफलता प्राप्त करता है।

6. Those who are honest gets respect. जो ईमानदार होते हैं, वे आदर पाते हैं।

Points to Remember

1. Who का प्रयोग मनुष्य के लिए होता है, या हम कह सकते हैं Subject और Object दोनो के लिए होता है।
2. Helping verb/Main verb who के तुरन्त बाद आती है, जो Subject के अनुसार प्रयोग होती है।
3. वाक्य मे "Definite Article" (The) का प्रयोग होता है।
4. Formula: The + person + who + Helping verb/main verb.
   Example: The boy + who + helped me is my friend.
5. Who: जो, जिसने।
6. Which: जो, जिसे, किसने।
7. That: जो, जिसने, जिसे।
8. In the case of restrive sentence या defining relative clause subject, we can use 'that' in place of who or which.

Examples:-

(a) The person who gave me money is my father.
    The person that gave me money is my father.

(b) The car which hit me was red.
    The car that hit me was red.

Which: (जो, जिसने, किसने) Which का प्रयोग मानव जाति को छोड़कर अन्य सभी के लिए होता है Which का प्रयोग जानवर के साथ और इसे non-living things के साथ प्रयोग किया जाता है।

Examples:-

1.	The pen which is in your hand is mine.	जो, पैन आपके हाथ में है, वह मेरा है।
2.	The laptop which you gave me last year is working well.	लैपटॉप जो आपने पिछले साल मुझे दिया था, वह बहुत ठीक काम कर रहा है।
3.	I have seen the movie which you gave me.	मैं वह फिल्म देख चुका हूँ, जो आपने मुझे दी थी।
4.	The shirt which I bought was blue.	जो कमीज़ मैंने खरीदी थी, वह नीली थी।
5.	The book which I purchased yesterday is torn.	वह किताब जो मैंने कल खरीदी थी, वह फटी हुई है।
6.	He asked me which way to go.	उसने मुझसे पूछा कि किस तरफ जाना है।

Points to Remember

For place, time or reason, we use 'where' 'when' or 'why' however, we should use 'which' with prepostion. It becomes more professional.

* The library where we met. (Informal)
* The library at which we met. (Formal)
* The day when we met. (Informal)
* The day on which we met. (Formal)
* The reason why I was at the library. (Informal)
* The reason for which I was at the library. (Formal)

Exercise-9

Translate into English:

1. वह कार जो लाल रंग की है, वह मेरी है।

   ……………………………………………………

2. वह घर जो नदी के उस पार है, वह बहुत सुंदर है।

   ……………………………………………………

3. वह किताब जिसे आप घर में ढूँढ रहे हो, वह मेरे पास है।

____

4. वह पेन जो मेज़ पर पड़ा है, मेरा है।

____

5. जो पर्स मुझे कल मिला, उसका है।

____

6. जो कुत्ता उसने खरीदा, मर गया है।

____

7. क्या मैं वो मोबाईल देख सकता हूँ, जो आपने कल खरीदा था?

____

8. जो मोबाईल मैंने खो दिया था, वह मुझे मिल गया है।

____

9. जो चाकू किचन में है, वह बहुत तेज़ है।

____

10. जो घर आपने खरीदा है, वह बहुत पुराना है।

____

Rule 2: Relative Pronoun 'whom' का प्रयोग subordinate clause में verb के object के रूप में होता है।

Examples:-

1. I have a son whom I love very much.	मेरा एक बेटा है, जिसे मैं बहुत प्यार करता हूँ।
2. The girl whom I love doesn't love me.	जिस लड़की को मैं प्यार करता हूँ वह मुझसे प्यार नहीं करती है।
3. The boy whom you beat was my brother.	जिस लड़के को आपने मारा था, वह मेरा भाई था।
4. The boy whom my father teaches is very intelligent.	वह लड़का जिसको मेरे पिता जी पढ़ाते हैं, वह बहुत अकलमंद है।
5. The man whom the police arrested was a dangerous thief.	वह आदमी जिसको पुलिस ने गिरफ्तार किया, बहुत खतरनाक था।

Whom: (जिसको, जिनको)

Whom का प्रयोग मनुष्य के लिए होता है, जो केवल Object के लिए इस्तेमाल होता है।

The person whom I gave pen is my brother. (✓)
The person who I gave pen is my brother. (×)

Exercise-10

Translate into English:

1. ये ही पुस्तकें हैं, जिन्हें मैंने पुस्तक मेले से पिछले साल खरीदी थीं।
2. यही पत्र है, जो मैंने, लिखा है।
3. जो सोता है, वह खोता है।
4. वह आदमी जो अंग्रेज़ी जानता है, आदर पाता है।
5. जो किताबें सस्ती हैं, वे बहुत बिकती हैं।
6. जो लड़का गिर गया, वह मेरा भाई था।
7. यही पुस्तक है, जो मेरे पिता जी ने रविवार को दी थी।
8. यही गाय है, जो बहुत दूध देती है।
9. जो शिक्षक मन से पढ़ाते हैं, वे आदर पाते हैं।
10. जो छात्र सड़क पर भटकते हैं, वे परीक्षा के समय रोते हैं।
11. जो आलू अभी खेत में हैं, वह स्वादिष्ट हैं।
12. जो आज छात्र है वह कल देश का नागरिक होगा।

13. जो लड़का मेहनत नहीं करता है, वह जीवन में असफल होता है।

____

14. जो मोबाईल उसने मुझे दिया था वह खो गया है।

____

15. जो छात्र तेज़ होते हैं, वे उच्च अंक पाते हैं।

____

Note: That जो इसका, जिसने, जिसे प्रयोग सभी के साथ होता है।

Rule 3: हम 'that' का प्रयोग living or non-living things दोनों के लिए कर सकते हैं। साथ ही कुछ खास शब्द- all, some, only, everything, nothing, the only, any, everyone, none, no, nobody, much, little, the some, the few, the little, any के बाद that का प्रयोग करना चाहिए।

Examples:-

1.	My father has given me everything that I needed.	जो मुझे ज़रूरत थी, वे सब कुछ मेरे पिता जी ने मुझे दिया।
2.	This is the only pen that I bought yesterday.	केवल यही पेन है, जो मैंनें कल खरीदा।
3.	My wife has spent the little money that I gave her.	मेरी पत्नी ने कुछ ही पैसे खर्च किए, जो मैंने उसे दिए थे।
4.	All that succeeds is always not fair.	जो सफल होता है वह हमेशा निष्पक्ष नहीं होता है।
5.	All that glitters is not gold.	हर चीज़ जो चमकती है, सोना नहीं होती।
6.	This is the same dog which I saw yesterday.	यह वही कुत्ता है, जो मैंने कल देखा था।

Points to Remember

1. All + Uncountable Noun के बाद that का प्रयोग होता है, जब All का प्रयोग वस्तु के लिए हो।

Examples:-

(a) All the money that I gave her has been spent.
(b) All that glitters is not gold.

2. **लेकिन जब All का प्रयोग व्यक्ति के लिए होता है, तो इसके बाद who/that का प्रयोग होता है।**

Example:- All who/that are interested to do this work can start now. 'That' is used for singular or plural noun.

Rule 4: Superlative Degree के बाद 'that' का प्रयोग होता है।

Examples:-

1. This is the best that we should do.	यह सब से अच्छा है, जो हमें करना चाहिए।
2. Ravi is the most hard-working boy that I have ever met.	रवि सबसे मेहनती लड़का है, जिससे मैं कभी मिला हूँ।
3. He is the greatest man that I have ever seen.	वो सबसे महान आदमी है, जिसे मैंने कभी देखा है।

Rule 5: The Relative Pronoun 'that' is used after two antecedents, one denoting a person and the other denoting an animal or a thing.

अगर 'and' से जुड़कर दो antecedents का प्रयोग हो, जिनमें से एक मनुष्य तथा दूसरा जानवर या वस्तु हो, तो इसके बाद relative pronoun 'that' का प्रयोग होता है।

Examples:-

1. The man and his dog that I saw yesterday have been kidnapped.	वह आदमी और उसका कुत्ता जिसको मैंने कल देखा था, वे अपहरण हो गए।
2. The girl and her belongings have been affected	लड़की और उसकी चीज़ें प्रभावित की गई हैं।

Rule 6: The Relative Pronoun 'that' is used after the interrogative pronouns- who- what- whose- whom.

Examples:-

1.	What is the reason that he has not come here?	क्या कारण है, जो वह यहाँ नहीं आया है?
2.	What is it that he should not do?	क्या है, जो उसे नहीं करना चाहिए?
3.	What is it that you can't do?	क्या है, जो आप नहीं कर सकते हो?
4.	Whose painting is this that looks beautiful?	यह किसकी चित्रकारी है, जो सुंदर दिखती है?
5.	Who was he that was playing with you?	वह कौन था जो आपके साथ खेल रहा था?

Whose (जिसका, जिसके, जिनको)

(The possessive form of who) is used for persons, animals and also things.

Examples:-

1.	I have a friend whose father is a doctor.	मेरा एक दोस्त है, जिसके पिता एक डॉक्टर हैं।
2.	The shirt whose colour is black looks cute.	शर्ट जिसका रंग काला है, वह सुँदर दिखती है।
3.	The book whose pages are yellow and torn is mine.	वह पुस्तक जिसके काग़ज़ पीले और फटे हुए हैं, वह मेरी है।
4.	The chair whose leg is broken, please bring it.	वह कुर्सी जिसकी एक टाँग टूटी हुई है, कृपया करके इसे लेकर आएँ।

Points to Remember

1. 'Whose' is better than 'of which':

Examples:-

(a) The book whose name is "War and Peace" is very nice.

(b) The book of which name is "War and Peace" is very nice.

2. In case of things we can use 'whose' as well as 'of which' as a possessive case.

Example:-

(a) The truck whose driver jumped out before the accident has completely destroyed.

OR

The truck of which driver jumped out before the accident has completely destroyed.

3. In other words whose = of which, but whose is more formal than of which.

Examples:-

(a) The police were looking for the car whose driver was drunk.

(b) The police were looking for the car of which driver was drunk.

What (जो, जो कुछ)

What refers to things only when it is used without an antecedent.

What का प्रयोग वस्तुओं (non-living) के लिए किया जाता है लेकिन इससे पूर्व कोई भी Antecedent नहीं आता।

Examples:-

1. What cannot be cured must be endured.	जिसका इलाज नहीं हो सकता, उसे सहना ही पड़ता है।
2. What he says is right.	वह जो कहता है, वह सही है।
3. What I have said has been said.	मैंने जो कह दिया है, सो कह दिया है।
4. Life is what we make it.	जीवन वही है, जो हम बनाते हैं।

Note: यदि sentence में Antecedent के प्रयोग होने पर 'what' की जगह 'that'/ 'which' का प्रयोग होता है।

Example:- The disease that/which cannot be cured must be endured.
जिस बिमारी का इलाज नहीं हो सकता, उसे सहना ही पड़ता है।

When and Where (जब, जहाँ)

We can use "When" with time and "Where" with place to make it clear what time or what place we are talking about:

Examples:-

1. The place where I live is very beautiful.	वो नगर जहाँ मैं रहता हूँ वह बहुत सुंदर है।
2. The place where he used to live is so far from here.	वह जगह जहाँ वह रहता था यहाँ से बहुत दूर है।
3. This is the place where he lives.	यही वह जगह है जहाँ वह रहता है।
4. This is the day when we met first time.	यह वही दिन है जब हम पहली बार मिले थे।
5. It was Diwali when I gave this gift to you.	वह दिवाली का दिन था जब मैंने आपको गिफ्ट दिया था।

Let us help you:-

- Relative pronoun should be placed as near as possible to its antecedent.
- Antecedent: वह शब्द noun या pronoun जिसके लिए हम relative pronoun का प्रयोग करते हैं, उसे antecedent कहते हैं।

Examples:-

(a) The girl who won the match in hockey is the daughter of Mr. Raj Verma.

(b) The girl is the daughter of Mr. Raj Verma who won the match in hockey.

In the first example (a) The girl won the match whereas in the second example (b) Mr. Raj Verma won the match, therefore we should use relative pronoun just after its antecedent.

Let's understand with another examples:-

(c) The furniture which we saw last week is made of sandal. (✓)

(d) The furniture is made of sandal which we saw last week. (×)

Here we are talking about sandalwood but not furniture.

(e) Amit Saxena, who is the student of Mr. Raj Kumar, wrote an English Grammar book. (✓)

(f) Amit Saxena is the student of Mr. Raj Kumar who wrote an English Grammar book. (×)

वाक्य (e) में "Amit Saxena" ने English Grammar की book लिखी। जबकि वाक्य (f) में Mr. Raj Kumar ने book लिखी का अर्थ दिया जा रहा है जो बिलकुल गलत है।

Exercise-11

Translate into English:

1. यहाँ कुछ भी नहीं है, जो दर्शकों के ध्यान को आकर्षित कर सके।

____

2. कुछ भी नहीं है, जो मुझे वहाँ जाने से रोक सकता है।

____

3. क्या यह वही घर है, जो आप बता रहे थे?

____

4. मुझे पता था, जो वह उसे देना चाहता था।

____

5. जिसे कहा नहीं जा सकता, कभी नहीं कहना चाहिए।

____

6. जो ठीक नहीं किया जा सकता है, सहन करना पड़ता है।

____

7. वह तुम्हारे बारे में जो कहता है, सही है।

____

8. जिस बिमारी का इलाज नहीं हो सकता, उसे सहना पड़ता है।

9. वह जो कहता है, अच्छा है।

10. ये तो वही कार है, जिसका कल एक्सीडेंट हुआ था।

11. यही वो किताब है, जिसकी हमें ज़रूरत थी।

12. सब जो तुम्हे अपना लगता है, वो तुम्हारा नहीं है।

13. यही एक किताब है, जो मैंने अभी तक नहीं पढ़ी है।

14. यह वही किताब है, जो मुझे सबसे ज़्यादा पंसद है।

15. जो एक बार कहा जाता है, अनसुना नहीं किया जा सकता।

16. वह जो भी चाहेगा, उसे मैं तत्काल दूँगा।

17. वे लोग जो रिक्शा चलाते हैं, बड़े मज़बूत होते हैं।

18. जिस घर में वह रहती है, वह पुराना है।

19. जो तुम्हारे लिए अच्छा है, वह मेरे लिए खराब हो सकता है।

20. वे लड़के जिनके घर स्कूल से दूर होते हैं, वे बस से आते हैं।

Translation helps to form sentences but we will speak English by speaking only.

13 Use of 'This', 'That', 'These', 'Those'

This/That/These/Those का प्रयोग तब किया जाता है, जब किसी व्यक्ति या वस्तु की ओर इशारा करते हुए उसे दर्शाना हो।

Examples:-

That is a big house.	वह एक बड़ा घर है।
This is Rahul.	वह राहुल है।
Those are stars.	वे तारे हैं।
These are pencils.	ये पेंसिले हैं।

ऊपर दिये गए उदाहरणों से यह पता चलता है कि This/That के साथ singular noun और singular verb का प्रयोग किया जाता है। These/Those के साथ plural noun और plural verb का प्रयोग किया जाता है।

This/That/These/Those का प्रयोग Demonstrative Pronoun के रूप में:

This is a hen.
यह एक मुर्गी है।

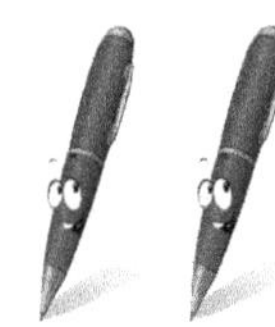

These are two pens.
ये दो कलम हैं।

These are bells.
ये घंटियाँ हैं।

That is a bed.
वह पंलग है।

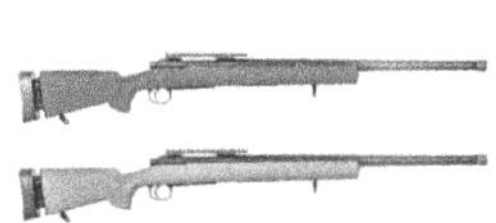

Those are guns.
वे बदूंके हैं।

Those are dogs.
वे कुत्ते हैं।

Let us help you:-

1. **निकट की एक वस्तु के लिए 'this' का प्रयोग होता है, जबकि दो या दो से ज़्यादा वस्तुओं के लिए 'these' का प्रयोग होता है।**

	Singular	Plural
For Nearness:	This (यह)	These (ये)

2. **दूर की एक वस्तु के लिए that का प्रयोग होता है, जबकि दो या दो से ज़्यादा वस्तुओं के लिए 'those' का प्रयोग होता है।**

	Singular	Plural
For Distance:	That (वह)	Those (वे)

Exercise-1

(A) Translate the following into Hindi:

1. This is a cat.
____
2. This is an egg.
____
3. This is a bed.
____
4. This is a dog.
____

(B) Translate the following into English:

1. यह एक कुर्सी है।
____
2. यह एक डिब्बा है।
____
3. यह एक बस है।
____
4. यह एक ग्लास है।
____

Exercise-2

(A) Translate the following into Hindi:

1. That is a cow.

2. That is a window.

3. That is a tree.

4. That is a map.

(B) Translate the following into English:

1. वह एक सूरज है।

2. वह एक पेड़ है।

3. वह एक मुर्गी है।

4. वह एक चम्मच है।

Exercise-3

(A) Translate the following into Hindi:

1. These are eggs.

2. These are goats.

3. These are cats.

4. These are beds.

(B) Translate the following into English:

1. ये कुर्सियाँ हैं।

2. ये गाय हैं।

3. ये किताबें हैं।

4. ये कम्प्यूटर हैं।

Exercise-4

(A) Translate the following into Hindi:

1. Those are stars.

2. Those are trees.

3. Those are bushes.

4. Those are tables.

(B) Translate the following into English:

1. वे किताबें हैं।

2. वे तारे हैं।

3. वे घोड़े हैं।

4. वे गाय हैं।

This, That, These and Those का प्रयोग Demonstrative Adjective के रूप में:

This house is big.
यह एक बड़ा घर है।

These books are good.
ये किताबें अच्छी हैं।

These children are innocent.
ये बच्चे मासूम हैं।

That shop is small.
वह दुकान छोटी है।

Those cows are useful.
वे गाय लाभदायक हैं।

Those rooms are empty.
वे कमरें खाली हैं।

Exercise-5

Translate into English:

1. वह घर गंदा था।

   ____

2. ये फल मीठे हैं।

   ____

3. वह लड़का आई. ए. एस. बनेगा।

   ____

4. यह लड़की तेज़ है।

   ____

5. वह कमरा खाली होगा।

   ____

6. वे घर कमज़ोर हैं।

   ____

7. ये कुर्सियाँ पुरानी नहीं हैं।

____

8. क्या यह पानी गंदा है।

____

9. क्या वे लड़के ईमानदार नहीं थे?

____

10. क्या वे रोटियाँ बासी नहीं होंगी?

____

Differences between Demonstrative Adjective and Demonstrative Pronoun.

Demonstrative Adjective	Demonstrative Pronoun
यदि this, that, these, those के तुरंत बाद noun है, तो ये शब्द Demonstrative Adjective होते हैं। **Examples:-** This girl is good. That pen is new. These shirts are white.	यदि इनके तुरंत बाद verb है तो ये शब्द Demonstrative Pronoun होते हैं। **Examples:-** This is a good girl. This is a new pen. These are white shirts.

Let us help you:-

1. This, These, That, Those are used for demonstration.
2. किसी की ओर इशारा करने के लिए This, These, That, Those का प्रयोग होता है।
3. Demonstrative Words are of two types:

(a) Demonstrative Adjective

Example:- That moon is looking nice.

(b) Demonstrative Pronoun

Example:- That is a nice pen.

Test Paper-1

"Test of your honesty"

पूरा टेस्ट करने के बाद ही अपने 'Answers' को Match करें।

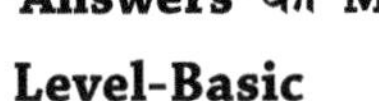

Level-Basic

Subject:	**English Grammar**
Maximum Marks:	**100**
Time Allowed:	**90 Minutes**

Important Instructions:

1. All the answers should be in words.
2. Not to use any number for answers.
3. All the questions are compulsory to attempt.
4. Marks are given before each question.

1. Fill in the blanks with the given words. (3)
(Cricket, Newspaper, Pizza, Amit, Twenty, Red)

(a) His name is ____________ .
(b) He is ____________ years old .
(c) His favourite colour is ____________ .
(d) His hobby is playing ____________ .
(e) His favourite food is ____________ .
(f) He likes to read ____________ .

2. How many letters are in the alphabet? (1)

____

3. How many vowels are in the alphabet and name them? (1)

____________ , ____________

4. Fill in the blanks with vowels (a, e, i, o, u) to complete the words? (3)

(a) L ________ ck
(b) F ________ sh
(c) M ________ t
(d) F ________ n
(e) ________ gg
(f) ________ mbrella

5. Fill in the blanks with consonants to complete the words. (3)

(a) Bu ________

(b) Su ________

(c) ________ en

(d) ________ oon

(e) ________ ar

(f) Ta ________

SCHOOL BUS

6. Write the missing letters between: (3)

(a) : A , ___ , ___ , ___ , E (b) : L , ___ , ___ , ___ , P

7. Arrange the names of these places in alphabetical order. (4)

Red Fort, Taj Mahal, Qutub Minar, Lotus Temple.

(a) ________, (b) ________ , (c) ________ , (d) ________ .

8. Circle the words which start with vowels. (3)

(a) Book, Temple, Sun, Ant

(b) Ostrich, Hen, Tiger, Fish

(c) Computer, Metro, Intelligence, Moon

9. Underline the subjects of the following sentences. (4)

(a) Tina has gone to the market.

(b) Intelligent boys work nicely.

(c) The moon shines in the sky.

(d) My friends gave me a pen.

(e) I saw Mohan's brother.

(f) My brothers and my sisters are not at home.

(g) The foolish boy lost the race.

(h) The daughter of Mr. Gupta is an intelligent girl.

10. Write the types of the following sentences: (10)

(a) Did he go there? ____________
(b) Let me do the work. ____________
(c) Was she at home? ____________
(d) What a view! ____________
(e) They are coming here. ____________
(f) Close the door. ____________
(g) Give me that bottle. ____________
(h) How beautiful the building is! ____________
(i) They are not watching T.V. ____________
(j) She has no time. ____________

11. Re-arrange the following words to make meaningful sentences. (4)

(a) Doctor he a became. ____________
(b) Nicely sang he. ____________
(c) Playing the children were. ____________
(d) Questions difficult very are these. ____________

12. Tick (✓) the sentences and cross (×) those which are not. (3)

(a) It's ten o'clock. ☐
(b) Book on the table. ☐
(c) Dancing chair. ☐
(d) You were watching T.V. ☐
(e) Your T.V. ☐
(f) We have a book. ☐

13. Match the group of words given in the two columns. (5)

Column 1	Column 2
(i) Pintu	(a) goes to office everyday.
(ii) Tinku and Timmu	(b) live in the forest.
(iii) The mother	(c) is an intelligent student.
(iv) Animals	(d) are playing ludo.
(v) My father	(e) cooks food.

(i) ________ (ii) ________ (iii) ________ (iv) ________ (v) ________

14. Circle the nouns in the following sentences. (2)

(a) Father brought broom and milk.
(b) Put the glass of milk on the table.
(c) We get energy from the sun.
(d) She has a beautiful mobile.

15. Circle the words which are not nouns. (3)

(a) Thick, book, copy, school, pen, college.
(b) Child, dog, Khushbu Khan, listen, radio.
(c) Lion, strong, elephant, tea, milk, orange.

16. Tick (✓) the correct words to complete the sentences. (2)

(a) (A few, A little, much) persons were in hospital.
(b) I purchased (many, a little, much) pens from the shop.
(c) She has (few, little, many) milk.
(d) Milkmen add (few, many, much) water in milk.

17. Write the possessive forms of the following. (8)

(a) The house owned by Mohan. ____________________
(b) The stick of his grandfather. ____________________
(c) The shop of Kartar Singh. ____________________
(d) The intelligence of students. ____________________
(e) The salaries of the employees. ____________________
(f) The hostel for women. ____________________
(g) The work of the teachers. ____________________
(h) The office of Mr. Das. ____________________

18. Read the following sentences and tick the correct ones. (3)

(a) Monika is the most tallest girl in the class. ☐
(b) Anil is more stronger than Sunil. ☐
(c) The sun is bigger than the moon. ☐
(d) This book is the most thickest book in the library. ☐
(e) Meena is more beautiful than her elder sister. ☐
(f) This pen is more darker than that pen. ☐

19. Write the comparative and superlative degrees of these adjectives. (8)

	Positive	Comparative	Superlative
(a)	Beautiful	________	________
(b)	Old	________	________
(c)	Far	________	________
(d)	Little	________	________
(e)	Intelligent	________	________
(f)	Black	________	________
(g)	Late	________	________
(h)	Healthy	________	________

20. Fill in the blanks with the correct forms of nouns. (3)

(a) She brought five ________ from the stationary. (books, book)

(b) My sister is putting her ________ in the case. (spectacle, spectacles)

(c) She has two ________ . (child, children)

(d) I have ________ . (scissor, scissors)

(e) My father brought new ________ . (furnitures, furniture)

(f) Five ________ were played between India and Australia. (match, matches)

21. Fill in the blanks with opposite genders of the given nouns. (4)

	Masculine	Feminine
(a)	________	aunt
(b)	________	women
(c)	lion	________
(d)	________	bull
(e)	________	sister
(f)	________	niece
(g)	horse	________
(h)	he	________

22. Write the plural forms of the following singular nouns. (5)

S. No.	Singular	Plural	S. No.	Singular	Plural
(a)	Box	________	(f)	Leaf	________
(b)	Spy	________	(g)	Diagnosis	________
(c)	Woman	________	(h)	Criterion	________
(d)	Child	________	(i)	News	________
(e)	Mouse	________	(j)	Kidney	________

23. Tick the correct words of the following options. (2)

(i) (a) Mr. Rakesh (b) Mr. Rakesh Gupta
(ii) (c) Mrs. Ritu Arora (d) Mrs. Ritu
(iii) (e) Miss Nisha (f) Miss Nisha Verma
(iv) (g) Ms. Alka Kumar (h) Ms. Alka

24. Madam, Sister, Niece, Grandmother, Mother, Waitress, Princess, Fiancee. Write the female words in the female group. (8)

Male group	Female Group
(a) Brother	________
(b) Sir	________
(c) Prince	________
(d) Waiter	________
(e) Nephew	________
(f) Father	________
(g) Grandfather	________
(h) Fiance	________

25. Name the persons who do the things listed below. Choose from the table: (5)

Tailor	Teacher	Nurse	Milkman
Pilot	Washerman	Cobbler	Postman
Carpenter	Barber		

(a) A ________ is a person who brings us milk.

(b) A ________ is a person who flies an aeroplane.

(c) A ________ is a person who makes things from wood.

(d) A ________ is a person who looks after the sick people.

(e) A ________ is a person who makes clothes for us to wear.

(f) A ________ is a person who mends our shoes.

(g) A ________ is a person who teaches us.

(h) A ________ is a person who cuts our hair.

(i) A ________ is a person who brings our letters to our homes.

(j) A ________ is a person who washes our dirty clothes.

बादाम-अखरोट खाने से दिमाग़ तेज़ नहीं होता।

Tests & Exercises से तेज़ होता है।

जब **Environment** से **Hindi** सीख सकते हैं, तो **English** क्यों नहीं?

14 Use of To Be (Use of Am, Is, Are)

'Be' is a very important verb. It has many forms. 'Be' is just like a tree which has many branches.

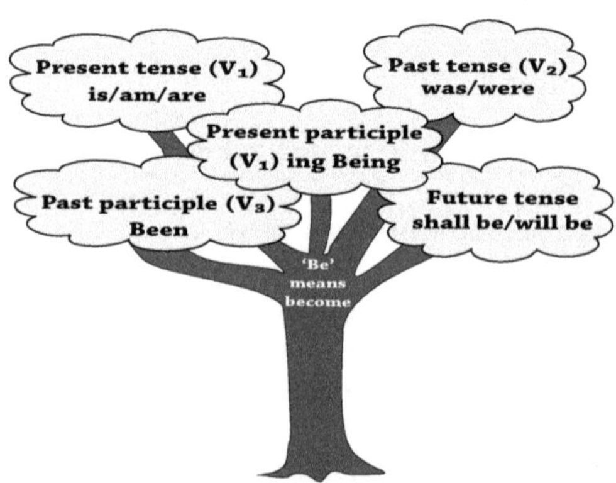

जब हम किसी व्यक्ति या वस्तु के बारे में उसकी **(position/situation)** स्थिति/परिस्थिति, **(state)**, **(condition)** हालत किसी चीज़ के होने या न होने को बताते हैं, तो **'Be'** का प्रयोग होता है।

Use of Am, Is and Are

Read the following sentences.

I am a doctor.
मैं एक डॉक्टर हूँ।

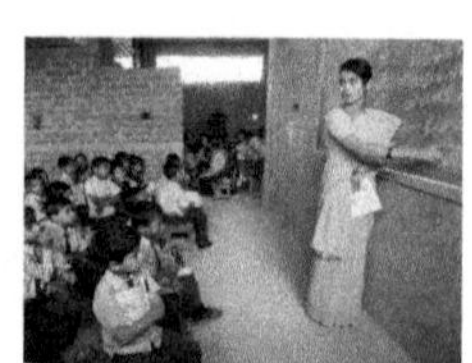

She is a teacher.
वह एक शिक्षक है।

Children are intelligent.
बच्चे समझदार हैं।

The words 'am', 'is' and 'are' are helping verbs. These words tell us about a person, an animal or a thing. We use 'Am' with I (1st person) 'Is' with she (3rd person singular noun) and 'Are' with children (plural noun or more than one person or a thing.)

Let us read some sentences to understand their usage.

Am: It is used only with I

Examples:-

I am Mohan. मैं मोहन हूँ।

I am a doctor. मैं एक डॉक्टर हूँ।

I am Neetu. मैं नीतू हूँ।

I am a teacher. मैं एक शिक्षक हूँ।

Note: Helping verbs helps the main verb to express time and there are thirteen helping verbs.

Is: It is used with He, She, It or Name, Singular Countable Noun and Uncountable Noun.

Examples:-

He is Ram Singh. यह राम सिंह है।

He is a postman. वह एक डाकिया है।

She is Pooja. वह पूजा है।

She is a nurse. वह एक नर्स है।

It is a book. यह एक किताब है।

It is a story book. यह एक कहानी की किताब है।

Amit Singh is a potter. अमित सिंह एक कुम्हार है।

He is a laborious man. वह एक मेहनती आदमी है।

Are: It is used with You, They, We and plural nouns.

Examples:-

Are you Seema?	क्या आप सीमा हो?
Yes! I am Seema.	हाँ! मैं सीमा हूँ।
Are you a doctor?	क्या आप डॉक्टर हो?
Yes! I am a doctor.	हाँ! मैं डॉक्टर हूँ।

They are Ram and Shyam.	वे राम और श्याम हैं।
They are students.	वे छात्र हैं।
We are friends.	हम दोस्त हैं।

Look at the box given below and understand the correct use of am, is and are.

Person	First Person	Second Person	Third Person
Singular	I → am	You → are	He, She, It, Name → is
Plural	We → are	You → are	They → are

जब हम किसी व्यक्ति या चीज़ की presence/existence, quality/disquality, position/condition की बात करते हैं, या फिर किसी चीज़ या व्यक्ति के होने या न होने की बात करते हैं, तो Is/Am/Are का प्रयोग होता है Present Tense में।

कुछ लोग हिंदी से अंग्रेज़ी में (Translation) करते हैं। जब वाक्य के अंत में (ह/हूं/है) आता है या (था/थे/थी) का प्रयोग हो, तो Is/Am/Are या Was/Were प्रयोग होता है लेकिन यह तरीका Spoken English में गलत है 'Completely Fail' है। हम translation कर के English को Fluently नहीं बोल सकते इसलिए English का 'sense' या 'theme' develop करें ताकि लिखने के साथ-साथ बोलना भी आए।

Read the following sentences:-

Pen is on the table.	कलम मेज़ पर रखी हुई है।
Watch is on the wall.	घड़ी दिवार पर टंगी हुई है।
Mobile is upside down.	मोबाइल उल्टा पड़ा हुआ है।
Books are in the bag.	थैले में किताबें रखी हुई हैं।

ऊपर दिये गये उदाहरणों से 'concept clear' करें जैसे 'रखा हुआ', "टंगी हुई", पड़ा हुआ ये सब English को बहुत मुश्किल और कठिन बनाता है। अगर हम केवल 'sense' या 'theme' को समझे किसी भी वाक्य में किसी presence/existence या किसी चीज़ या व्यक्ति का होना या न होना हो, तो Is/Am/Are प्रयोग होता है present tense में। In short में, लगे हुए, चिपके हुए, टंगे हुए जैसे translation base तरिकों में न उलझे, sense को create और develop करें।

Let's understand the formation of sentences.
आओ वाक्यों की रचना करना सीखते हैं।

Affirmative Sentence

Subject + is/am/are + noun/adjective

Examples:-

Geeta is a teacher.	गीता एक शिक्षक है।
Mohan is my friend.	मोहन मेरा दोस्त है।
They are my friends.	वे लोग मेरे दोस्त हैं।
Ram and Balram are brothers.	राम और बलराम भाई हैं।
I am at home.	मैं घर पर हूँ।
It is a book.	यह एक किताब है।
There is water in the tank.	टंकी में पानी है।

Exercise-1

(A) Fill in the blanks with the correct forms of the verbs:

1. I ____________ (am/is/are) a teacher.
2. My father ____________ (am/is/are) a doctor.
3. Our country ____________ (am/is/are) very beautiful.
4. They ____________ (am/are/is) helpful persons.

(B) Fill in the blanks with is, are or am.

Hello, Good Evening. I 1. ____________ Rahul and she 2. ____________ Geeta, she 3. ____________ my neighbour. 4. We ____________ good friends. 5. Sheetal and Anil ____________ also my friends.

Exercise-2

Fill in the blanks with is, am or are.

1. It __________ a watch.
2. The books __________ on the table.
3. She __________ a doctor.
4. I __________ a student.
5. We __________ friends.
6. You __________ my friend.

Exercise-3

Translate into English:

1. मैं अपने वचन का पक्का हूँ।

   ____

2. यह घर किराये के लिए खाली है।

   ____

3. माता जी घर पर हैं।

   ____

4. आज धूप बहुत तेज़ है।

5. वे लोग बहुत मेहनती हैं।

6. मैं समय का पाबंद हूँ।

7. मैं बिमार हूँ।

8. मेरा भाई बहुत दयालु है।

9. हम विद्यार्थी हैं।

10. यह छाता है।

Negative Sentence

Subject + is/am/are + not + noun/adjective

Examples:-

(a) I am not a doctor. मैं एक डॉक्टर नहीं हूँ।
(b) She is not here. यहाँ वह नहीं है।
(c) They are not farmer's sons. वे किसानों के बच्चे नहीं हैं।
(d) Sunita and Sunil are not poor. सुनीता और सुनील गरीब नहीं हैं।

Exercise-4

Translate into English:

1. पूजा मेरी बहन नहीं है।

2. मोहन आपका दुश्मन नहीं है।

3. आप वफादार नौकर नहीं हो।

4. चीनी डिब्बे में नहीं है।

5. मैं तैयार नहीं हूँ।

6. अनील और सुनील दोस्त नहीं हैं।

7. यह ठीक से नहीं रखा हुआ है।

8. वे लोग स्कूल में नहीं हैं।

9. उसकी माँ बीमार नहीं हैं।

10. टंकी में पानी नहीं है।

Interrogative Sentence

is/am/are + subject + noun/adjective

Examples:-

(a) Am I your good friend?	क्या मैं आपका अच्छा दोस्त हूँ?
(b) Is he your father?	क्या वह आपके पिता हैं?
(c) What is it?	यह क्या है?
(d) Where is your mother?	अपकी माँ कहाँ हैं?
(e) Are they doctors?	क्या वे डॉक्टर हैं?

Helping (is/am/are) Subject से पहले आता है interrogative Sentence में:

Exercise-5

Translate into English:

1. क्या फोन उल्टा है?

2. क्या मैं आपके साथ हूँ?

3. क्या रवि अनील के पिता जी हैं?

4. क्या वह लोग चोर हैं?

5. क्या यह ठीक है?

6. क्या बच्चे गली में हैं?

7. क्या कपड़े अलमारी में हैं?

8. क्या आप घर पर हैं?

9. क्या हम ज़िम्मेदार हैं, इस गलती के?

10. क्या मैं गुनेहगार हूँ?

Negative + Interrogative Sentence

is/am/are + subject + not + noun/adjective

Examples:-

(a) Am I not with you? क्या मैं आपके साथ नहीं हूँ?
(b) Are we not honest? क्या हम लोग ईमानदार नहीं हैं?
(c) Is she not your mother? क्या वह आपकी माँ नहीं हैं?

जब वाक्यों में हैरानी या गुस्सा हों सवाल पूछते समय, तो हम पूछते समय मना भी करते हैं, जो आश्चर्य, गुस्से का भाव दर्शाता है।

Exercise-6

Translate into English:

1. क्या मैं एक होशियार विद्यार्थी नहीं हूँ?

2. क्या मैं आपका दोस्त नहीं हूँ?

3. क्या पिता जी गुस्से में नहीं हैं?

4. क्या यह लाल रंग नहीं है?

5. क्या वे लोग घर पर नहीं हैं?

6. क्या हम लोग आपके साथ नहीं हैं?

7. क्या यह गलत नहीं है?

8. क्या वह लड़का शादी-शुदा नहीं है?

9. क्या आप सही नहीं हो?

10. क्या चाय में चीनी नहीं है?

 Let us help you:-

1. Is/am/are are also used for existence/presence or non-existence. (किसी चीज़ का होना या न होना बताते हैं)

2. Am I not की short form aren't I होती है।
   Example: Am I not a teacher?
   Aren't I a teacher?

3. We use 'am' with I. **Example:** I am an honest person.

4. We use 'is' with, he, she, it, name or uncountable nouns in present whereas "was" is used in past.

5. We use 'are' with, you, they, we, or plural countable nouns in present whereas 'were' is used in past.

6. We use 'shall'/'will' with I and we whereas we use 'will' with he, she, it or name.

Use of was, were

जब हम **past tense** में, किसी व्यक्ति या चीज़ की **presence/existence, quality/disquality, position/ condition** की बात करते हैं, या फिर उनके होने या न होने की बात करते हैं, तो **was/were** का प्रयोग करते हैं।

Read the sentences given below.

Abhishek was ill yesterday.
कल अभिषेक बीमार था।

Now, you are thin but you were fat earlier.
अभी, आप पतले हो, पर पहले मोटे थे।

We use 'was' in place of 'is/am' whereas 'were' in place of 'are' when we talk about past action. Some more sentences to understand the usage of 'was' and 'were'.

Was: It is used with I, He, She, It, Name

Examples:-

I was in the temple on last Tuesday.	पिछले मंगलवार को मैं मंदिर में था।
He was a football player.	वह एक फुटबॉल खिलाड़ी था।
She was ill yesterday.	कल वह बीमार थी।
It was a small puppy earlier.	पहले, यह एक छोटा पिल्ला था।
Mr. Jawaharlal Nehru was the first Prime Minister of India.	जवाहरलाल नेहरू, भारत के पहले प्रधानमंत्री थे।

'was' is also used for uncountable nouns of past.
जो चीज़ें गिनी न सकें उस के लिए **past tense** में **was** का प्रयोग होता है।
Example: There was little milk in the jar.

Were: It is used with you, they, we and plural noun.

Examples:-

You were tired yesterday. कल आप थके हुए थे।

Mohit and Babbar were in jail in 2010. 2010 में मोहित और बब्बर जेल में थे।

We were in school in 1974. 1974 में हम लोग स्कूल में थे।

Look at the box given below and understand the correct use of 'was' and 'were'.

Person	First Person	Second Person	Third Person
Singular	I → was	You → were	He, She, It or Name → was
Plural	We → were	You → were	They → were

Let's understand the formation of sentences.
आओ वाक्यों की रचना करना सीखते हैं।

Affirmative Sentence

subject + was/were + noun/adjective

Examples:-

(a) I was at home on last Sunday. रविवार को, मैं घर पर था।

(b) She was with her friend. वह अपने दोस्त के साथ थी।

(c) Sohan was naughty in his childhood. सोहन अपने बचपन में शरारती था।

(d) They were tired yesterday. कल वह थके हुए थे।

Exercise-7

Fill in the blanks with the correct forms of the verbs.

(1) I _________ (was/were) too late yesterday.

(2) You _________ (was/were) in hospital last week.

(3) We _________ (was/were) at home yesterday.

(4) Sheetal _________ (was/were) naughty in her childhood.

Exercise-8

Fill in the blanks with 'was' or 'were'.

Once upon a time, there 1. ________ a king who 2. ________ very kind. Three members 3. ________ in his family. His son 4. ________ cruel. One day the king punished his son and sent him in jail, therefore the king 5. ________ sad in his whole life.

Exercise-9

Translate into English:

1. मोहन बहुत बड़ा झूठा था।

____

2. पिता जी बहुत दुःखी थे।

____

3. मैं तैयार था।

____

4. गरीब बेघर थे।

____

5. पजांब के किसान गरीब थे।

____

6. अभिजीत और रवि दोस्त थे।

____

7. मेरे चाचा डॉक्टर थे।

____

8. बच्चे खुश थे।

____

9. पूजा कल गैर-हाजिर थी।

____

10. उसकी बहन अमीर थी।

____

Negative Sentence

subject + was/were + not + noun/adjective

Examples:-

(a) We were not at home. हम घर पर नहीं थे।

(b) Sunita and Ram were not ready. सुनीता और राम तैयार नहीं थे।

(c) I was not aware. मैं बेखबर था।

(d) You were not in the party yesterday. कल आप पार्टी में नहीं थे।

Exercise-10

Translate ino English:

1. क्लास गंदी नहीं थी।

____

2. वह लाल रंग नहीं था।

____

3. मैं तैयार नहीं था।

____

4. इमारत छोटी नहीं थी।

____

5. किताब उल्टी नहीं थी।

____

6. मैं किसी का दुश्मन नहीं था।

____

7. उसका बचपन कठिन नहीं था।

____

8. बच्चे घर पर नहीं थे।

____

9. लोग वहाँ नहीं थे।

____

10. वह ठीक नहीं था।

____

Interrogative Sentence

was/were + subject + noun/adjective

Examples:-

(a) Were we right that time? क्या हम ठीक थे उस समय?

(b) Was Mohan with Sunita yesterday? क्या कल मोहन, सुनीता के साथ था?

(c) Was it right? क्या वह ठीक था?

(d) Were they neighbours in childhood? क्या वे लोग बचपन में पड़ोसी थे?

Exercise-11

Translate into English:

1. क्या संतोष वकील थी?

2. क्या आप दिल्ली में थे?

3. क्या पुस्तक अच्छी थी?

4. क्या हम लोग सही थे?

5. क्या स्कूल खाली था?

6. क्या आपकी साड़ी पर कुछ लगा हुआ था?

7. क्या कपड़े गीले थे?

8. क्या बच्चे समझदार थे?

9. क्या केले मीठे थे?

10. क्या दरवाज़े पर कोई था?

Negative + Interrogative Sentence

was/were + subject + not + noun/adjective

Examples:-

(a) Were we not with you? क्या हम आपके साथ नहीं थे?

(b) Was I not a good doctor? क्या मैं अच्छा डॉक्टर नहीं था?

(c) Were they not on the way? क्या वे लोग रास्ते में नहीं थे?

(d) Was she not right? क्या वह सही नहीं थी?

Exercise-12

Translate into English:

1. क्या प्राचीन काल में लोग अशिक्षित नहीं थे?

____

2. क्या स्त्रियाँ स्वस्थ नहीं थी?

____

3. क्या वह राजा अत्याचारी नहीं था?

____

4. क्या पुरानी फिल्में अच्छी नहीं थी?

____

5. क्या मैं आप के साथ नहीं था?

____

6. क्या फोन उल्टा नहीं था?

____

7. क्या कपड़े गीले नहीं थे?

____

8. क्या हम लोग सही नहीं थे?

____

9. क्या इस किताब में पचास पन्ने नहीं थे?

____

10. क्या किताब पर कवर नहीं चढ़ा हुआ था?

____

"Use of Shall be/Will be"

जब हम **Future Tense** में, किसी व्यक्ति या चीज़ की **presence/existence, quality/disquality, position condition** की बात करते हैं, तो **shall be/ will be** का प्रयोग करते हैं।

We use 'shall be' and 'will be' to show the presence/existence of something or some body in future.

Read the following sentences.

She will be a doctor.
वह डॉक्टर बनेगी।

We shall be hungry in the late evening.
देर रात तक, हमलोग भूखें होंगे।

Some more sentences to understand the usage of "shall be" and "will be".

Shall be: It is used with I and We:

Examples:-

When I grow up, I shall be a teacher.
मैं बड़ा होकर मैं एक शिक्षक बनूँगा।

We shall be married after ten years.
दस साल बाद हम शादी-शुदा होंगे।

Will be: It is used with You, He, She, It or Name.

You speak well, you will be a leader.
आप अच्छा बोलते हो, आप नेता बनोगे।

He/She will be a journalist in future.
वह भविष्य में पत्रकार बनेगी/बनेगा।

Look at this table:

Person	First Person	Second Person	Third Person
First Person	I → shall be	You → will be	He, She, It or Name → will be
Second Person	We → shall be	You → will be	They → will be

Let's understand the formation of sentences.
आओ वाक्यों की रचना करना सीखते हैं।

Affirmative Sentence

subject + shall be/will be + noun/object

Examples:-

(a) He will be educated. वह शिक्षित बनेगा।

(b) I shall be a doctor. मैं एक डॉक्टर बनूँगा।

(c) We shall be there. हम लोग वहाँ रहेंगे।

(d) They will be busy. वे लोग व्यस्त रहेंगे।

In case of commitment or determination of any situation in future we use 'shall'.

ध्यान दें: जब हम वाक्य में भाव से प्रतिज्ञा या दृढ़, निश्चय का बोध हो तब हम कुछ shall be or will be का प्रयोग करते हैं।

Examples:-

(a) Mohan shall be a doctor. मोहन अवश्य डॉक्टर बनेगा।

(b) You shall be a leader. आप अवश्य नेता बनोगे।

(c) We will be advocates. हमलोग अवश्य वकील बनेंगे।

(d) They shall be busy. वे लोग अवश्य व्यस्त रहेंगे।

(e) I will be present there. मैं अवश्य वहाँ उपस्थित रहूँगा।

Exercise-13

Translate into English:

1. यह बच्चा कुछ बनेगा।
2. ये दोनों शादी के बाद खुश रहेंगे।
3. कल मैं अवश्य रहूँगा एक बजे वहाँ पर।
4. यह ठीक रहेगा।

Negative Sentence

subject + shall/ will + not + be + noun/object

Examples:-

(a) He will not be a scientist. वह वैज्ञानिक नहीं बनेगा।
(b) Ram will not be a teacher. राम शिक्षक नहीं बनेगा।
(c) I shall not be busy. मैं व्यस्त नहीं रहुँगा।
(d) We will not be guilty. हम लोग अवश्य दोषी नहीं होंगे।

Exericse-14

Translate into English:

1. हम लोग अवश्य दुःखी नहीं होंगे।
2. यह ठीक नहीं रहेगा।
3. कल मैं घर पर नहीं रहूँगा।
4. वह लोग व्यस्त नहीं रहेंगे।

Interrogative Sentence

shall/will + subject + be + noun/object

Examples:-

(a) Will you be absent tomorrow? क्या कल आप अनुपस्थित रहेंगें?

(b) Shall we be unhappy? क्या हम लोग दु:खी रहेंगें?

(c) Shall Mohan be a doctor? क्या मोहन अवश्य डॉक्टर बनेगा?

(d) Will they be hungry? क्या वे लोग भूखे रहेंगें?

Exercise-15

Translate into English:

1. क्या आप मेरे साथ अवश्य रहोगे?

____

2. क्या वे लोग डॉक्टर बनेंगे?

____

3. क्या कल स्कूल खुले रहेंगे?

____

4. क्या चाय एक मिनट में गर्म हो जाएगी?

____

Negative + Interrogative Sentence

shall/will + subject + not + be + noun/object

Examples:-

(a) Will Renu not be an actress? क्या रेनू एक अभिनेत्री नहीं बनेगी?

(b) Shall I not be a journalist? क्या मैं एक पत्रकार नहीं बनूँगा?

(c) Will you not be honest? क्या आप ईमानदार नहीं रहेंगे?

(d) Shall we not be ready by 6 pm? क्या हम लोग 6 बजे तैयार नहीं होंगे?

Exercise-16

Translate into English:

1. क्या वह लड़का डॉक्टर नहीं बनेगा?

 ____

2. क्या कल आप घर पर नहीं रहोगे?

 ____

3. क्या हम लोग तैयार नहीं रहेंगे?

 ____

4. क्या बिलकुल वह दु:खी नहीं रहेगा?

 ____

Let us help you:-

7. In case of determination or commitment we use 'shall be' or 'will be' oppositely.
   (a) We will be there definitely.
   (b) Mohan shall be silent 100%.
8. In modern English mostly 'will' is commonly used with all subjects.

Speaking English is an art.

It depends on environment.
No Environment , No English

15 Use of To Have (Use of Has, Have and Had)

'Have' is a very important verb. It has many forms. 'Have' is just like a house which has many rooms.

Look at this picture and understand its forms.

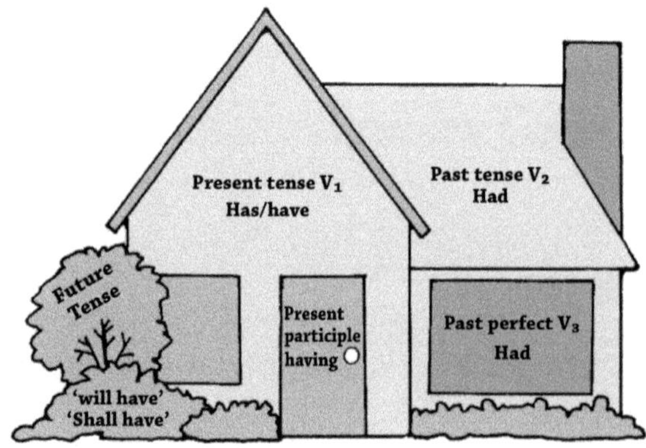

किसी व्यक्ति या वस्तु के पास किसी अन्य व्यक्ति पर या वस्तु का अधिकार (possession) मालिकाना हक (ownership) हो, तो has/have का प्रयोग किया जाता है।

Use of 'has' and 'have'

Read the following sentences.

Mohan has a book. मोहन के पास एक किताब है।
She has a bag. उसके पास एक थैला है।
I have a new ball. मेरे पास एक नई गेंद है
They have umbrellas. उन लोगो के पास छाते हैं।

We use 'has' when we talk about one person, place, thing, animal or he, she, it, name but when we talk about more than one person, place, thing, animal or I, you, they then we use 'have'.

Some more sentences to understand the usage of 'Has' and 'Have'.

Has: It is used with, He, She, It or Name

Examples:-

He is Sunil. He has a suitcase in his hand.
वह सुनील है और उसके हाथ में सूटकेस है।

She is Tina. She has a doll in her hand.
वह टीना है, उसके हाथ में एक गुड़िया है।

It is a cow, it has four legs.
यह गाय है, इसके चार पैर होते हैं।

Ravi is a carpenter, he has an axe.
रवि बढ़ई है, उसके पास एक कुल्हाड़ी है।

Have: It is used with I, You, They, We and plural noun.

Examples:-

I am Mukesh. I have a car.
मैं मुकेश हूँ मेरे पास एक कार है।

You are a goldsmith. You have gold.
आप एक सुनार हो, आपके पास सोना है।

They are students. They have books.
वे लोग विद्यार्थी हैं, उनके पास किताबें हैं।

We are doctors. We have responsibilities.
हम लोग डॉक्टर हैं हम पर ज़िम्मेदारियाँ हैं।

Sunita and Geeta are friends.
They have balloons.
सुनीता और गीता दोस्त हैं। उनके पास गुब्बारे हैं।

Look at the box given below and understand the correct use of has and have.

Person	First Person	Second Person	Third Person
Singular	I → have	You → have	He, She, It or Name → have
Plural	We → have	You → have	They → have

Let's understand the formation of sentences.
आओ वाक्यों की रचना करना सीखते हैं।

Affirmative Sentence

subject + has/have + object/noun

Examples:-

I have a pen.	मेरे पास एक कलम है।
She has an apple.	उसके पास एक सेब है।
You have a book.	आप के पास एक किताब है।
He has a computer.	उसके पास एक कम्प्यूटर है।
This is a chair, it has four legs.	यह कुर्सी है, इसके चार टांगे हैं।
Mohit has a beautiful car.	मोहित के पास एक सुंदर कार है।

Exercise-1

(A) Fill in the blanks with the correct verb in the bracket.

1. I ________ a new book. (has/have)
2. He ________ one cousin. (has/have)
3. We ________ five books. (has/have)
4. The train ________ many facilities. (has/have)
5. The car ________ four wheels. (has/have)
6. Children ________ beautiful pens. (has/have)
7. They ________ a good time together. (has/have)
8. You ________ a lovely smile. (has/have)

(B) Fill in the blanks with has or have:

This is my school. It 1. ________ a big bell. It 2. ________ many classrooms. All classes 3. ________ chairs, doors and white boards. Teachers 4. ________ attendence registers. We 5. ________ school i-cards. It 6. ________ a big park.

(C) Tick (✓) the correct words.

1. The girls (has/have) new dolls.
2. I (has/have) a new pencil.
3. These houses (has/have) no windows.
4. Mohit (has/have) a ring.

(D) Translate into English:

1. मेरे पास कम्प्यूटर है।

____

2. तुम्हारे पास एक किताब है।

____

3. उस के पास दो नौकर हैं।

____

4. उस के पास एक बड़ा मकान है।

____

5. बकरी की दो सींगे होती हैं।

____

6. उस के पास एक तोता है।

____

7. मोहन के पास एक गाय है।

____

8. आप लोगो के पास बहुत काम है।

____

9. हर एक के पास किताबें हैं।

____

10. बच्चों के पास बहुत सारे खिलौने हैं।

____

Negative Sentence

(A) subject + has/have + not + noun/object

Examples:-

(a) She has no water. उसके पास पानी नहीं है।

(b) He has no old pen. उसके पास पुरानी कलम नहीं है।

(c) I have no pen. मेरे पास कलम नहीं है।

(d) They have not a sack of rice. उन लोगो के पास चावल का कट्टा नहीं है।

(B) subject + does/do + not + have + noun/object

Examples:-

(a) She does not have water. उसके पास पानी नहीं है।

(b) He does not have an old pen. उसके पास एक पुरानी कलम नहीं है।

(c) I do not have a pen. मेरे पास कलम नहीं है।

(d) They do not have a sack of rice. उन लोगों के पास चावल का कट्टा नहीं है।

In modern English, we use this formula (subject + does/do + not + have + noun/object). In case of this formula, we use only 'have' for making a negative sentence.

ध्यान दें: जब हम negative sentence बनाने के लिए इस formula (subject + does/do + not + have + noun/object) का प्रयोग करते हैं, तो negative sentence की रचना करना बहुत सरल or आसान हो जाता है। यहाँ एक बात स्पष्ट रूप से बताना चाहूँगा कि इस नियम में केवल 'Have' का ही प्रयोग होता है।

How to use 'do'/'does'

'Do' और 'Does' का प्रयोग सीखना यहाँ बहुत जरूरी है, अब हम 'Do/Does का प्रयोग एक टेबल द्वारा सीखेंगे।

Look at the table given below and understand the correct use of 'Do' and 'Does'.

Person	First Person	Second Person	Third Person
Singular Plural	I → do We → do	You → do You → do	He, She, It or Name → does They → do

जब हम Negative Sentence की रचना करते हैं,
तो 'not' शब्द का प्रयोग do or does के बाद लगाते हैं।

Examples:-

(a) She does not have money. उसके पास पैसे नहीं हैं।
(b) They do not have enough time. उन लोगों के पास ज़्यादा समय नहीं है।

अगर हम Negative Sentence की रचना इस नियम
(subject + has/have + not + noun/object) से करें।

Examples:-

(a) She has no money. उसके पास पैसे नहीं हैं।
(b) They have not enough time. उन लोगों के पास ज़्यादा समय नहीं है।

ऊपर दिये गये उदाहरणों से यह बात स्पष्ट होती है कि वाक्य का अर्थ नहीं बदलता, तो आप लोग दोनों में से कोई एक नियम का प्रयोग कर सकते हैं या दोनों नियमों का भी।

Exercise-2

(A) Fill in the blanks with the correct verb from the brackets.

1. Children ________ time for playing. [does not have or do not have]
2. He ________ water. [has no or have no]
3. I ________ a new idea. [does not have or do not have]
4. We ________ two pens in the geometry box. [have no or have not]
5. Mohan ________ money. [does not have or do not have]
6. I ________ an old computer. [have no or have not]
7. Tinku ________ manners. [has no or have no]
8. Mohan and Pinki ________ cooler in their home. [has no or have no]

(B) Tick (✓) the correct word from the brackets.

1. These factories (does not have/do not have) strict rules and regulations.
2. I (has no/have no) idea.
3. She (has no/has not) two new dolls.
4. Rahul and his friends (has no/have no) homework.
5. We (does not have/do not have) toys.
6. They (does not have/do not have) mobiles.
7. Rinku (has no/has not) five books in his bag.
8. You (has no/have no) internet in your mobiles.
9. This fan (has no/have not) big blades.
10. This is a nice AC. It (has no/has not) a big wire in it.

(C) Translate into English:

1. तुम्हारे पास एक चावल का बोरा नहीं है।

   ____

2. मोहन के पास पुरानी चाबी नहीं है।

   ____

3. उन लोगों के पास पुरानी कार नहीं है।

   ____

4. उसके पास पानी नहीं है।

   ____

5. मेरे पास समय नहीं है।

   ____

6. अनिल के पास बहुत दौलत नहीं है।

   ____

7. इसका कोई उपाय नहीं है।

   ____

8. बच्चों के पास एक भी खिलौना नहीं है।

   ____

9. हम लोगों के पास आत्मविश्वास नहीं है।

   ____

10. किसानों के पास ज़्यादा साधन नहीं हैं।

   ____

Interrogative Sentence

(A) has/have + subject + noun/object

Examples:-

(a) Has he a pen? — क्या उसके पास एक कलम है?
(b) Have you a house? — क्या आपके पास घर है?
(c) Have I a suitcase? — क्या मेरे पास सूटकेस है?
(d) Has the lady a saree? — क्या महिला के पास साड़ी है?

(B) does + do + subject + have + noun/object

Examples:-

(a) Does he have a pen? — क्या उसके पास एक कलम है?
(b) Do you have a house? — क्या आपके पास घर है?
(c) Do I have a suitcase? — क्या मेरे पास सूटकेस है?
(d) Does the lady have a saree? — क्या महिला के पास साड़ी है?

'Do'/'Does' comes before the subject to make an interrogative sentence and we use only 'have' in the sentence.

ध्यान दें: जब हम 'Do' या 'Does' का प्रयोग करते हैं 'to have' के Case में, तो 'Has' का प्रयोग केवल 'Affirmative Sentence' में ही प्रयोग होता है। दूसरे शब्दों में Negative और Interrogative वाक्यों में 'Have' का प्रयोग होता है।

Exercise-3

Translate into English:

1. क्या आपको कमर दर्द है?

____

2. क्या उसके पास घर है?

____

3. क्या आपके पास कलम है?

____

4. क्या नौकरों के पास आज़ादी है?

____

5. क्या हम लोगों के पास समय है?

____

6. क्या उन लोगों के पास चावल का बोरा है?

____

7. क्या उन बच्चों के पास मिठाइयाँ हैं?

____

8. क्या गरीबों के पास खाना है?

____

9. क्या बिमला के पास झाड़ू है?

____

10. क्या उसके पिता के पास स्कूटर है?

____

Negative - Interrogative Sentence

(A) have/has + subject + not + noun/object

Examples:-

Have I no house?	क्या मेरे पास घर नहीं है?
Has he no water?	क्या इसके पास पानी नहीं है?
Has Sunita not an umbrella?	क्या सुनीता के पास छाता नहीं है?
Have we not two cars?	क्या हम लोगों के पास दो कार नहीं हैं?

(B) does/do + subject + not + have + noun/object

Examples:-

Do I not have house?	क्या मेरे पास घर नहीं है?
Does he not have water?	क्या उसके पास पानी नहीं है?
Does Sunita not have an umbrella?	क्या सुनीता के पास छाता नहीं है?
Do we not have two cars?	क्या हमारे पास दो कार नहीं हैं?

ध्यान दो: **negative-interrogative sentence** में **subject** के बाद **not** आता है और **Do** या **Does** से वाक्य शुरू करते हैं, फिर **have** और अंत में **noun** आता है।

Example: Do + they + not + have + time?

क्या उन लोगो के पास समय नहीं है?

Exercise-4

Translate into English:

1. क्या आपके पास समय नहीं है?

____

2. क्या उन लोगों के पास थैला नहीं है?

____

3. क्या गधों के सींग नहीं होते?

____

4. क्या उन लोगों के पास ज़्यादा शहद नहीं है?

____

5. क्या हम लोगों के पास कम्प्यूटर नहीं है?

____

6. क्या पिता जी के पास चाबी नहीं है?

____

7. क्या शिवम के पास चाय की पत्तियाँ नहीं हैं?

____

8. क्या तुम्हें न्यौता नहीं है?

____

9. क्या उस आदमी के पास कम्बल नहीं है?

____

10. क्या उस लड़के के पास दिल नहीं है?

____

Read loudly:

I don't have time.	मेरे पास समय नहीं है।
She doesn't have time.	उसके पास समय नहीं है।
They don't have time.	उन लोगों के पास समय नहीं है।
You don't have time.	आपके पास समय नहीं है।
Don't I have time?	क्या मेरे पास समय नहीं है?
Doesn't she have time?	क्या उसके पास समय नहीं है?
Don't they have time?	क्या उन लोगों के पास समय नहीं है?
Don't you have time?	क्या आपके पास समय नहीं है?

ऊपर दिये गये वाक्यों में 'doesn't/don't का प्रयोग किया गया है, जो 'Spoken English' को "fluently and attractively" बोलने में बहुत अहम भूमिका निभाते हैं।

Let us help you:-

1. We use 'no' before noun or adjective but 'not' is used before the noun after which article or (any, two, much, many, enough) is given.
2. With (I, you, they, we) we use 'have' whereas, (he, she, it, name) we use 'has'.
3. In modern English, we use 'do' or 'does' in negative sentences and interrogative sentences.

   (a) She does not have pen. (b) Does she have pen?

   (c) They do not have time. (d) Do they have time?
4. With he, she, it, name, we use 'does' whereas I, you, they, we, we use 'do'.
5. 'Not' comes after 'do'/'does' in negative sentences.
6. 'Do'/'Does' comes before subject in interrogative sentences.
7. 'Had' is the past form of has/have.

8. In negative + interrogative doesn't/don't + subject + have + noun/ adjective.

   Examples: (a) Doesn't Ritu have time? (b) Don't they have money?

9. The above formula which is point number '8' is mostly used in our modern English.

10. We use 'shall have' with I and We whereas He, She, It or Name we use 'will have'.

11. In modern English, 'will' is most commonly used in our daily life.

'Use of Had'

जब हम **past tense** में किसी व्यक्ति या वस्तु के पास किसी अन्य व्यक्ति या वस्तु का अधिकार **(possession)** या मालिकाना हक **(ownership)** होने की बात करते हैं, तब **'Had'** का प्रयोग किया जाता है।

Read the sentences given below:

Mohit was in the army. मोहित फौज में था।
Mohit had a gun. मोहित के पास एक बंदूक थी।

Deepali was good at study. दीपाली पढ़ाई में अच्छी थी।
Deepali had many books. दीपाली के पास बहुत सारी किताबें थीं।

She had fever yesterday. उसे बुखार था।

Had is used in place of have or has when we talk about past tense. We use 'had' with I, We, You, He, She, It, They or Name.

Let's understand the formation of sentences.
आओ वाक्यों की रचना करना सीखते हैं।

Affirmative Sentence

subject + had + noun/object

Examples:-

I had a car.	मेरे पास एक कार थी।
We had an information.	हमारे पास एक खबर थी।
He had a cow.	उसके पास एक गाय थी।
They had enough money.	उन लोगों के पास पर्याप्त पैसा था।

Exercise-5

(A) Fill in the blanks with 'Had', 'Has' or 'Have'.

1. An elephant _________ four legs and one tail.
2. They _________ a beautiful kitchen in their house.
3. He _________ a brown paper to cover over his copy.
4. I _________ an apple in my hand.
5. Mohit _________ fever the day before yesterday.
6. A month _________ four weeks.
7. When my mother was young, she _________ big dreams.
8. Last year we _________ a new year party at my home.
9. When I was small, I _________ a bicycle.
10. You _________ a last chance now.

(B) Choose the correct words from the brackets.

1. He (has/had) a brand new mobile but I lost it yesterday.
2. Manohar (has/have) an innocent face.
3. We (have/had) a small get together last night.
4. She (has/had) many relatives when she was in Gujarat.
5. An elephant (has/have) big teeth.
6. I (have/had) a test last friday.
7. My mother (has/have) long hair.
8. Renu (has/had) anger yesterday.

(C) Translate into English:

1. उन लोगों को आशा थी।

2. मुझे विश्वास था।

3. हमारे पास एक पुस्तक थी।

4. उसके पास बहुत समय था।

5. राम और मनोहर के पास साईकल थी।

Negative Sentence

(A) subject + had + not + noun/object

Examples:-

They had no house.	उन लोगों के पास घर नहीं था।
You had no old mobile.	आपके पास पुराना मोबाइल नहीं था।
I had not a pen.	मेरे पास एक कलम नहीं थी।
Seema had not three rooms in her house.	सीमा के घर में तीन कमरे नहीं थे।

(B) subject + did + not + have + noun/object

Examples:-

They did not have a house.	उन लोगों के पास घर नहीं था।
You did not have an old mobile.	आपके पास पुराना मोबाइल नहीं था।
I did not have a pen.	मेरे पास एक कलम नहीं थी।
Seema did not have three rooms in her house.	सीमा के घर में तीन कमरे नहीं थे।

In modern English, we use this formula [subject + did + not + have + noun/object]. We use "did not have" just after subject to make a negative sentence.

ध्यान दें: जब हम इस नियम के अनुसार 'did' का प्रयोग करते हैं, तो 'did' के बाद 'have' का प्रयोग होता है। 'had' का प्रयोग affirmative sentence में होता है।

उदाहरणों से Concept Clear करें

I had no water or I did not have water.	मेरे पास पानी नहीं था।
They had not little water or They did not have little water.	उन लोगों के पास थोड़ा-सा भी पानी नहीं था।

यहाँ यह बात स्पष्ट होती है, वाक्यों के अर्थ में कोई फर्क नहीं है, लेकिन जब हम 'did' का प्रयोग करते हैं तो नियम के अनुसार 'have' का प्रयोग होता है।

Exercise-6

Translate into English:

1. मेरे पास पानी नहीं था।

____

2. उसके पास कॉपी नहीं थी।

____

3. मोहन के पास एक बोतल नहीं थी।

____

4. हमें शांति नहीं थी।

____

5. पहले तुम्हें तहज़ीब नहीं थी।

____

6. उन लोगों के पास ज़्यादा किताबें नहीं थीं।

____

Interrogative Sentence

(A) had + subject + noun/objcet

Examples:-

Had I money? क्या मेरे पास पैसे थे?
Had they two sons? क्या उन लोगों के दो बेटे थे?
Had she a cooker? क्या उसके पास कूकर था?

(B) did + subject + have + noun/object

Examples:-

Did I have money? क्या मेरे पास पैसे थे?
Did they have two sons? क्या उन लोगों के दो बेटे थे?
Did she have a cooker? क्या उसके पास कूकर था?

'Did' comes before subject to make interrogative sentence and we use 'have' in the sentences.

ध्यान दें: जब हम 'did' का प्रयोग करते हैं, तो negative sentence and interrogative sentence में 'have' का प्रयोग होता है।

Exercise-7

Translate into English:

1. क्या उन लोगों के पास इत्र था?

____

2. क्या मनोहर के पास नई कार थी?

____

3. क्या किसानों की अपनी भूमि थी?

____

4. क्या उसके पास सिंगार-मेज़ थी शादी से पहले?

____

5. क्या उसके पिता जी की सम्पति थी?

____

6. क्या तब मेरे पास मौका था?

---

7. क्या आपके पास मच्छरदानी थी?

---

8. क्या हम लोगों के पास आत्मसंयम था?

---

9. क्या पूजा के पास नई फ्रॉक थी?

---

10. क्या मम्मी के पास दो छुट्टियाँ थीं?

Negative + Interrogative Sentence

(A) had + subject + not + noun/object

Had we no time?	क्या हमारे पास समय नहीं था?
Had I no water?	क्या मेरे पास पानी नहीं था?
Had he not three bags?	क्या उसके पास तीन थैले नहीं थे?
Had Sunita not a big house?	क्या सुनीता के पास बड़ा घर नहीं था?
Had they not an umbrella?	क्या उन लोगों के पास छाता नहीं था?

(B) did + subject + not + have + noun/object

Did we not have time?	क्या हमारे पास समय नहीं था?
Did I not have answer?	क्या मेरे पास जवाब नहीं था?
Did he not have three bags?	क्या उसके पास तीन थैले नहीं थे?
Did Sunita not have a big house?	क्या सुनीता के पास बड़ा घर नहीं था?
Did they not have an umbrella?	क्या उन लोगों के पास छाता नहीं था?

ध्यान दें: negative + interrogative sentence में 'did' को subject से पहले रखते हैं और 'not' को subject के बाद, उसके बाद have और अंत में noun आता है।

Example:- Did + we + not + have + time?

क्या हम लोगों के पास समय नहीं था?

Exercise-8

Translate into English:

1. क्या मम्मी के पास दुपट्टा नहीं था?

2. क्या पिताजी के सिर पर पगड़ी नहीं थी?

3. क्या हम में आत्म-विश्वास नहीं था?

4. क्या आप में क्षमता नहीं थी?

5. क्या 1969 में भूटान में सुविधा नहीं थी?

6. क्या तुम्हें ज़रूरत नहीं थी?

7. क्या उन लोगों पर क़र्ज़ था?

8. क्या सन् 1947 के बाद हिंदुस्तानियों के पास रज़ाईयाँ नहीं थीं?

9. क्या सीमा के पास चप्पल नहीं थी?

10. क्या आपको कोई ज्ञान नहीं था?

Read loudly:

I didn't have money.	मेरे पास पैसे नहीं थे।
She didn't have money.	उसके पास पैसे नहीं थे।
They didn't have money.	उन लोगो के पास पैसे नहीं थे।
You didn't have money.	आपके पास पैसे नहीं थे।
Didn't I have money?	क्या मेरे पास पैसे नहीं थे?
Didn't she have money?	क्या उसके पास पैसे नहीं थे?
Didn't they have money?	क्या उन लोगों के पास पैसे नहीं थे?
Didn't you have money?	क्या आपके पास पैसे नहीं थे?

ध्यान दें: ऊपर दिये गये वाक्यों में 'didn't शब्द का प्रयोग किया गया है, जो 'Spoken English' को 'fluently' and 'attractively' बोलने में बहुत अहम भूमिका निभाता है।

Let us help you:-

1. We use 'did' with all subjects.
2. We use 'had' in affirmative sentence.
3. We use 'didn't' which is a contraction of 'did not'.
4. We use 'have' in case of using 'did' with negative and interrogative sentences.

Use of Shall have/Will have

जब हम Future Tense में किसी व्यक्ति या वस्तु के पास किसी अन्य व्यक्ति या वस्तु का अधिकार (possession) या मालिकाना हक (ownership) होने की बात करते हैं, तो 'shall have'/'will have' का प्रयोग किया जाता है।

Read the sentences given below:

I shall have a car on my birthday.
मेरे जन्मदिन पर, मुझे कार मिलेगी।

We shall have a new computer.
हमारे पास नया कम्प्यूटर होगा।

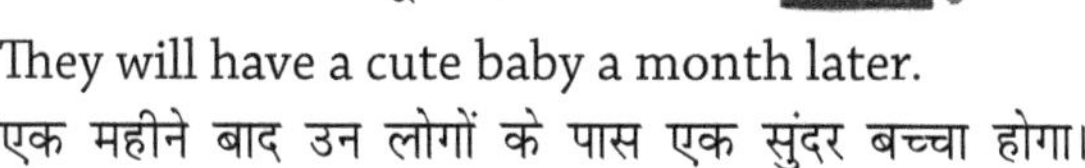

They will have a cute baby a month later.
एक महीने बाद उन लोगों के पास एक सुंदर बच्चा होगा।

You will have a good job within a month. Don't worry.
फिक्र मत करो! आपके पास एक महीने के अंदर एक अच्छी नौकरी होगी।

When we talk about someone keeps something or someone in future then we use 'shall have' and 'will have'.

Some sentences to understand the usage of shall have/will have.

Shall have: It is used with I and We

Examples:-

I shall have a new shirt in the evening. — शाम को मुझे नई कमीज़ मिलेगी।
We shall receive good news today. — आज हमें अच्छी खबर मिलेगी।

Will have: It is used with You, They, He, She, It or Name

You will have success soon. — आपको सफलता जल्दी मिलेगी।

He/She will have share in the property. — उसे संपत्ति में हिस्सा मिलेगा।

ध्यान दें: 'shall' और 'will' के साथ हमेशा 'have' प्रयोग होता है।

Look at the box given below and understand the correct use of shall have and will have.

Person	First Person	Second Person	Third Person
Singular	I → shall have	You → will have	He, She, It or Name → will have
Plural	We → shall have	You → will have	They → will have

Affirmative Sentence

subject + shall have/will have + noun/object

Examples:-

Mohan will have a new car in this year.	इस साल मोहन के पास नई कार होगी।
I shall have peace now.	अब मुझे शांति मिलेगी।
They will have a cute child.	उन लोगों को सुंदर बच्चा होगा।
We shall have a new rule.	हमें एक नया कानून मिलेगा।
Farmers will have many resources.	किसानों के पास बहुत सारे साधन होंगे।

Exercise-9

Translate into English:

1. मेरे पास नया कम्प्यूटर होगा अगले हफ्ते।

 ____

2. हम लोगो के पास आज़ादी होगी।

 ____

3. लड़कियों को सरकारी नौकरियाँ मिलेगी।

 ____

4. बेरोज़गारों को रोज़गार मिलेगा।

 ____

5. मेरे पास अच्छा मौका होगा।

 ____

Negative Sentence

subject + shall not have/will not have + noun/object

Examples:-

Mohan and Sohan will not have time.
मोहन और सोहन के पास समय नहीं होगा।

I shall not have new shoes by Sunday.
रविवार तक मेरे पास नये जूते नहीं होंगे।

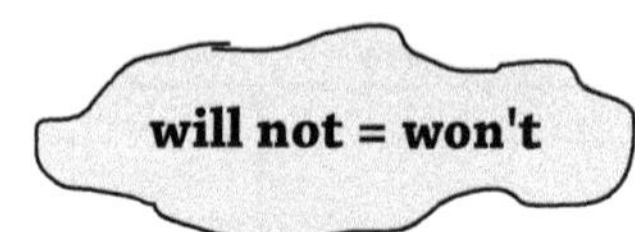

They will not have anything.
उन लोगों के पास कुछ नहीं होगा।

Hospitals will not have medicines.
अस्पतालों में दवाइयाँ नहीं होंगी।

We shall not have our property.
हमारी अपनी संपति नहीं होगी।

Exercise-10

1. मोहन को इस महीने कोई सुविधा नहीं मिलेगी।

___

2. हमें रोज़गार नहीं मिलेगा।

___

3. किसानों को सरकारी सहायता नहीं मिलेगी।

___

4. मेरे पास दवाईयाँ नहीं होंगी।

___

5. मार्केट में ज़्यादा मुकाबला नहीं होगा।

___

Interrogative Sentence

will/shall + subject + have + noun/object

Examples:-

Will you have an answer?	क्या आपके पास जवाब होगा?
Shall we have something?	क्या हम लोगों के पास कुछ होगा?
Will she/he have a job?	क्या उसको नौकरी मिलेगी?
Shall I have fame?	क्या मुझे प्रसिद्धि मिलेगी?
Will animals have freedom?	क्या जानवरों को आज़ादी मिलेगी?

Exercise-11

Translate into English:

1. क्या कल तुम्हारे पास पुस्तक होगी?

____

2. क्या मेरी ज़िदंगी में मुझे कामयाबी मिलेगी?

____

3. क्या इसमें बुरे तत्व होंगे?

____

4. क्या हम लोगों को शांति मिलेगी?

____

5. क्या उसके पास नया घर होगा?

____

Negative + interrogative sentence

will + shall + subject + not + have + noun/object

Examples:-

Will ladies not have their rights?
क्या महिलाओं के पास अपने अधिकार नहीं होंगे?

Shall I not have money?
क्या मुझे पैसे नहीं मिलेंगे?

Will Indians not have source of employment?
क्या भारतीयों को रोज़गार के साधन नहीं मिलेंगे?

Shall we not have anything?
क्या हम लोगों को कुछ नहीं मिलेगा?

Will she/he not have tea?
क्या उसे चाय नहीं मिलेगी?

Exercise-12

Translate into English:

1. क्या मुझे वेतन नहीं मिलेगा?

   ____

2. क्या हम लोगों को मतदान करने का अधिकार नहीं मिलेगा?

   ____

3. क्या उसे नौकरी नहीं मिलेगी?

   ____

4. क्या उन लोगों को कम्प्यूटर नहीं मिलेगा?

   ____

5. क्या अनाथ बच्चों को शिक्षा नहीं मिलेगी?

   ____

Let us help you:-

1. In modern and 'Spoken English' we use "won't" which is a short form of 'will not'.

(a) She won't have time.

(b) He won't have money.

(c) Won't you have food?

(d) Won't they have mobiles?

2. Won't is used in negative and negative + interrogative sentences of future.

Test Paper-2

"Test of your honesty"

पूरा टेस्ट करने के बाद ही अपने **'Answers'** को **Match** करें।

Level-Basic

Subject: **English Grammar**
Maximum Marks: **100**
Time Allowed: **90 Minutes**

Important Instructions:

1. This test is divided into two sections.
   Section A: Multiple Choice Questions:
   Section B: Translation Based Questions:
2. All the answers should be in words.
3. Not to use any number for answers.
4. All the questions are compulsory to attempt.
5. Marks are given before each question.
6. Each question carries 1/2/0.5 Marks.

Multiple Choice Questions: **(83 marks)**

Section-A

1. Using 'a', 'an', the or [0] nothing to complete the text. (5)

Chandan lives in (a) ________ Canada. It is (b) ________ big country. Ottawa is (c) ________ capital of (d) ________ Canada. It is (e) ________ expensive city but Chandan has (f) ________ good job. He is (g) ________ doctor. He has (h) ________ big house near (i) ________ Mattawa River (j) ________ house is very expensive but is beautiful.

2. Write 'a' or 'an' next to the job. (4)

(a) ________ electrician (e) ________ shop assistant
(b) ________ dentist (f) ________ university professor
(c) ________ secretary (g) ________ teacher
(d) ________ housewife (h) ________ engineer

3. Fill in the blanks with 'a', 'an', 'the' or (0) nothing. (8.5)

(a) ______ Ottawa is (b) ______ big city. (c) ______ centre is very busy. (d) ______ Byward is (e) ______ good place for shopping. You can also go to (f) ______ departmental store like 'Walmart'. (g) It ______ very famous shop. If (h) ______ weather is nice, you can go in (i) ______ boat on (j) ______ Matta river or walk in (k) ______ park. It is difficult to find (l) ______ cheap hotel in (m) ______ Ottawa but if you are rich you can stay in (n) ______ expensive hotel like the west in Ottawa. with (o) ______ restaurant on (p) ______ top floor of (q) ______ hotel.

4. Complete the form with 'is' or 'are'. (2)

(a) This class ______ beautiful.

(b) That book ______ mine.

(c) These ______ students in the class.

(d) Those ______ bags on the desks.

5. Make negative statements and questions from the following: (5)

(a) This is your book. ______________, ______________?

(b) That is your daughter. ______________, ______________?

(c) These are his keys. ______________, ______________?

(d) Those are our bikes. ______________, ______________?

(e) This house is Mohan's. ______________, ______________?

6. Choose the subject or object pronoun and write them: (4)

Mohan: (a) Rohan wants I/me to accompany he/him. What do you think?
Mohan's father: (b) Do you like he/him?
Mohan: (c) I like he/him.
Mohan's father: (d) Well he/him seldom visits we/us.
Rohan: (e) Mohan's father doesn't want him to accompany I/me.
Sohan: (f) Oh! I don't like he/him. He/his is boring.
Rohan: (g) He/his is very good and I like he/him.
Sohan: (h) Maybe but there are many good friends look at they/them.

Ans 6: (a) ____________ (b) ____________
(c) ____________ (d) ____________
(e) ____________ (f) ____________
(g) ____________ (h) ____________

7. Underline the mistakes and correct those in the following sentences: (4)

(a) Sohan thinks Mohan is boring. He doesn't like he.
(b) Sohan likes other boys. He thinks them are friendly.
(c) I like you, do you like I?
(d) Rohan likes Mohan and him thinks he is friendly.

Ans 7: (a) ____________ (b) ____________
(c) ____________ (d) ____________

8. Make the sentences by using who/which/that. (4)

(a) A wife is a woman. She has a husband.

____

(b) A mechanic is a person. He/she repairs cars.

____

(c) A car is a vehicle. It has four wheels.

____

(d) Camel is the ship of desert. It runs very fast.

____

9. Choose the correct relative pronouns of the following sentences. (3)

(a) I don't like people (which/who) are unfriendly.

____

(b) Volvo is a bus (that/who) goes fast.

____

(c) I know someone (that/which) can play the DJ well.

____

(d) I like the children (who/which) are not rigid.

____

(e) Do you know the girl (which/that) lives upstairs?

____

(f) He likes films (which/who) have suspense.

____

10. Complete the sentences with who/that/which. (3)

(a) An elephant is an animal _________ has a long trunk.

(b) A laptop is an electronic device _________ business people use.

(c) Flowers are something _________ make the environment beautiful.

(d) A suitcase is a bag _________ people take on a holiday.

(e) Do you know the children _________ live in Shahdara.

(f) The man _________ works in this factory is not friendly.

11. Join the two sentences using which/who/that. (2.5)

(a) Chips are potatoes. They are cut and fried.

____

(b) Cricket is a game. It has eleven players.

____

(c) A wife is a person. He/She does all the domestic work.

____

(d) Coffee is a drink. People drink in winter.

____

(e) A cobbler is a person. He makes shoes.

____

12. Fill in the blanks with I, She, He, You, It, We, They. (3.5)

(a) _________ am a boy.

(b) Tina is in school. _________ is a teacher.

(c) Rohit is in hospital. _________ is a doctor.

(d) _________ is a bus.

(e) Rohit and Renu are neighbours. _________ are friends.

(f) Mohit, Ahmed and I are in school. _________ are students.

(g) I am with you because _________ are my brother.

13. Replace the possessive adjectives and noun with the possessive pronouns. **(5)**

Possessive adjectives	Possessive pronouns
(a) Is this your mobile?	________________
(b) 'No', I think it is his mobile.	________________
(c) This is not my bag.	________________
(d) Is it your bag?	________________
(e) 'No', it is not my bag.	________________
(f) Perhaps it is their bag.	________________
(g) Have you got our bags?	________________
(h) 'No', I have got my bag.	________________
(i) This is not my mobile.	________________
(j) 'No', it is their mobile.	________________

14. Choose the correct word. **(4)**

(a) Could you help me carry (my/mine/computer?

(b) Is that (her/hers)?

(c) Their/Theirs houses are beautiful.

(d) This is not (mine/my) mobile. (my/mine) is a black one.

(e) Are there (your/yours) pens on the table?

(f) That is (your/yours).

(g) Has she got (her/hers) pen?

(h) She thought (her/hers) pen is missing.

Ans 14: (a) ________ (b) ________ (c) ________
(d) ________ (e) ________ (f) ________
(g) ________ (h) ________

15. Fill in the blanks with is, am, are to complete the following sentences. (5)

(a) Karishma ________ busy with her freinds.

(b) The stars ________ in the sky.

(c) The moon ________ smaller than the sun.

(d) There ________ sugar in the jar.

(e) I ________ happy with my toys.

(f) The children ________ fond of pizza.

(g) There ________ fresh grapes in the fruit basket

(h) There ________ no water in the tank.

(i) I ________ not Mohan's best friend.

(j) Mohan and his brother ________ not real brothers.

16. Fill in the blanks with 'is' , 'am' or 'are'. (3.5)

I (a) ________ Mukul. Sonia (b) ________ my friend. Tina (c) ________ also my friend. Both the girls (d) ________ my cousins, Sonia (e) ________ a student in six standard and Tina (f) ________ in seventh standard. We (g) ________ very close to one another.

17. Fill in the blanks with the correct verbs in the brackets. (2.5)

(a) We ________ (has/have) two books.

(b) A week ________ (has/have) seven days.

(c) She ________ (has/have) one brother.

(d) This company ________ (has/have) many employees.

(e) You ________ (has/have) two beautiful cars.

18. Fill in the blanks with the words given in the box. **(2.5)**

(am, are, is, has, have)

(a) I ________ Sonu. He ________ one brother, Tanuj.

(b) Tina ________ our little sister.

(c) She ________ fever.

(d) We ________ sad for her.

(e) We ________ love for each other.

19. Tick the right words to complete the sentences. **(3.5)**

(a) India is/are a very beautiful country.

(b) We are/is Indians.

(c) This/These are my parents.

(d) The people is/are happy.

(e) The men is/are at home.

(f) Are you a doctor? No, I am/I'm not.

(g) What's that/those?

Ans 19. (a) ________ (b) ________ (c) ________ (d) ________
(e) ________ (f) ________ (g) ________

20. Tick the correct words in the brakets. **(2)**

(a) Mohan (am, was) in the street.

(b) My father and mother (was, were) in Delhi last week.

(c) The Taj Mahal (is, was) in Agra.

(d) The Red Fort and Qutub Minar (are, were) in Delhi.

Ans 20. (a) ________ (b) ________ (c) ________ (d) ________

21. Tick the correct words in the brackets. **(2.5)**

(a) My father (has/had) long hair.

(b) He (has/had) fever last month.

(c) I (has/had) many toys when I was in Delhi.

(d) An elephant (has/had) a long trunk.

(e) They (have/had) exams in the last month.

Ans 21. (a) ________ (b) ________ (c) ________

(d) ________ (e) ________

22. Choose the correct words from the brackets. **(2)**

(a) They (were/was) in the street in the evening.

(b) Chetak (was/were) a very popular scooter in 1990.

(c) Mohan and Sohan (was/were) friends.

(d) She (was/were) with her friends.

Ans 22. (a) ________ (b) ________ (c) ________ (d) ________

23. Fill in the blanks 'was' or 'were'. **(2)**

(a) The girls ________ late.

(b) The film ________ very funny.

(c) The children of that class ________ naughty.

(d) The farmer ________ very hardworking.

....

Section-B

Translation Based Questions. **(7)**

24. Translate into English.

(a) अंधेरा है।

(b) वह नेक है।

(c) धरती गोल है।

(d) हिंदुस्तान एक महान देश है।

(e) मोहन और सोहन लाचार नहीं हैं।

(f) क्या पंडित जवाहरलाल नेहरू भारत के पहले प्रधानमंत्री थे।

(g) वे लोग व्यापारी नहीं हैं।

(h) क्या रोहन का भविष्य उज्जवल नहीं है?

(i) क्या हम लोग ईमानदार नहीं हैं?

(j) क्या आसमान में तारें नहीं हैं?

(k) क्या पिताजी घर पर थे?

(l) क्या आपका स्कूल लक्ष्मी नगर में नहीं था?

(m) क्या पानी ज़मीन पर नहीं पड़ा हुआ था?

(n) क्या कविता मोहन के साथ नहीं थी?

25. Translate into English. (10)

(a) कल मैं वहाँ रहूँगा।

____

(b) रविवार को वह व्यस्त नहीं रहेगा।

____

(c) क्या वह तैयार नहीं होगी?

____

(d) हम लोगो के पास समय है?

____

(e) उसके पास पुस्तक है।

____

(f) मोहन के पास पुरानी कार नहीं है।

____

(g) उन लोगो के पास पांच कलम नहीं हैं।

____

(h) मेरे पास कम्प्यूटर नहीं है।

____

(i) मेरे पास पांच कम्प्यूटर नहीं हैं।

____

(j) क्या मोहन के पास मोबाईल नहीं है?

____

(k) क्या उन लोगों के पास एक घर नहीं है?

____

(l) उस लड़की के पास एक कार थी।

____

(m) रोहन के पास पैसे नहीं थे।

____

(n) क्या मोहन के पिताजी के पास तीन गाय नहीं थीं।

____

(o) क्या आपके पास जवाब नहीं था?

____

(p) क्या उस आदमी के पास अच्छे कपड़े नहीं थे?

____

(q) क्या एक साल बाद आपके पास चार कारें नहीं होंगी?

____

(r) क्या इस साल के बाद बेरोज़गार के पास रोज़गार नहीं होगा?

____

(s) क्या शिक्षित लोगों के पास नौकरियाँ नहीं होंगी?

____

(t) क्या दिवाली के दिन आपके पास समय नहीं होगा?

____

Grammar is an engine of English.

Vocabulary is the petrol of English.

Then English will run.

No Environment No English.

16 Introductory

When a sentence has no subject, then 'It' and 'There' are used as introductory words.

जब वाक्य में Subject नहीं होता, तो 'It' और There को Subject के स्थान पर Subject की तरह प्रयोग किया जाता है। जब 'It' और There को Subject की तरह प्रयोग किया जात है, तो 'It' और 'There' शब्दों का कोई विशेष अर्थ नहीं होता।

Use of It

(i) Non-living things:

'It' का प्रयोग निर्जीव वस्तुओं के लिए होता है।

Examples:-

It is an umbrella.	यह एक छाता है।
It is an aeroplane.	यह एक जहाज़ है।
It is a well.	यह एक कुआँ है।

(ii) Time, weather, situation and seasons:

Examples:-

It is 7 o'clock.	सात बज रहे हैं।
It is noon.	दोपहर का समय है।
It is Monday.	सोमवार का दिन है।
It was 2010.	सन् 2010 का वर्ष था।
It was winter.	सर्दियों के दिन थें।
It is in bad condition.	यह खराब हालत में है।
It is raining.	बारिश हो रही है।
It is thundering.	बिजली गरज रही है।
It snows in January.	जनवरी में बर्फ गिरती है।
Is it 5 o'clock.	क्या पाँच बज रहे हैं?

(iii) Eunuch (हिजड़ा), birds/animals, very small child.

Examples:-

It is an eunuch at the door.	दरवाज़े पर हिजड़ा खड़ा है।
It is a cute child.	बहुत सुन्दर बच्चा है।
Who is it a boy or a girl?	क्या यह लड़का है या लड़की?
It is a fox.	यह लोमड़ी है।
It is a parrot.	यह तोता है।

Exercise-1

Translate the following into English:

1. यह एक खिड़की है।

___

2. यह एक किताब है।

___

3. यह एक कुत्ता है।

___

4. चार बजे हैं।

___

5. बर्फ गिर रही है।

___

6. दरवाज़े पर एक हिजड़ा था।

___

7. आज शनिवार का दिन है।

___

8. वह बहुत सुन्दर बच्चा था।

___

(iv) Emphasizing and stressing on human being or doer in the sentence.

यदि वाक्य में ज़ोर दिया (Stress) हुआ हो, तो वाक्य मे दो clauses बनते हैं, जिनमें पहले (Clause) में It से शुरू होता है, और दूसरा Clause Who, Which, What या That से शुरू होता है।

Examples:-

Was it you?	क्या वह आप ही थे?
Is it they?	क्या वे लोग ही हैं?
Is it I?	क्या वह मैं ही हूँ?
It is I who am with you.	वह मै ही हूँ जो आपके साथ हूँ?
It is Ashok who helped you.	अशोक ने ही आप की मदद की थी
It is the girl who wrote this book.	यही लड़की है, जिसने यह किताब लिखी
Who was it at the door?	दरवाज़े पर कौन था?
Who was it that stole my book?	कौन था जिसने मेरी किताब चुराई थी?

Let us help you:-

We should use singular verb with 'It' in first clause, then subject after subject we put relative pronouns(who, which, that, what) finally, we add verb as per antecedent.

Look at this formula:-
It is/was + subject + who/which/that + verb

(Note: Noun/Pronoun को महत्त्व देने के लिए)

Examples:-

It is I who am with you.	मैं ही हूँ जो आप के साथ हूँ।
It is you who are laborious here.	वह आप ही हो, जो यहाँ मेहनती हो।
Who was it that broke my phone?	कौन था, जिसने मेरा मोबाइल तोड़ा?
It is we who have done it.	हमने ही किया है यह।
It is the child who called everyone.	यही बच्चा है, जिसने सबको बुलाया।
It is I who am responsible for this.	मैं ही हूँ, जो इसके लिए ज़िम्मेदार हूँ।

Exercise-2

Translate into English:

1. उससे बात करना मूर्खता है।
2. किसानों को शिक्षित करना ज़रूरी है।
3. उस लड़की से पीछा छुड़ाना मुश्किल है।
4. भूखों को खाना खिलाना अच्छी बात है।
5. अंग्रेजी सीखना बहुत आसान है।
6. यह तो शर्म की बात है।
7. संभव है।
8. कोई फर्क नहीं पड़ता है।
9. फर्क पड़ता है।
10. दो मिनट लगेंगे।
11. दो मिनट लगते हैं।
12. मुझे मिले हुए दो दिन हो गये हैं।
13. माँ को देखे हुए कई साल हो गये हैं।

14. हमें अच्छा खाना खाये हुए पाँच साल हो गये हैं।

15. मुझे यह किताब पढ़ते हुए दो साल हो गये हैं।

16. दस दिन हो गये।

17. कई साल हो चुके थे।

18. मोहन को देखे दस साल हो गये।

19. शाम हो गई है।

20. लॉकडाऊन में बाहर निकले कई दिन हो गये।

21. मैंने ही आप को उकसाया था?

22. क्या यही लड़की है, जिसने आपके भाई को शादी का प्रस्ताव दिया?

23. क्या यही लड़का नही है, जिसने हमारी कार पर टक्कर मारी थी?

24. वहाँ केवल मैं ही नहीं गया था।

25. चावल सिर्फ हमने ही नही खाये थे।

26. उसी ने इस मोबाइल को नहीं खरीदा है।

27. क्या उसी ने इस किताब को पढ़ा है?

28. क्या तुमनें ही इस फिल्म को नहीं देखा है?

29. उस लड़की ने ही शिकायत की है।

30. किसी स्त्री ही ने इस आदमी को मारा है।

31. क्या पिता ही ने हमारी मदद नहीं की थी।

32. कौन है जिसने इस परेशानी का हल निकाला है?

Introductory 'There'

The word 'there' is used for existence or non-existence of something or somebody.

वाक्य में किसी व्यक्ति या वस्तु के होने या न होने की बात हो, किसी चीज़ के अस्तित्व की बात हो, तो 'There' का प्रयोग किया जाता है। 'There' के बाद जो subject हो उसके अनुसार singular verb या plural verb का प्रयोग होता है।

There is a fan on the table.	मेज़ पर एक पंखा है।
There is a chair here.	यहाँ एक कुर्सी है।
There are many trees in the garden.	बगीचें में बहुत पेड़ हैं।
There are two pens in my bag.	मेरे थैले मे दो कलम हैं।

ऊपर दिये गए वाक्यो से यह पता चलता है कि Introductory 'there' का प्रयोग किसी व्यक्ति/वस्तु की अस्तित्व/मौजूदगी या स्थिति को दर्शाने के लिए किया जाता है।

(i) One thing/person, uncountable thing refer to "there is".

किसी single person, एक वस्तु या जिन वस्तुओं को गिना न जा सके, तो 'there is' का प्रयोग होता है।

Examples:-

There is a girl. एक लड़की है।
There was a doctor. एक डॉक्टर था।
There will be a game here. यहाँ एक खेल होगा।
There is less sugar in the tea. चाय में चीनी कम है।
There is water in the tank. टंकी में पानी है।
There is a college in my village. मेरे गाँव में एक कॉलेज है।

(ii) Plural nouns/two or more than two things refer to 'there are'.

दो या दो से ज़्यादा वस्तुओं के लिए 'there are' का प्रयोग किया जाता है।

Examples:-

There are two doctors. दो डॉक्टर हैं।
There were many beggars. कई सारे भिखारी थे।
There are trees in the garden. बगीचे में पेड़ हैं।

Exercise-3

Look at the pictures and fill in the blanks using there is/was or there are/were.

1. ______________ a boy under the tree.

2. ______________ four windows of this house.

3. ______________ tea in the cup.

4. ____________ six eggs in the basket yesterday.

But ____________ an egg in the basket today.

5. ____________ 366 days in 2016 but ____________ 365 days usually in every year.

(B) Fill in the blanks using 'is' or 'are' with there:

(1) There ____________ three pencils in the box.

(2) There ____________ biscuits in a jar.

(3) There ____________ water in the tank.

(4) There ____________ air in the room.

(5) There ____________ hair on the head.

(6) There ____________ stars in the sky.

Affirmative Sentence

There + is/are/was/were/shall be/will be + noun/object

Examples:-

There is a book in my bag.	मेरे थैले में एक किताब है।
There are some problems in life.	जीवन में कुछ कठिनाईयाँ होती हैं।
There was a boy.	एक लड़का था।
There were many mobiles in the shop.	दुकान में बहुत सारे मोबाईल थे।
There will be an election in March.	मार्च में चुनाव होंगे।
There shall be a magic in my life.	मेरे जीवन में अवश्य एक जादू होगा।

Exercise-4

Translate into English:

1. यहाँ आज शाम को शांति अवश्य रहेगी।

2. इसमें एक समस्या है।

3. मंदिर के सामने एक मस्जिद है।

4. मेरे गांव में एक पुस्तकालय होगा।

5. यहाँ एक लड़का था।

6. दो लड़के गली में थे।

Negative Sentence

In negative sentence, we use' no' before a noun and uncountable noun without article or adjective of number. Quantity (much, many, any, little, two, all) however we use 'not' when article or adjective of number/quantity comes before a noun.

जब noun से पहले article या संख्यासूचक नहीं हो, तब no लगता है यदि noun से पहले article या संख्यासूचक शब्द हो तब not लगाते हैं।

(i) There + is/are/was/were + no/not + noun/object

(ii) There + will/shall + be + no + noun/object

लेकिन article या adjective of number/quantity comes before a noun (any/ much/many/enough/two) then.

(iii) There + will + shall + not + article/any/much+ noun/object

Examples:-

There is no pen in my hand. There is not a pen in my hand.	मेरे हाथ में, कलम नहीं है।
There is no cat in the room. There is not a cat in the room.	कमरे में बिल्ली नहीं है।
There is no air in the room. There is not little air in the room.	कमरे में, न के बराबर भी हवा नहीं है।
There are no holidays in this month.	इस महिने में छुट्टियां नहीं हैं।
There are not many holidays in this month.	इस महिने में ज़्यादा छुट्टियां नहीं हैं।
There was no water in the tank.	टंकी में पानी नहीं था।
There will be no fruits in the market.	मार्केट में फल नहीं होंगे।
There will not be enough fruits in the market.	मार्केट में ज़्यादा फल नहीं होंगे।
There shall be no problem now. There shall not be any problem now.	अब अवश्य कोई परेशानी नहीं होगी।

Exercise-5

1. ग्लास में पानी नहीं है।

   ____

2. क्लास में एक भी बच्चा नहीं है।

   ____

3. आसमान में तारें नहीं थे।

   ____

4. मेरे हाथ में दो पुस्तक नहीं थी।

   ____

5. कल घर पर कोई नहीं होगा।

   ____

Interrogative Sentence

(i) Is/are/was/were + there + noun/object

(ii) Shall/will + there + be + noun/object

Examples:-

Is there a pen in your bag?	क्या आपके थैले में एक कलम है?
Is there any boy at the door?	क्या कोई लड़का है दरवाज़े पर?
Are there two teachers in the school?	क्या स्कूल में दो शिक्षक हैं?
Will there be students on Sunday?	क्या रविवार को छात्र होंगे?
Was there a monkey in that house?	क्या उस घर में बंदर था?

Exercise-6

(A) Look at the pictures and fill in the blanks using 'is there'/ 'are there' or 'was there'/'were there'.

1. ________ pen in our hand?

2. ________ trees in the garden?

3. ________ water in the well?

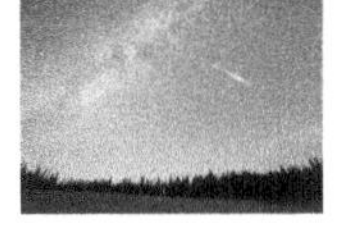

4. ________ stars in the sky yesterday night?

5. ________ computer before 1947?

(B) Fill in the blanks using 'is' or 'are'.

1. ____________ there many people in the programme?
2. ____________ there humanity among the people of this era?
3. ____________ there five students in the class?
4. ____________ there biscuits in the jar?
5. ____________ there hair on his head?

(C) Translate into English:

1. क्या आपके घर में T.V. है।

____

2. क्या बोरे में चावल नहीं थे?

____

3. क्या उस बर्तन में पानी था?

____

4. क्या आकाश में चाँद था?

____

5. क्या स्कूल में साठ बच्चे थे?

____

6. क्या अगले महिने चुनाव होगा?

____

7. क्या मोबाइल में five calls नहीं थीं?

____

8. क्या उस घर में चार कमरे नहीं हैं?

____

Negative + Interrogative Sentence

(i) Is/are/was/were + there + not/no + noun/object

(ii) Will/shall + there + be + no + noun/object

Examples:-

Is there no hospital in Patna? or Is there not a hospital in Patna?	क्या पटना में हॉस्पिटल नहीं है?
Will there be no water in the tank?	क्या टंकी में पानी नहीं होगा?
Were there not four trees near the well?	क्या कुँए के पास चार पेड़ नहीं थे?

Use of Let

The word 'let' is used for permission, it is a word which gives the meaning of 'allow'. In this chapter, we will learn a very important thing that subject becomes the cause of action but does not do any action.

Let शब्द का प्रयोग permission लेने या देने के लिए किया जाता है। Let का मतलब 'allow' भी होता है। Let शब्द के प्रयोग से हम एक बात और सीखेंगे के इसमें 'Subject' काम नहीं करता बल्कि "करने देता" है।

(i) Taking or giving permission:
आज्ञा लेना या देने के लिए:

Examples:-

They let me go.	वे लोग मुझे जाने देते हैं।
I let you eat first.	मैं आपको पहले खाने देता हूँ।
My father is letting my sister work in the night shift.	मेरे पिता, मेरी बहन को रात की शिफ्ट में काम करने दे रहे हैं।
My teacher let me sit in the class yesterday.	कल मेरे शिक्षक ने मुझे कक्षा में बैठने दिया।

Note: Forms of 'Let'

V^1	V^2	V^3	V + S	V + ing
Let	Let	Let	Lets	Letting

There are subjective case and objective case as shown below.

Subjective Case	Objective Case
I	Me
We	Us
You	You
They	Them
He	Him
She	Her
It	It

Affirmative Sentence

Examples:-

Ram lets his sister play games with boys.	राम अपनी बहन को लड़को के साथ खेल खेलने देता है।
My mother lets me go out with my friends.	मेरी माँ मुझे मेरे दोस्तों के साथ जाने देती है।
I am letting you sleep early.	मैं आपको जल्दी सोने दे रहा हूँ।
We are letting our tenant live without taking rent during lockdown.	लॉकडाऊन में, हम अपने किरायेदार को बिना किराया लिये रहने दे रहे हैं।
My father let me enter in the house yesterday night.	कल रात को मेरे पिता ने मुझे घर में घुसने/आने दिया।
I let you go yesterday first, I will go today.	कल मैंने आपको पहले जाने दिया था, आज मैं जाऊँगा।
She was letting me use her mobile.	वह लड़की मुझे अपना मोबाईल इस्तेमाल करने दे रही थी।
He will let his brother ride cycle is the morning.	सुबह को, वह अपने भाई को साईकल चलाने देगा।

"Allow" शब्द "let" से ज़्यादा formal होता है जो किसी पदको या महत्वता को दर्शता है। लेकिन दोनों शब्दों के मतलब में कोई फर्क नहीं है।

(a) Government allows farmers to take loan without documents.
सरकार किसानों को बिना दस्तावेज़ों के कर्ज़ा लेने देती है।

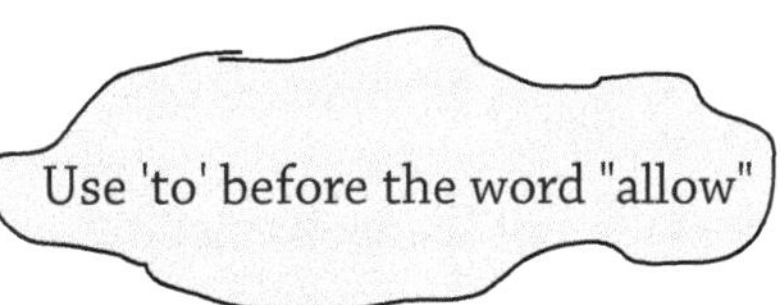

(b) Father does not allow my sister to work in call centre.
पिता जी मेरी बहन को कॉल सेंटर में काम करने नहीं देते।

Exercise-7

Translate into English:

1. वे लोग मुझे काम करने देंगे।

____

2. मोहन अपने भाई को टी.वी. देखने देता है।

____

3. गांव में माँ ने पिता को खाना बनाने दिया था।

____

4. छुट्टियों में मेरे घर वाले देर तक सोंने दे रहे थे।

____

5. पुलिस ने चोरों को जाने दिया।

____

6. वे लोग हमें चैन से अब जीने दे रहे हैं।

____

7. हीरा लाल अब अपनी बेटी को पढ़ने देता है।

____

Negative Sentence

Examples:-

She does not let me use laptop.	वह मुझे लैपटॉप इस्तेमाल करने नहीं देती है।
My landlord does not let us cook non-veg.	मेरा मकान मालिक हमें non-veg बनाने नहीं देता।
Some people are not letting innocent persons live peacefully.	कुछ लोग मासूम लोगो को चैन से जीने नहीं दे रहे हैं।
My sister will not let me touch her mobile.	मेरी बहन मुझे अपना मोबाईल छूने नहीं देगी।
I did not let my father drink alcohol.	मैनें अपने पिता को शराब पीनें नहीं दी।

Exercise-8

Translate into English:

1. मोहन ने अपनी बहन की शादी उस लड़के से होने नहीं दी।

   ____

2. गाँववाले किसानों को फसल जलाने नहीं दे रहे थे।

   ____

3. हमारे बुरे कर्म हमें चैन से जीने नहीं देंगे।

   ____

4. कविता किसी भी लड़के को अपने पास बैठने नहीं देती।

   ____

5. माँ-बाप अपने बच्चों को फोन पर बात करने नहीं दें रहे थे।

   ____

6. मैं आपको यह घर खरीदनें नहीं दूँगा।

   ____

7. कल रात मोहन ने किसी को सोने नहीं दिया।

   ____

Interrogative Sentence

Examples:-

Will your family members let your brother live like this?	क्या आपके घरवाले आपके भाई को ऐसे ही जीने देंगे?
Does every father let his daughter study?	क्या हर एक पिता अपनी बेटी को पढ़ने देता है?
Why did you not let me watch T.V yesterday?	कल आपने क्यू मुझे टी. वी. देखने नहीं दिया?
Was your step-mother not letting you eat food?	क्या आपकी सोतेली माँ आपको खाना खाने नहीं दे रही थी?

Exercise-9

(i) Translate into English.

1. क्या मोहन अपनी पत्नी को नौकरी करने नहीं देता?

   ____

2. क्या अमीर, गरीबों को अपने सामने खड़ा होने नहीं देते?

   ____

3. क्या आप मुझे अपनी शादी (attend) करने नहीं दोगे?

   ____

4. क्या पुलिस चोरों को चोरी करने देती है?

   ____

5. क्या सरकार किसानों को गन्ने की खेती करने दे रही है?

   ____

6. क्या कविता आपको काम करने नहीं दे रही थी?

   ____

7. क्या आपके पिता जी हमें नाचने नहीं देंगे?

   ____

8. क्या उन लोगों की बुरी आदतों ने उन्हें जीने नहीं दिया?

____

9. क्या लड़की का भाई मोहन को उस लड़की से मिलने देता है?

____

10. क्या आप मुझे एक बात नहीं जानने दोगे?

____

(ii) Expression of disturbance, hindrance or problem not about permission:

Let शब्द का प्रयोग ज़रूरी नहीं केवल आज्ञा के लिए ही हो, बल्कि इसका प्रयोग कोई रूकावट, किसी चीज़ में परेशानी के भावों को भी दर्शता है। इस तरह के वाक्यों में Subject नहीं होता है और यह दो तरह के होते हैं (a) Positive और (b) Negative.

Examples:-

Let + object + v^1	Don't + let + object + v^1
Let me sleep. मुझे सोने दो।	Don't let that girl go. उस लड़की को मत जाने दो।
Let him play. उसे खेलने दो।	Don't let me die. मुझे मत मरने दो।
Let the kids swim. बच्चों को तैरने दो।	Don't let your children close to animals. बच्चों को जानवरों के पास मत जाने दो।
Let it be like this. इसे ऐसे ही रहने दो।	Don't let anyone touch it. किसी को इसको छूने मत दो।
Let the mobile be on charging. मोबाईल को चार्ज होने दो।	Don't let Mohan eat this. मोहन को यह खाने मत दो।

Exercise-10

Translate the following into English:

1. मोहन को जाने दो।

2. अपनी बहन को पढ़ने दो।

3. मुझे बोलने दो।

4. सुनिता को पहले अपनी बात पूरी करने दो।

5. उस लड़के को पानी पीने दो।

6. देर से आने वालो को कक्षा में आने मत दो।

7. पेड़ों को मरने मत दो।

8. रोहित को अपनें ही जिस्म में इन्जेक्शन लगाने मत दो।

9. उस लड़के को प्लग से चार्जर निकालने मत दो।

10. मुझे एक चीज़ जानने दो।

(iii) Suggestion, giving an instruction, idea, किसी मश्वरें या सुझाव, किसी को अपने साथ शामिल करना, तब let's का प्रयोग होता है, जो let us है।

Examples:-

(a) Let's go. — चलो, चलते हैं।
(b) Let's watch a movie. — चलो, फिल्म देखते हैं।
(c) Let's do rest. — चलो, आराम करते हैं।
(d) Let's eat a pizza. — चलो, पिज़्ज़ा खाते हैं।

Exercise-11

(A) Read the sentences, then fill in the blanks by using let's. One example for you:

Mohan wants to eat food. He says to Mohit let's eat food.

1. Danish wants to play cricket. He says to Rohit. ____________
2. I want to dance. I say to my friends. ____________
3. Himanshu wants to enjoy outside in the rain. He says to his sister. ____________
4. Father wants to watch T.V. He says to his son. ____________
5. Pooja wants to celebrate a party. She says to her mother. ____________

(B) Match the following:

1. She is very hungry.	(a) Let's switch on the T.V.
2. It's my birthday today.	(b) Let's take an umbrella.
3. Sheetal wants to watch T.V.	(c) Let's study.
4. It's raining.	(d) Let's eat food.
5. My exams will start from Monday.	(e) Let's arrange a party.

Let us help you:-

1. We use 'it' for the confusion of gender,
   Examples: (a) It is a naughty eunuch. (b) Who is it, a boy or a girl.
2. 'It' is used for emphasizing a human being.
   Example: It is my father who gave my fees.
3. We use 'there is' for singular noun or uncountable noun in present tense whereas 'there was' is used in past tense.
4. We use 'there are' for plural noun or two or more than two countable nouns in present tense whereas 'there were' in the past tense.
5. 'Let' is used for giving and taking permission.
   Example: I let him eat food.
6. Let's = Let us.
   Example: Let's go there.

17 Short Forms

Read these sentences:

(i) She is cooking food.

(ii) She's cooking food.

In sentence (i) we used "she is" but in sentence (ii) we used "She's" here, we would like to say that 'she's' is the short form of she is.

जब हम वाक्यों में **'short forms'** का प्रयोग करते हैं, तो वाक्यों की रचना बहुत आकर्षित होती है और **Spoken English** में **'short forms'** बहुत अधिक प्रयोग होती हैं, यह **fluency** से अंग्रेज़ी बोलने में बहुत उपयोगी और सहायक होती है।

Examples:-

(a) I am – I'm (b) You are – you're
(c) We will – we'll (d) They are – they're

ध्यान दे: Short forms का प्रयोग लिखने और बोलने में बहुत अधिक किया जाता है, और इसे Contraction कहते हैं।

There are short forms of am – are – is – was – were – will – in positive:

In present		In past		In future	
Singular		Singular		Singular	
Long form	Short form	Long form	Short form	Long form	Short form
I am	I'm	I was	–	I will	I'll
He is	He's	He was	–	He will	He'll
She is	She's	She was	–	She will	She'll
It is	It's	It was	–	It will	It'll

Plural		Plural		Plural	
Long form	**Short form**	**Long form**	**Short form**	**Long form**	**Short form**
You are They are We are	You're They're We're	You were They were We were	– – –	You will They will We will	You'll They'll We'll

There are short forms of am – are – is – was – were – will – in negative:

In present		In past		In future	
Singular		**Singular**		**Singular**	
Long form	**Short form**	**Long form**	**Short form**	**Long form**	**Short form**
I am not He is not She is not It is not	I'm not He isn't She isn't It isn't	I was not He was not She was not It was not	I wasn't He wasn't She wasn't It wasn't	I will not He will not She will not It will not	I won't He won't She won't It won't
Plural		**Plural**		**Plural**	
Long form	**Short form**	**Long form**	**Short form**	**Long form**	**Short form**
You are not They are not We are not	You aren't They aren't We aren't	You were not They were not We were not	You weren't They weren't We weren't	You will not They will not We will not	You won't They won't We won't

Let us help you:-

Person	Positive	Negative	
Singular	–	Shall not	Shan't
Plural	–	Shall not	Shan't

There are short forms of 'do' and 'does' in positive:

Positive in present			
(Singular)		(Plural)	
Long form	**Short form**	**Long form**	**Short form**
I do He does She does It does	– – – –	You do They do We do None	– – – None

Here are some more short forms of 'Do' and 'Does' in negative:

Negative in present			
(Singular)		(Plural)	
Long form	**Short form**	**Long form**	**Short form**
I do not He does not She does not It does not	I don't He doesn't She doesn't It doesn't	You do not They do not We do not None	You don't They don't We don't None

Let us help you:-

Long form	Short form
1. Shall not 2. Am I not?	Shan't Aren't I ?

ध्यान दें: जब "Am" की short form का प्रयोग interrogative sentence में किया जाता है, तो वह "Aren't I" बन जाता है।

Examples:- Am I not with you = Aren't I with you?
क्या मैं आपके साथ नहीं हूँ?

Am I not honest = Aren't I honest?
क्या मैं ईमानदार नहीं हूँ?

There are short forms of 'did' in positive:

Positive in past			
Singular		**Plural**	
Long form	**Short form**	**Long form**	**Short form**
I did	–	You did	–
He did	–	They did	–
She did	–	We did	–
It did	–	None	None

Here are some more short forms of 'did' in Negative:

Negative in past			
Singular		**Plural**	
Long form	**Short form**	**Long form**	**Short form**
I did not	I didn't	You did not	You didn't
He did not	He didn't	They did not	They didn't
She did not	She didn't	We did not	We didn't
It did not	It didn't	None	None

There are short forms of 'Has' and 'Have' in positive in present tense:

Positive in present			
Singular		**Plural**	
Long form	**Short form**	**Long form**	**Short form**
I have	I've	You have	You've
He has	He's	They have	They've
She has	She's	We have	We've
It has	It's	None	None

'Here' are some more short forms of 'Has' and 'Have' in negative in present tense:

Negative in present			
Singular		**Plural**	
Long form	**Short form**	**Long form**	**Short form**
I have not	I haven't	You have not	You haven't
He has not	He hasn't	They have not	They haven't
She has not	She hasn't	We have not	We haven't
It has not	It hasn't	None	None

They are short forms of 'had' in positive in the past tense:-

Positive in past			
Singular		**Plural**	
Long form	**Short form**	**Long form**	**Short form**
I had	I'd	You had	You'd
He had	He'd	They had	They'd
She had	She'd	We had	We'd
It had	It'd	None	None

Here are some more short forms of 'had' in negative in the past tense:

Negative in Past			
Singular		**Plural**	
Long form	**Short form**	**Long form**	**Short form**
I had not	I hadn't	You had not	You hadn't
He had not	He hadn't	They had not	They hadn't
She had not	She hadn't	We had not	We hadn't
It had not	It hadn't	None	None

Exercise-1

(A) Match the words with their short forms:

1.	He is	(a)	They'll
2.	They will	(b)	I'm
3.	He will	(c)	We're
4.	I am	(d)	They're
5.	We are	(e)	He's
6.	You are	(f)	He'll
7.	They are	(g)	You're

(B) Write the full forms of these short forms:

1.	Wasn't	________	9.	It's	________
2.	Aren't	________	10.	She isn't	________
3.	They're	________	11.	I wasn't	________
4.	I'm	________	12.	I won't	________
5.	Isn't	________	13.	She wasn't	________
6.	He'll	________	14.	We'll	________
7.	Won't	________	15.	She won't	________
8.	You're	________	16.	You weren't	________

Exercise-2

(A) Write the full forms of these short forms:

1.	Don't	________	4.	Hasn't	________
2.	Doesn't	________	5.	Haven't	________
3.	Didn't	________	6.	Hadn't	________

(B) Write the short forms of these full forms:

1.	I have	________	8.	She has not	________
2.	She has	________	9.	It has not	________
3.	It has	________	10.	You have not	________
4.	I had	________	11.	They had	________
5.	He had	________	12.	They had	________
6.	It had	________	13.	We have	________
7.	I have not	________	14.	We had not	________

18 Telling the Time

How to tell the time in English:

There are a number of people who get confused in telling the time. As we know, it's very important to have knowledge about time. Here we should have some basic knowledge about 'clock'. There are many numbers in the clock and three needles.

The three needles are called hands.

Second hand: The hand which is very thin and moves very fast, is called 'Second hand'.

Minute hand: The hand which is thick and moves a bit when a minute has gone by, is called 'Minute hand'.

Hour hand: The hand which is the thickest and smallest and moves when an hour has gone by is called 'Hour hand'.

There are some words which are very important to understand.

Clockwise: When the three hands travel around a circle in the same direction on a clock it's called "clockwise." There is counting from 1 to 12.

Noon: It means 12 : 00 PM.

Midday: It means between 11 : 00 AM and 2 : 00 PM.

Afternnon: It means after 12 : 00 PM.

AM: Ante meridiem- before noon (12 : 00 midnight to 11 : 59.

PM: Post meridiem-after noon (12 : 00 noon to 11 : 59)

At: We use "At" (preposition) before time.

Examples:- (a) The class ends at ten o' clock.
(b) The train arrives at half past two.

It is or it's: What time is it or what's the time?

Examples:- It is eleven o'clock.
It is quarter to one.

Simple way: (Hour + minutes) here, we use simple numbers for telling time.

Examples:- (a) 7 : 05 - It's seven o five or It's five past seven.
(b) 6 : 38 - It's six thirty-eight.
(c) 10 : 12 - It's ten twelve.

Other way: (minutes + past/to + hour) here, we use past after 1 - 30 minutes, whereas we use 'to' after 31 - 59 minutes.

Examples:- (a) 9 : 15 - It's quarter past nine.
(b) 9 : 50 - It's ten to ten.
(c) 1 : 20 - It's twenty past one.

O'Clock: It means "of the clock" when we say 0 : 00.

Example:- 12 : 00 - It's twelve o'clock.

Quarter past: It means, the minute hand comes exactly at 3 - it's called quarter past.

Quarter = 15 minutes

Example:- 11 : 15 - It's quarter past eleven.

Quarter to: It means, the minute hand comes exactly at 9, it's called quarter to.

Example:- 11 : 45 - It's quarter to twelve.

How to tell the time in English:

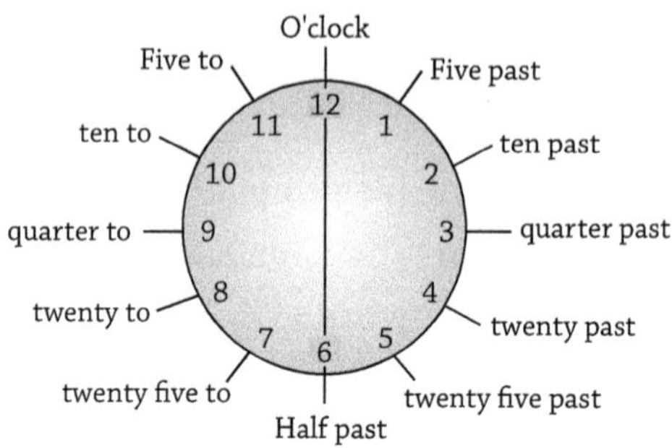

Exercise-1

Fill in the blanks by using the pictures.

1. What time does your class start?

Rohan: My class starts at 1. ________ o'clock.

Mohan: What time do you come back home?

Rohan: I come back home at 2. ________

Mohan: What time do you have your lunch?

Rohan: I have my lunch at 3. ________

Mohan: What time do you take rest?

Rohan: I take rest at 4. ________

Mohan: What time do you go for tuition?

Rohan: I go for tuition at 5. ________

Mohan: What time do you come from your tuition?

Rohan: I come from tuition at 6. ________

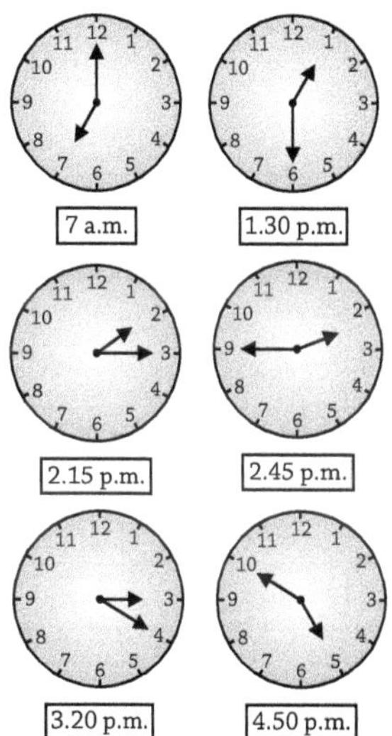

Exercise-2

Match the following:

1.	It's twenty five past ten.	(i)	10 : 00
2.	It's ten past one.	(ii)	10 : 30
3.	It's ten to ten.	(iii)	10 : 25
4.	It's a quarter to twelve.	(iv)	10 : 15
5.	It's ten o'clock.	(v)	1 : 10
6.	It's half past ten.	(vi)	9 : 50
7.	It's a quarter past ten.	(vii)	11 : 45

Exercise-3

Draw the clock:

1.	**2.**	**3.**
It's ten to nine.	It's twelve past five.	It's five to eleven.
4.	**5.**	**6.**
It's seven o'clock.	It's ten past nine.	It's a quarter past one.
7.	**8.**	**9.**
It's twenty to two.	It's a quarter to four.	It's half past eleven.
10.	**11.**	**12.**
It's ten to ten.	It's twelve o'clock.	It's twenty five to three.

Exercise-4

Fill in the blanks with number:

1. It's twenty five to two ________ .
2. It's half past ten ________ .
3. It's ten to twelve ________ .
4. It's one o'clock ________ .
5. It's a quarter to five ________ .
6. It's five past five ________ .
7. It's a quarter to seven ________ .

Exercise-5

(A) Tick on the correct option:

1. 5 : 05

(a) It's five to five.
(b) It's five o'clock.
(c) It's five past five.

2. 6 : 25

(a) It's twenty five to six.
(b) It's twenty five past six.
(c) It's twenty five past nine.

3. 10 : 30

(a) It's half past ten.
(b) It's ten past nine.
(c) It's twenty to ten.

4. 10 : 00

(a) It's ten to ten.
(b) It's ten o'clock.
(c) It's ten past ten.

5. 3 : 45

(a) It's a quarter past three.
(b) It's a quarter to four.
(c) It's a quarter to two.

6. 8 : 50

(a) It's eight to nine.
(b) It's ten to nine.
(c) It's ten past eight.

(B) What time is it?

1. 12 : 15 It is ______________ .
2. 7 : 35 It is ______________ .
3. 8 : 45 It is ______________ .
4. 12 : 00 It is ______________ .
5. 4 : 05 It is ______________ .
6. 9 : 50 It is ______________ .
7. 11 : 15 It is ______________ .
8. 11 : 20 It is ______________ .

Exercise-6

Translate into English:

1. सात बज रहे हैं।

____

2. साढ़े सात बज रहे हैं।

____

3. सवा सात बज रहे हैं।

____

4. पौने सात बज रहे हैं।

____

5. पाँच बजकर दस मिनट हो गये हैं।

____

6. आठ बजने में पाँच मिनट बाकी हैं।

____

7. पाँच नहीं बजे हैं।

____

8. क्या पाँच बज गए?

____

9. क्या पाँच नहीं बजे हैं?

____

10. चार बजने में पंद्रह मिनट बाकी हैं।

____

11. पाँच बजकर पंद्रह मिनट हुए हैं।

____

Let us help you:-

1.	**Asking time:**	What time is it- tell me time, please.
2.	**Answer:**	For telling time we use 'it is'.
3.	**O'clock means:**	0 : 00 or 12 : 00 or 12 o'clock.
4.	**A quarter means:**	15 minutes.
5.	**Half past:**	30 minutes.
6.		We use 'at' with time.
	Example:-	She goes to class at 4 pm.
7.	**Half:**	30 minutes.
	Example:-	1 : 30 - It's half past one.
8.	**Dots:**	We should use dots.
	Example:-	7 : 05 - It's 5 past seven.
9.	**'a':**	We should use 'a' before quarter.
	Example:-	7 : 15 - It's a quarter past seven.
10.	**Minute:**	The word minute is not necessary to be used.
	Example:-	7 : 05 - It's five minutes past seven. It's five past seven.
11.	**'O' - oh:**	2 : 05 (It's two oh five/It's two o two)

19 Interrogative Sentences

Interrogative Sentences are those in which we ask questions and have question marks at the end.

Examples:-

Are you a doctor? क्या आप डॉक्टर हो?
Yes, I am a doctor. हाँ, मैं डॉक्टर हूँ।

Do you have a pen? क्या आपके पास कलम है?
Yes, I have a beautiful pen. हाँ, मेरे पास एक सुंदर कलम है।

ऊपर दिये गये दो उदाहरणों में हमें यह पता चलता है कि जब हमें किसी से कुछ पूछना होता है, तो हमें Interrogative Sentences का प्रयोग करना होता है। Questions या Interrogative Sentences दो प्रकार के होते हैं।

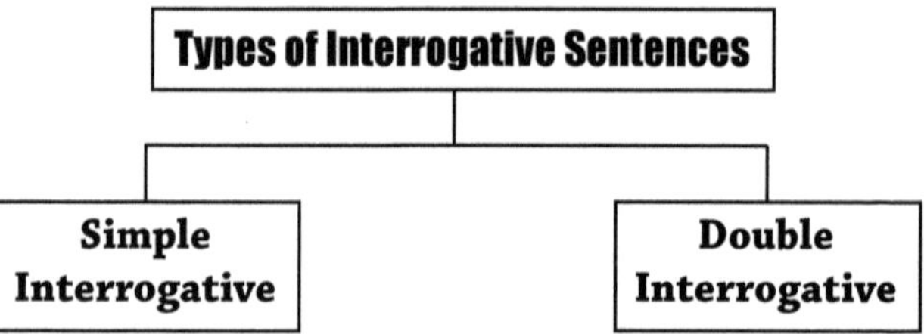

Simple Interrogative: When auxiliary verb/helping verb comes before a subject in a sentence to make question and there are many auxiliary verbs like Is/am/are, was/were, has/have/had, do/does/did, shall/will it is called a simple interrogative sentence.

ध्यान दें: Simple Interrogative वाले questions का जवाब Yes/No से दिया जाता है।

Here are some examples:

(a) [Is] Mohan happy [?] → Put the question mark at the end.

↓ Put the helping verb before the subject.

(b) [Were] they students [?] → Put the question mark at the end.

↓ Put the helping verb before the subject.

ऊपर दिये गये उदाहरणों से हमने सीखा कि कैसे हम helping verbs/auxiliary verbs को वाक्यों के शुरू में रखते हैं Subject से पहले।

2. Double Interrogative: Double interrogative sentences are those in which we use question words before subjects to make interrogative sentences. Here are some question words like:

1. What
2. When
3. Who
4. Where
5. Whom
6. Which
7. Whose
8. Why
9. How
10. How much
11. How many
12. How far
13. How long
14. How often/How many times
15. What kind of /What type of/ What sort of

1. What

What we ask about things or name of things. In other 'words' we use 'What' to find out subject or object of sentences.

Subject या Object का नाम पूछना, तब हम 'What' का प्रयोग करते हैं, 'What' का अर्थ है क्या।

Let's understand the formation of sentences.
आओ वाक्यों की रचना करना सीखते हैं।

Examples:-

Mohan : What are these?

Mohan's guess (मोहन ने सोचा) : Hens.

Rohan's response : No, these are not hens.

Rohan's reply : These are ducks.

Mohan : What is that?

Mohan's guess (मोहन ने सोचा) : Truck.

Roha's response : No, that is not a truck.

Rohan's reply : That is a bus.

Here are some more examples:

What are you doing?	आप क्या कर रहे हो?
What does your father do?	आपके पिता क्या करते हैं?
What is your mother?	आपकी माता क्या हैं?
What happened?	क्या हुआ?
What did you see yesterday?	कल आपने क्या देखा?

Exercise-1

Translate into English:

1. क्या हुआ?

____

2. आप क्या चाहते हो?

____

3. उसने तुमसे क्या कहा?

____

4. मैं आपके लिए क्या करूँ?

____

5. आपका भाई क्या है?

____

6. क्या समस्या है?

____

7. हम क्या कर रहे हैं?

____

2. When

When we ask about time of action, then we use 'When'.

जब हम किसी action का time पूछते हैं, तो 'when' का प्रयोग किया जाता है, और इसका अर्थ 'कब' होता है।

Let's understand the formation of sentences.
आओ वाक्यों की रचना करना सीखते हैं।

Examples:-

Ram : When do you catch the bus?
Ram's guess (राम ने सोचा) : At 9 o' clock in the morning.
Rahim's response : No, I do not catch the bus by 9 : 00 am.
Rahim's reply : I catch the bus by 10 : 30 am.

Ram : When is your meeting?
Ram's guess (राम ने सोचा) : At 10 : 00 am.
Rahim's response : No, it is not at 10 : 00 am.
Rahim's reply : It is at 11 : 30 am.

Here are some more examples:

When do you sleep?	आप कब सोते हो?
When is his marriage?	उसकी शादी कब है?
When was she dancing?	वह कब नाच रही थी?
When will Anil come?	अनील कब आएगा?
When is Diwali?	दिवाली कब है?

Exercise-2

Translate into English:

1. मोहन कब उठता है?

   ____

2. तुम कब स्कूल जाते हो?

   ____

3. वह कब खाता है?

   ____

4. आपका जन्मदिन कब है?

   ____

5. वे लोग कब समझेंगे?

   ____

6. आप अपना काम कब करोगे?

   ____

7. हम लोग वहाँ कब गए थे?

   ____

3. Who

When we ask about person or people 'who' is used to find out subject or object.

जब हम किसी व्यक्ति को पूछते हैं तो 'who' का प्रयोग किया जाता है। 'who' का प्रयोग केवल व्यक्ति के लिए होता है।

Let's understand the formation of sentences.
आओ वाक्यों की रचना करना सीखते हैं।

Examples:-

Pushpa	: Who is Mohan?
Pushpa's guess (पुष्पा ने सोचा)	: A teacher.
Kavita's response	: No, he is not a teacher.
Kavita's reply	: He is a doctor.
Pushpa	: Who invented the bulb?
Pushpa's guess (पुष्पा ने सोचा)	: Amos Emerson.
Kavita's response	: No, Amos Emerson did not invent.
Kavita's reply	: Thomas Edison invented the bulb.

Here are some more examples:

Who is mad here?	यहाँ कौन पागल है?
Who found my pen?	किसे पेन मिला?
Who will be the next P.M.?	अगले प्रधानमंत्री कौन बनेंगे?
Who is watching T.V.?	कौन टी.वी. देख रहा है?
Who is talking in the class?	कक्षा में कौन बात कर रहा है?

Exercise-3

Translate into English:

1. यह कौन है?

____

2. भारत के प्रधानमंत्री कौन हैं?

____

3. आपके साथ कौन है?

____

4. टी. वी. का अविष्कार किसने किया?

____

5. मुख्य अतिथि कौन बनेंगे?

____

6. कौन दूध लेकर आएगा?

____

7. किसने मेरा कलम तोड़ा था?

____

4. Where

When we ask about place.

जब हम किसी जगह के बारे में कुछ पूछते हैं, तो 'Where' का प्रयोग किया जाता है। Where का अर्थ 'कहाँ' होता है।

Let's understand the formation of sentences.
आओ वाक्यों की रचना करना सीखते हैं।

Examples:-

Ratan Lal : Where are cows?
Ratan Lal's guess (रतन लाल ने सोचा) : In the dairy.
Kishan Singh's response : No, they are not in the dairy.
Kishan Singh's reply : They are in the field.

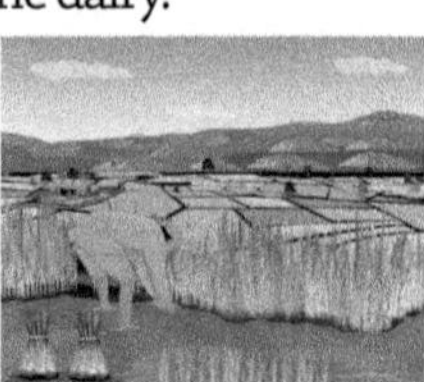

Ratan Lal : Where are you?
Ratan Lal's guess (रतन लाल ने सोचा) : At home.
Kishan Singh's response : No, I am not at home.
Kishan Singh's reply : I am in the field.

Here are some more examples:

Where are you?	आप कहाँ हो?
Where is his school?	उसका स्कूल कहाँ है?
Where is Mohan living?	मोहन कहाँ रह रहा है?
Where are they coming from?	वे लोग कहाँ से आ रहे हैं?
Where is the hospital?	यहाँ अस्पताल कहाँ है?

Exercise-4

Translate into English:

1. आपका घर कहाँ है?

___

2. मोहन कहाँ है?

___

3. पूजा कहाँ की रहने वाली है?

___

4. आपके पिताजी कहाँ के रहने वाले हैं?

___

5. ताजमहल कहाँ है?

___

6. लक्ष्मी नगर कहाँ है?

___

7. वे लोग कहाँ रहते हैं?

___

5. Whom

When we talk about a person and ask the indirect object then we use 'Whom'. It is used only with human beings.

जब उस व्यक्ति की बात हो जिस पर किसी अन्य व्यक्ति ने कुछ कार्य किया हो, तो जिस व्यक्ति पर काम हुआ उसको पूछने के लिए 'Whom' शब्द का प्रयोग किया जाता है।

Let's understand the formation of sentences.
आओ वाक्यों की रचना करना सीखते हैं।

Examples:-

Mahipal Yadav : With whom are you?
Mahipal Yadav's guess (महिपाल यादव ने सोचा) : With a policeman.
Pawan Kumar's response : No, I am not with a policeman.
Pawan Kumar's reply : I am with a lawyer.

Mahipal Yadav : For whom is Rani buying a doll?
Mahipal Yadav's guess (महिपाल यादव ने सोचा) : For her daughter.
Pawan Kumar's response : No, she does not have any daughter.
Pawan Kumar's reply : She is buying a doll for an orphan girl.

Mahipal Yadav : To whom will you give this gift?
Mahipal Yadav's guess (महिपाल यादव ने सोचा) : To the doctor.
Pawan Kumar's response : No, I will not give this gift to the doctor.
Pawan Kumar's reply : I will give this gift to a wardboy for encouraging him.

Here are some more examples:

For whom are you buying this?	आप यह किसके लिए खरीद रहे हो?
With whom are you?	आप किसके साथ हो?
To whom was she talking?	वह किससे बात कर रही थी?
Whom does she know here?	वह यहाँ किसे जानती है?
Whom do you believe?	आप किस पर विश्वास करते हो?

Exercise-5

Translate into English:

1. आप किसे खोज रहे हो?

____

2. वह किससे मिलना चाहता है?

____

3. सुरेश किससे बात कर रहा है?

____

4. आप यह गिफ्ट किसको दोगें?

____

5. आप की मम्मी किसके लिए खाना बना रही है?

____

6. मैं किसके साथ जाउँगा?

____

7. हम लोग किससे डर रहे हैं?

____

6. Which

When we talk about selection or choice of a thing or a person, we can use 'Which' for thing and person but only for selection or choice.

जब भी किसी व्यक्ति या वस्तु के चुनाव (चुन्ने) की बात हो, तो 'Which' शब्द का प्रयोग होता है।

Let's understand the formation of sentences.
आओ वाक्यों की रचना करना सीखते हैं।

Examples:-

Pooja : Which is your pen?
Pooja's guess (पूजा ने सोचा) : This one.
Kavita's response : No, this one is not.
Kavita's reply : That one is mine.

Pooja : Which is Sonia's favourite hero?
Pooja's guess (पूजा ने सोचा) : Arjun Kapoor.
Kavita's response : No, Sonia's favourite hero is not Arjun Kapoor.
Kavita's reply : Sonia's favourite hero is Shahid Kapoor.

Here are some more examples:

Which boy have you liked for marriage?
आपने शादी के लिए किस लड़के को पंसद किया है?

Which of them was more handsome?
उन लोगों में से ज़्यादा सुंदर कौन था?

Which of those houses did you see?
उन घरों में से आपने कौन से घर देखे थे?

Which is her favourite ice-cream?
उसकी पंसदीदा आईसक्रीम कौन-सी है?

Which state have you come from?
आप कौन से राज्य से आए हो?

Exercise-6

Translate into English:

1. कौन-सी टीम टूर्नामेंट जीती थी?

____

2. इनमें से मेरा मोबाइल कौन-सा है?

____

3. वे लोग किस शहर में रहते हैं?

____

4. आपकी पत्नी कौन से फलों का रस सबसे ज़्यादा पंसद करती है?

____

5. उनमें से कौन-सा लड़का जीतेगा?

____

6. हम लोग कौन-सा समाचार पत्र पढ़ते हैं?

____

7. उसने आखिरी फिल्म कौन-सी देखी थी?

____

7. Whose

When we ask about possession or ownership of something or somebody, we use 'Whose'. It shows the something belongs to something or somebody.

जब हम किसी व्यक्ति या वस्तु का रिश्ता किसी अन्य व्यक्ति या वस्तु से पूछते हैं, तो 'Whose' का प्रयोग किया जाता है, इससे 'मालिकाना हक' का भी बोध होता है।

Let's understand the formation of sentences.
आओ वाक्यों की रचना करना सीखते हैं।

Examples:-

Fazil : Whose daughter are you?

Fazil's guess (फाज़िल ने सोचा) : Kashif Ji's.

Fatima's response : No, I am not the daughter of Kashif Ji.

Fatima's reply : I am the daughter of Kamil.

Fazil : Whose pen is this?

Fazil's guess (फाज़िल ने सोचा) : Yours.

Fatima's response : No, this pen is not mine.

Fatima's reply : This is my father's pen.

Here are some more examples:

Whose house is that?	वह घर किसका है?
Whose colours are these?	ये रंग किसके हैं?
Whose car are they using?	वे लोग किसकी कार इस्तेमाल कर रहे हैं?
Whose son is Mohan?	मोहन किसका लड़का है?
Whose mobile is on the table?	मेज़ पर किसका मोबाइल रखा हुआ है?

Exercise-7

Translate into English:

1. वह किसकी चाय है?
2. वह किसकी कुर्सी है?
3. आप किसका घर खरीद रहे हो?
4. वह घर किसका है?
5. किसके पिताजी बीमार थे?
6. वे लोग किसकी कार चला रहे थे?
7. वह किसका बेटा है?

8. Why

When we ask about reason of something then we use 'Why'. It also denotes purpose of something.

जब किसी चीज़ का **reason** या **purpose** पूछते हैं, तो **'Why'** शब्द का प्रयोग होता है।

Let's understand the formation of sentences.
आओ वाक्यों की रचना करना सीखते हैं।

Examples:-

Mohit Malhotra : Why is Poonam Deewan in hospital?
Mohit Malhotra's guess (मोहित मलहोत्रा ने सोचा) : For her treatment.
Kartar Singh's response : No, she is not in the hospital for treatment.
Kartar Singh's reply : She is a doctor here.

Mohit Malhotra : Why is Monika learning English?
Mohit Malhotra's guess (मोहित मलहोत्रा ने सोचा) : For job.
Kartar Singh's response : No, she is not learning English for a job.
Kartar Singh's reply : She is learning English for enhancing her confidence level and for self-development.

Here are some more examples:

Why do you lie?	आप झूठ क्यों बोलते हो?
Why is this book here?	यह किताब यहां क्यों है?
Why is that country so poor?	वह देश इतना गरीब क्यों है?
Why are you happy?	आप खुश क्यों हो?
Why does she speak so much?	वह इतना क्यों बोलती है?

Exercise-8

Translate into English:

1. आप वहाँ क्यों आए थे?

2. वह झूठ क्यों बोलता है?

3. बच्चे आज इतने गुस्सा क्यों हैं?

4. वे लोग सरकारी नौकरी क्यों करना चाहते हैं?

5. आप क्यों क्रोधित हैं?

6. हमारे पिताजी ने हमें क्यों पढ़ाया था?

7. आप यहाँ क्यों हो?

9. How

When we ask about the process or method of something then we use 'How'.

जब हम किसी चीज़ का 'Process' या 'Method' पूछते हैं, तो 'How' का प्रयोग होता है।

Let's understand the formation of sentences.
आओ वाक्यों की रचना करना सीखते हैं।

Examples:-

Shanti : How is she washing clothes?

Shanti's guess (शांति ने सोचा) : By using a washing machine.

Meena's response : No, she is not washing clothes by using a washing machine.

Meena's reply : She is washing clothes by her hands.

Shanti : How is your mother?

Shanti's guess (शांति ने सोचा) : Fine.

Meena's response : No, she is not fine.

Meena's reply : She has a cough and fever.

Here are some more examples:

How is your father?	आपके पिताजी कैसे हैं?
How is tea prepared?	चाय कैसे बनती है?
How does she come?	वह कैसे आती है?
How did his uncle become a doctor?	उसके चाचा डॉक्टर कैसे बने?
How are you?	आप कैसे हो?

Exercise-9

Translate into English:

1. मैं यहाँ कैसे आया हूँ?

 ____

2. सब कुछ कैसा चल रहा है?

 ____

3. वह कैसे अपराधी बना था?

 ____

4. वह कैसे वहाँ जीता है?

 ____

5. आपने वह कैसे किया था?

---

5. वहाँ का मौसम कैसा है?

---

6. आपके पिताजी कैसे हैं?

---

10. How much

When we ask about quantity and uncountable things then we use 'How much'.

किसी चीज़ की quantity पूछने के लिए या अगणनीय वस्तुओं के लिए 'How much' का प्रयोग किया जाता है।

Let's understand the formation of sentences.
आओ वाक्यों की रचना करना सीखते हैं।

Examples:-

Mother : How much water is in the tank?
Mother's guess (माँ ने सोचा) : It is full.
Son's response : No, it is not full.
Son's reply : It is half filled with water.

Mother : How much sugar is in the tea?
Mother's guess (माँ ने सोचा) : There is less sugar.
Son's response : No, it is not less.
Son's reply : It is perfectly ok.

Here are some more examples:

How much rice should I serve in your plate?	आपकी थाली में कितने चावल डालूँ?
How much water does she drink in a day?	वह एक दिन में कितना पानी पीती है?
How much time does it take to sleep?	सोने में कितना समय लगता है?
How much does this mobile cost?	इस मोबाईल की कितनी कीमत है?
How much weight is of this thing?	इस चीज़ का वज़न कितना है?

Use how many with stars. This is an exception

Exercise-10

Translate into English:

1. उस बर्तन में कितना पानी था?

____

2. आप कितना पढ़ते हो?

____

3. वे लोग कितना दूध पीते हैं?

____

4. हम लोग कितना समय लेंगे इसे खत्म करने में?

____

5. कितनी फीस ली थी उसने?

____

6. उस डिब्बे में कितना घी होगा?

____

7. इस बाल्टी में कितना पानी है?

____

11. How many

When we ask about the number of countable things then we put 'How many'.

जब हम किसी चीज़ की मात्रा पूछते हैं तो 'How many' का प्रयोग होता है।

Let's understand the formation of sentences.
आओ वाक्यों की रचना करना सीखते हैं।

Examples:-

Father : How many horses are in the stable?
Father's guess (पिता ने सोचा) : Ten horses.
Son's response : No, there are not ten horses in the stable.
Son's reply : There are four horses in the stable.

Father : How many books are in the bag?
Father's guess (पिता ने सोचा) : Fifteen books.
Son's response : No, these are not fifteen.
Son's reply : These are only ten.

Here are some more examples:

How many states are in India?	भारत में कितने राज्य हैं?
How many students are in the class?	कक्षा में कितने छात्र हैं?
How many family members does she have?	उसके परिवार में कितने सदस्य हैं?
How many pages are in this book?	इस किताब में कितने पन्ने हैं?
How many stars are in the sky?	आकाश में कितने तारे हैं?

ध्यान दें: How many शब्द के बाद हमेशा noun का प्रयोग किया जाता है और इसके बाद helping verb आता है।

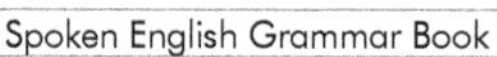

Exercise-11

Translate into English:

1. इस घर में कितनी खिड़कियाँ और कितने रसोई घर हैं?

2. मनोहर के पास कितनी गाड़ियाँ हैं?

3. इस बगीचे में कितने पेड़ हैं?

4. वे लोग कितनी भाषाएँ बोलते हैं?

5. हमारी क्लास में कितने छात्र हैं?

6. उसके कितने भाई-बहन हैं?

7. उस बस में कितनी सीट हैं?

12. How far

When we ask about distance, then we use 'How far'.

जब हम दूरी का पूछते हैं, तो 'How far' का प्रयोग किया जाता है।

Let's understand the formation of sentences.
आओ वाक्यों की रचना करना सीखते हैं।

Examples:-

Brother : How far is Red Fort from your house?
Brother's guess (भाई ने सोचा) : Ten kilometers.
Sister's response : No, it is not ten kilometers from our house.
Sister's reply : It is only five kilometers.

Brother : How far is the hospital from here?
Brother's guess (भाई ने सोचा) : It is far.
Sister's response : No, it is not far.
Sister's reply : It is near.

Here are some more examples:

How far is Mumbai from Gujarat?	मुंबई से गुजरात कितनी दूर है?
How far does your father walk?	आपके पिताजी कितनी दूर चलते हैं?
How far is office from your home?	दफ्तर से आपका घर कितना दूर है?
How far are you standing?	आप कितनी दूर खड़े हो?
How far can you throw it?	आप यह कितनी दूर फेंक सकते हो?

Exercise-12

Translate into English:

1. लालकिला यहाँ से कितनी दूर है?

____

2. एक दिन में आप कितनी दूरी तय करते हो?

____

3. मोहन ने पत्थर कितनी दूर फेंका था?

____

4. उन लोगों की सोंच कहाँ तक ठीक है?

____

5. हम लोग कितनी दूर तक चलते हैं?

---

6. मार्किट कितनी दूर है उसके घर से?

---

7. वह कितनी दूर तक गाड़ी चलाती है पूरे दिन में?

---

13. How long

When we ask about duration or period of time, then we use 'How long'.

जब हम समय की अवधि को पूछते हैं उसके period या distance को पूछते हैं? तो 'How long' का प्रयोग करते हैं।

Let's understand the formation of sentences.
आओ वाक्यों की रचना करना सीखते हैं।

Examples:-

Boss : How long have you been working on this project?
Boss' guess (बॉस ने सोचा) : For six years approximately.
Employee's response : No, I haven't been working for six years on this project.
Employee's reply : I have been working on this project for two years only.

Boss : How long will it take to complete this?
Boss' guess (बॉस ने सोचा) : Five days.
Employee's response : No, it will not take five days.
Employee's reply : It will take approximately ten days.

Here are some more examples:

How long has she been cooking?	वह कब से पका रही है?
How long will we take to reach there?	हमें वहाँ पहुँचने में कितना समय लगेगा?
How long did he take to finish his work?	उसने कितना समय लिया अपने काम को खत्म करने में?
How long can she sit without breathing?	वह बिना साँस लिये कितनी देर बैठ सकती है?
How long has Monika known you?	मोनिका आपको कब से जानती है?

Exercise-13

Translate into English:

1. आप दिल्ली में कब तक रूकोगे?

____

2. वे लोग यहाँ कब से रह रहे हैं?

____

3. वह आपको कब से जानता है?

____

4. मोहन वहाँ कब तक रहेगा?

____

5. वह कब से बिमार हो रही है?

____

6. हमें वहाँ पहुँचने में कितना समय लगेगा?

____

7. छात्र कब तक कक्षा में थे?

14. How often/How many times

When we ask about frequency of action then we use 'How often' or 'How many times'. The sense of 'How often' and 'How many times' is the same.

जब हम किसी action की frequency पूछते हैं, तो वह कितनी बार हुई तब हम 'How often' या 'How many times' का प्रयोग करते हैं, ये दोनों एक ही अर्थ देते हैं।

Let's understand the formation of sentences.
आओ वाक्यों की रचना करना सीखते हैं।

Examples:-

Salesman : How often do you take tea?

Salesman's guess (विक्रेता ने सोचा) : Four-five times in a day.

Customer's response : No, I don't take tea four or five times in a day.

Customer's reply : I take tea once in a day.

Salesman : How many times do you purchase tea in a month?

Salesman's guess (विक्रेता ने सोचा) : Approximately two times.

Customer's response : No, I don't purchase tea leaves two times in a month.

Customer's reply : I purchase it once in a month.

Here are some more examples:

How often does she go to her mother's house?	वह अपनी माँ के घर कितनी बार जाती है?
How many times do you take bath?	आप कितनी बार नहाते हो?
How often does your mother call you?	आपकी माँ आपको कितनी बार फोन करती है?
How many times do you eat in a day?	एक दिन में, आप कितनी बार खाते हो?
How often do ladies do shopping in a month?	महीनें में महिलाएँ कितनी बार खरीदारी करती हैं?

Exercise-14

Translate into English:

1. आप साल में कितनी बार मोबाइल बदलते हो?

____

2. मोहन महीनें में कितनी बार स्कूल जाता है?

____

3. हम एक मिनट में कितनी बार पलक झपकते हैं?

____

4. उसने यह फिल्म कितनी बार देखी है?

____

15. What kind of/What sort of or What type of

When we ask about type or kind of something then we use 'What kind of', 'What sort of', 'What type of'. They have the same meaning or sense.

जब हम किसी चीज़ की 'Variety' को पूछते हैं, उसके आकार-प्रकार को पूछते हैं, तो 'What sort of' का प्रयोग किया जाता है। ये तीनों 'What kind of', 'What sort of' or 'What type of' अर्थ में एक ही तरह का भाव प्रकट करते हैं।

Let's understand the formation of sentences.
आओ वाक्यों की रचना करना सीखते हैं।

Examples:-

Kalpana : What kind of dress are you looking for?

Kalpana's guess (कल्पना ने सोचा) : Western dress.

Teena's response : No, I am not looking for a western dress.

Teena's reply : I am looking for an Indian-western dress.

Kalpana : What kind of food does she eat?

Kalpana's guess (कल्पना ने सोचा) : Chinese.

Teena's response : No, she doesn't eat Chinese food.

Teena's reply : She eats North Indian food.

Here are some more examples:

What sort of a boy is your family looking for?	आपके घरवाले किस तरह का लड़का तलाश कर रहे हैं?
What kind of life do they live?	वे लोग किस प्रकार का जीवन जीते हैं?
What type of books do you like?	आप किस तरह की किताबे पसंद करते हो?
What sort of job does she want to do?	वह किस प्रकार की नौकरी करना चाहती है?
What type of movies does your father watch?	आपके पिताजी किस तरह की फिल्मे देखते हैं?

Exercise-15

Translate into English:

1. वह किस प्रकार का कम्प्यूटर खरीदेगी?

 ____

2. मोहन किस प्रकार के कपड़े पहनता है?

 ____

3. किस तरह की भाषा हमें सीखनी चाहिए?

 ____

4. आप किस तरह का व्यापार कर रहे हो?

 ____

 **Let us help you:-**

जैसे चाय की पत्ती के बिना चाय नहीं बन सकती वैसे ही 'Subject' से पहले, बिना Helping verb लगाए Interrogative Sentence नहीं बन सकता।

Examples:-

1. (a) You have money? (×)
   (b) Do you have money? (✓)

2. (a) You took class yesterday? (×)
   (b) Did you take class yesterday? (✓)

Question Tags

Read the following sentences:

(a) You are Mohan, **aren't you**?
(b) He is a good player, **isn'he**?

Again, read these sentences.

(c) We are not happy, **are we**?
(d) She is not beautiful, **is she**?

A question tag is a short question at the end of a statement. Question tags are used to ask for confirmation or agreement.

In examples (a) and (b) the question tags are negative because the statements are positive.

Example:-

(a) You are Mohan, **aren't you**?

Positive statement — Negative question tag

Now, see the example:

(d) She is not beautiful, **Is she**?

Negative statement — Positive question tag

ध्यान दें: जब statement (वाक्य) positive होता है, तो negative question tag आता है और जब statement वाक्य negative हो, तो positive question tag आता है।

The subject and the verb of the question tag should match with the subject and the verb of the statement.

Examples:-

(a) You are Mohan, **aren't you**?
(b) She is not beautiful, **is she**?

ध्यान दें: ऊपर दिये गये दो उदाहरणों में question tags के subjects और verbs match होते हैं statements के subjects और verbs से।

Why to use Question tag?

A question tag is used to confirm whether something is true or not or encourage the listener to reply.

Examples:-

(a) You are writing a book, **aren't you**? आप एक किताब लिख रहे हो, हूँ/न/हेना?

(b) It is not a very thick book, **is it**? यह बहुत मोटी किताब नहीं है, हूँ/न/हेना?

ध्यान दें: Statement के अंत में जो हम हूँ, हेना, न का expression देते हैं ताकि confirmation लें या सहमती मिलें।

Read the following sentences.

(a) He is not a doctor, **is he**?
(b) They are intelligent, **aren't they**?

In example (a) The statement is negative therefore, the question tag is positive and in example (b) The statement is positive therefore, the question tag is negative.

ध्यान दें: इस नियम को समझना बहुत महत्त्वपूर्ण है, जब 'statement' का रूप positive हो, तो इसके साथ negative question tag का प्रयोग होता है, यदि statement का रूप negative हो, तो positive queston tag का प्रयोग किया जाता है।

Note: We should always use contracted form of auxiliary verbs.

Here are some rules for question tag.

Rule 1: When the subject is a pronoun like:- I, you, they, we, he, she and it. Then we repeat the subject just after auxliary verb in the question tag.

Examples:-

(a) You will come tomorrow, **won't you**?
(b) She dances well, **doesn't she**?
(c) I saw him going there, **didn't I**?
(d) It is wrong, **isn't it**?
(e) Mohan and Rohan are playing, **aren't they**?

Note: In English question tag means auxiliary verb

Rule 2: When the subject is a noun, like:- Monika Laxman, Ram and Rohan, then we can't repeat a noun in the question tag but we change it into pronoun according to the gender.

Monika	→	She
Laxman	→	He
Ram and Rohan	→	They

Examples:-

(a) Monika was a good girl, **wasn't she**?

(b) Carman is a player, **isn't he**?

(c) Ram and Rohan did not have dinner, **did they**?

Exercise-16

Give the correct question tags of the following statements:

1. You are a student, ...
2. Abhishek Gupta isn't a teacher, ...
3. Mohan doesn't learn English, ...
4. They were happy, ...
5. She was with Rahul, ...
6. He is very angry, ...
7. I am late, ...
8. Mohan is in Delhi, ...
9. You aren't a teacher, ...
10. He isn't selfish, ...

11. She wasn't tired, ...

12. They weren't interested, ...

13. You haven't done your work, ...

14. You won't come on time, ...

15. He didn't study at all, ...

16. Anjum is not good at cooking, ...

17. His sister is a teacher, ...

18. Our father didn't come yesterday, ...

19. The audience were happy, ...

20. Children are innocent, ...

21. I am a teacher, ...

22. You don't like me, ...

23. They didn't hurt my heart, ...

24. You will tell her my name, ...

ध्यान दें: I am an English teacher, aren't I? यह exceptional case है।

Statements without auxiliary verbs

Examples:-

(a) You have worked all week , **haven't you**?
(b) He speaks English well, **doesn't he**?
(c) Drinking kills us slowly, **doesn't it**?

ध्यान दें: इस तरह की statements में verb first, s or es, and form पर ध्यान दें तो question tag बनाना सरल हो जाएगा।

Exericse-17

Write question tags of the statements given below:

1. You speak English, ...
2. She spoke a lie, ...
3. Harish lived in Gujarat, ...
4. Renu wants to marry Rohan, ...
5. He reads English newspaper, ...
6. Ritu likes shopping, ...
7. You eat non-veg, ...
8. The students read it every day, ...
9. I saw you in the temple, ...
10. They went to watch a movie, ...

Statements with modals

Examples:-

(a) You can speak, **can't you**?
(b) You should go now, **shouldn't you**?

Exericse-18

Put the correct question tags of the statements.

1. You would like to get success, ...
2. You wouldn't stop me, ...
3. She must cook food, ...
4. They should give education, ...

Rule 3: When subjects are like:- someone, somebody, no one, nobody, everyone, everybody, none, anyone, anybody, then the subject of the question tag becomes 'they' and plural verb is used. But for nothing, something, anything, everything we use 'it' in the question tag.

Examples:-

(a) Everyone saw the movie, **didn't they**?
(b) Nobody has done it, **have they**?
(c) No one is able to work now, **are they**?
(d) Everyone is happy, **aren't they**?
(e) No one was there, **were they**?
(f) Everything is dirty here, **isn't it**?
(g) Somebody has to take decision, **don't they**?

ध्यान दें: इस नियम के अनुसार अगर व्यक्ति है, तो 'they' लगाते हैं लेकिन अगर कोई वस्तु हो, तब 'it' का प्रयोग किया जाता है।

Example:- Nothing was there, was it?

Rule 4: When the statements are already negative like:- neither, never, no one, nobody, few, little, nothing, seldom, none, rarely, hardly, scarcely, then we use a positive tag.

Examples:-

(a) I know few number, **do I**?
(b) We seldom go to temple, **do we**?
(c) The girl has little water, **does she**?
(d) He hardly goes to market, **does he**?
(e) He hardly speaks, **does he**?
(f) They rarely go in restaurant, **do they**?
(g) Nothing is written on that wall, **is it**?
(h) Humans can never understand animals' feelings, **can they**?

Rule 5: When the subjects are:- there, one, this/that, these/those, then we put the subject of question tag like this.

Examples:-

(a) There - there
(b) One - one
(c) This/That - it
(d) These/Those - they

Examples:-

(a) That is yours, **isn't it**?
(b) This is mine, **isn't it**?
(c) One can't jump from here, **can one**?
(d) This girl came yesterday, **didn't she**?
(e) It is a lovely weather, **isn't it**?
(f) It was a great match, **wasn't it**?
(g) There is a ball under the table, **isn't there**?
(h) There aren't students in the class, **are there**?
(i) That's Punit's brother over there, **isn't he/Isn't it**?

> **Rule 6:** When the subjects of statements are like, all of us, either of them, neither of you, most of you, all of you then we put the subjects of question tags like this:

All of us → We
Either of them → They
All of you → You

Examples:-

(a) Neither of them helped me, **did they**?
(b) Either of you is a winner, **aren't you**?
(c) None of us has seen God, **have we**?

> **Rule 7:** Use of question tag with imperative.

(A) In imperative sentences we use 'will you'?

Examples:-

(a) Open the door, will you/**won't you**?
(b) Don't open the door, **will you**?
(c) Please, give me my pen, **will you/won't you**?

(d) Help him, **will you**?
(e) Don't tell a lie, **will you**?
(f) Explain the topic, **will you**?
(g) Don't forget me, **will you**?

After positive imperative we can use will you/won't you?
But after negative imperative we use "will you" only.

(B) Imperative with anger or irritation then we use "Can't you?"

Examples:-

(a) Shut up, **can't you**?
(b) Mind your own business, **can't you**?
(c) Hold your tongue, **can't you**?

(C) Let's = Let us, we use "Shall we"

Note: We use 'shall we' in the case of let's, it is an exception.

Examples:-

Let's dance, **shall we**?
Let's play, **shall we**?
Let's help him, **shall we**?
Let's discolse the secret, **shall we**?
Let's go to the party, **shall we**?

(D) Let + obj + v1 then we use "will you?"

Examples:-
Let him go, **will you**?
Let her cook, **will you**?

1. Firstly identify whether the statement is positive or negative.
2. Secondly, identify the subject and its pronoun of statement.
3. Finally, put the auxiliary verb according to the subject.
4. While making question tags, we should use contracted forms of auxiliary verbs.

20 Prepositions

A preposition is a word that shows the relationship of a noun or a pronoun with another word in a sentence.

Preposition वह शब्द होता है, जो किसी **noun** या **pronoun** से पहले आता है और इसका **relation** (संबंध) किसी और शब्द से बनाता है वाक्य में।

Read the sentences given below.

The teacher was angry **with** Kavita because she was irregular.
My father was very kind **to** me.
Mohan lives **at** Laxmi Nagar in East Delhi.
They live **near** Akshardham Mandir.

The word that shows relation of one thing with another word in a sentence is called preposition.

Object of Preposition

When a preposition comes before a noun or a pronoun it is called the object of a preposition.

Examples:-
Children are **in** the class.
I am happy **with** your behaviour.

Exercise-1

Circle the prepositions and underline the objects in the following sentences.

1. Mohan stays at the Taj Hotel.
2. Students went into an A.C. room.
3. The ladder was against the wall.
4. She was at home.
5. They were in the zoo.

Kinds of Prepositions

OF PLACE	OF TIME	OF DIRECTION

Preposition of Place: Prepositions which give information about the place, position or location of a noun or pronoun is preposition of place. Preposition of place are words like: **inside, outside, behind, in front of, next to, on, under, near, over, opposite, at, above, by, beside, between, among, across, in.**

Examples:-

The pen is **on** the table.
My house is **in front of** the temple.
My elder brother is **in** Mumbai.

Let's understand the prepositions of place with examples.

On

When the surfaces of two objects touch each other and upper object is in stable position.

जब दो वस्तुओं की सतह आपस में मिले और ऊपर वाली वस्तु स्थिर हो, तो (On) का प्रयोग किया जाता है, जिसका अर्थ ऊपर, लगा हुआ होता है।

Read the following sentences:

(A) For two surfaces:

The mobile is **on** the table.
The watch is **on** the wall.

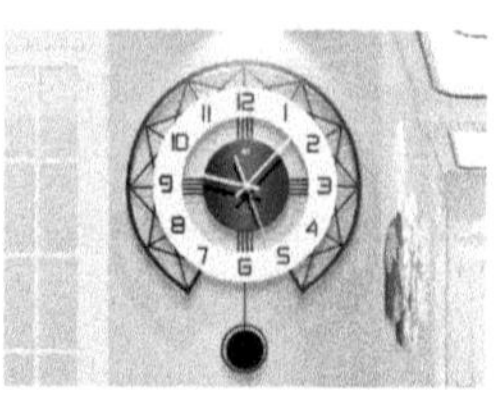

Note: When two things are attached to each other.
एक चीज़ किसी अन्य वस्तु के ऊपर है और स्थिर है।

(B) For a certain side:

The bus is **on** the left side.
I am **on** the right of father.

IN

When we talk about area, then we use 'In'.

जब हम बात करते हैं कोई चीज़ किसी Area के अंदर है, तब हम 'In' का प्रयोग करते हैं।

(A) For area, read the following sentences:

Water is **in** the bottle.
The pencils are **in** the box.

(B) For profession and identification:

I am **in** the army.
Mother is **in** a saree.

Note: The location of a thing that is inside a limited area.

At

We use 'At' when we talk about exact place or in case of object when something is near something.

जब हम exact place की बात करते हैं, तब हम 'At' का प्रयोग करते हैं। जिसका का अर्थ है (पर, के पास)

Read the following sentences:

(A) Exact place:

Sunil is **at** the metro-station.

She is **at** Aggarwal's shop.

(B) Something near something:

Mohan sits **at** the table.
The television is **at** the window.

(C) An action is done at place:

We are watching a movie **at/in** the cinema hall.
Students study **at/in** school.
I am enjoying **at/in** the party.

ध्यान दें: जब action किसी जगह पर होता है, तो 'In' और 'At' दोनों का प्रयोग हो सकता है।

Behind

When we talk about something that is partly or fully covered by something in front, then we use 'Behind'.

जब कोई वस्तु किसी अन्य वस्तु से थोड़ी या पूरी ढकी हो पीछे से (एक वस्तु आगे हो और दूसरी वस्तु उसके पीछे) इस का अर्थ है पीछे।

Read the following sentences:

Something is at the back of something:

Mohan is hidden **behind** the pillar.

The pen is kept **behind** the box.

In front of

We use 'In front of' when we talk about the part or side of something that faces forward.

जब एक वस्तु किसी अन्य वस्तु के सामने होती है, तो इसका अर्थ सामने होता है।

Read the following sentences:

Something is before something:

The tree is **in front of** the house.

The school is **in front of** the temple.

Near

We use 'Near' when we talk about something or someone that is close to something or someone.

जब एक व्यक्ति या वस्तु किसी अन्य व्यक्ति या वस्तु के करीब हो या पास हो, तो उसका अर्थ पास होता है।

Read the following sentences:

Close to the something:

The ball is **near** the table.

The bike is **near** the car.

Beside

When we talk about something by the side of something then we use 'Beside'.

जब एक वस्तु दायें और बायें हो, तो **'Beside'** का प्रयोग किया जाता है। इसका अर्थ निकट, बराबर में होता है।

Read the following sentences:

The bed is **beside** the window.

The pencil is **beside** the box on the table.

Use of '<u>Beside</u>' and '<u>Besides</u>'.

It is used for location or position of someone or something near someone/something.

जब हम बात करते हैं कोई व्यक्ति या वस्तु किसी अन्य व्यक्ति या वस्तु के बराबर में, तब हम 'Beside' का प्रयोग करते हैं।

Examples:-

The book is **<u>beside</u>** the bag.
The hospital is **<u>beside</u>** the office.

Besides is used to indicate 'In addition to', 'Apart from' as well.

Everyone went **<u>besides</u>**/**<u>except</u>**/**<u>apart from</u>** me.
I ate rice **<u>besides</u>** pulse and Chole Kulche.

Use of beside, next to, adjacent

Read the following sentences:

She stood **<u>beside</u>** her father.
She stood **<u>next to</u>** her father.
She stood **<u>adjacent</u>** to her father.
Ram's house and Raju's factory are **<u>adjacent</u>** to each other.

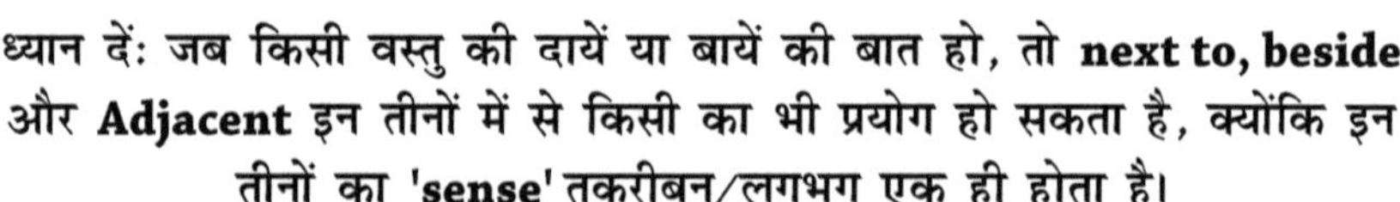

ध्यान दें: जब किसी वस्तु की दायें या बायें की बात हो, तो next to, beside और Adjacent इन तीनों में से किसी का भी प्रयोग हो सकता है, क्योंकि इन तीनों का 'sense' तकरीबन/लगभग एक ही होता है।

Below

We use 'Below' when we talk about somebody/someone at or to a lower position or level than somebody/something.

जब किसी व्यक्ति या वस्तु से नीचे या निचले स्तर पर किसी अन्य व्यक्ति या वस्तु हो, तो below शब्द प्रयोग होता है।

Read the following sentences:

(A) At a lower level:

The fish are **below** the surface.
Metro runs **below** the ground in Delhi.

(B) Lower level or lower position in comparison:

The temperature is **below** minus one degree in Kashmir.
The water level is **below** the danger point.

Above

We use 'Above' when we talk about somebody/something at or to a higher position or level than somebody/something.

जब हम किसी व्यक्ति या वस्तु से ऊपर किसी अन्य व्यक्ति या वस्तु को होना बताते हैं, तो 'above' शब्द प्रयोग होता है।

Read the following sentences:

(A) At a higher level:

The crow is flying **above** the head.
The watch is **above** the window.

(B) Higher level, higher position in comparison:

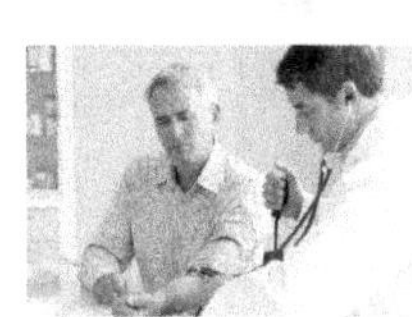

The blood pressure is **above** than normal.
Water level is **above** the danger point.

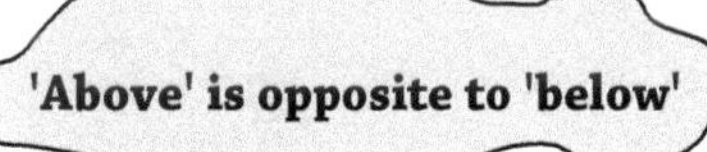

Under

We use 'Under' when we talk about somebody/something that is below the surface of somebody/something in case of covering or covered by.

जब किसी वस्तु की सतह के नीचे, किसी व्यक्ति या वस्तु का ढका होना जिसके ऊपर कोई और वस्तु हो।

Read the following sentences:

The bag is **<u>under</u>** the table.

A boat is passing **<u>under</u>** the bridge.

Mohan is sitting **<u>under</u>** the fan.

(B) For a particular limit or age:

Alcohol is not allowed **<u>to children</u>** 18 years old.

She is **<u>under</u>** weight in pregnancy.

We use 'Over' when we talk about somebody/something that is above something in case of covering or covered by.

जब किसी वस्तु से ढका हुआ होना किसी व्यक्ति या वस्तु का ऊपर से, तब हम **over** शब्द प्रयोग करते हैं, जो **'cover'** करती है, ऊपर से।

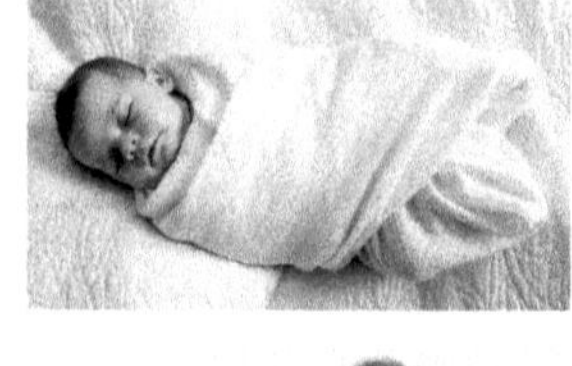

Read the following sentences:

(A) For something coverd by:

The blanket is **<u>over</u>** the child.

The fan is **<u>over</u>** the boy's head.

(B) For a particular limit or age:

The child is **<u>over</u>** 12 years old, so his ticket is necessary.

I sold **<u>over</u>** ten thousand copies of this book.

'Under' is opposite to 'over'

Comparison of below/above and under/over.

Below/Above	Under/Over
Lower/higher of something. Vertical position of something. Comparison of two things.	Covering something. For a particular limit or age. Not touching of two things.

Between

We use 'Between' when we talk about somebody/something that is in the middle of two persons, places or things.

जब कोई चीज़ या व्यक्ति दो चीज़ों या व्यक्तियों के बीच में होती है, तो **'between'** का प्रयोग किया जाता है। जिसका अर्थ बीच में होता है।

Read the following sentences:

Father is **between** the daughter and son.

There is a fight **between** Mohan and Rohan.

Among

We use 'Among' when we talk about somebody/something that is in the middle of more than two persons, things or places.

जब कोई चीज़ या व्यक्ति दो से ज़्यादा चीज़ो या व्यक्तियों के बीच में हो, तो **among** शब्द का प्रयोग किया जाता है।

Read the following sentences:

For there or more than three things:

Distribute the sweets **among** you all.

My house is **among** the trees.

The spinach is there **among** the vegetables in the basket.

Opposite

We use 'Opposites' when we talk about somebody/someone which is on the other side of somebody/something.

जब कोई चीज़ किसी व्यक्ति या वस्तु के सामने या दूसरी तरफ हो, तो opposite शब्द प्रयोग होता है, इसका अर्थ दूसरी तरफ होता है।

Read the following sentences:

On the other side of something or somebody:

The hospital is **opposite** the railway station.

Our house is **opposite** the temple.

'At'-'in'

When we talk about a small area of something then we use (at) but for bigger area we use (in)

जब एक वाक्य में दो 'area' की बात होती है, तब (At) किसी खास जगह के लिए जो 'area' में छोटा हो और बढ़े 'area' के लिए (In) का प्रयोग होता है।

Read the following sentences:

Mohan lives **at** Karol Bagh in Delhi.

Gandhiji was born **at** Porbandar in Gujarat.

By

We use 'By' when we talk about somebody/something which is near or beside somebody/something.

जब कोई व्यक्ति या वस्तु किसी चीज़ के करीब/पास हो, तो 'by' का प्रयोग होता है।

Read the following sentences:

Somebody/something near to:

Bed is **by** the window.

The trees are **by** the river.

Across

We use 'Across' when we talk about getting to the other side of something.

जब हम एक किनारे से दूसरे किनारे की ओर जाने की बात करते हैं, तो across का प्रयोग करते हैं। इसका अर्थ है उस पार।

Read the following sentences:

(A) For one side to another side:

This bridge is **across** the Yamuna river.

The farmer walks **across** the forest.

There is a clinic **across** the street.

Note: On the opposite side of something.

(B) For through out-every part of the place:

There are temples and mosques **across** India.

He is travelling **across** the city on foot.

Against

We use 'Against' when we talk about opposition to someone or something.

जब हम बात करते हैं, कोई चीज़ किसी के सहारे से है या उसके खिलाफ है, तो against शब्द प्रयोग किया जाता है।

Read the following sentences:

(A) Someone/something on something:

We should not stand **against** the Metro door.

The ladder was **against** the wall.

(B) Someone/something with disagreement:

Father gets angry when something goes **against** him.

They were protesting **against** British rule.

Around

We use 'Around' when we talk about someone/something that is encircled by someone/something.

जब कोई व्यक्ति या वस्तु के चारों तरफ किसी चीज़ का होना हो, तो 'around' शब्द का प्रयोग होता है, इसका अर्थ चारों तरफ है।

Read the following sentences:

Mother put her arm **around** her daughter.

Water and trees are **around** the city.

Sophiya has a scarf **around** her neck.

Beneath

When we talk about someone/something that is under someone/ something partly or completely then we use 'Beneath'.

जब कोई चीज़ या व्यक्ति किसी चीज़ या व्यक्ति के तले में, या नीचे दबा हुआ हो, तो beneath शब्द प्रयोग होता है।

Read the following sentences:

There are five persons **beneath** the debris of the building.

The snake was **beneath** the boat.

ध्यान दें: Beneath शब्द का प्रयोग (number) मात्रा के साथ नहीं होता है, beneath और underneath दोनों शब्द बराबर होते हैं, इन का अर्थ एक ही है।

Inside

When somebody or something is the 'inner part of something' or 'in the something' then we use 'Inside'.

जब कोई व्यक्ति या वस्तु किसी चीज़ के अदंरुनी हिस्से में हो, तो 'Inside' का प्रयोग होता है।

Read the following sentences:

Inner part of something:

The medicine is **inside** the bottle.

The letters are **inside** the letter box.

ध्यान दें: Inside = in.

Outside

When someone or something is out of something then we use 'Outside'.

जब कोई चीज़ किसी चीज़ के बाहर होती है, तो 'Outside' शब्द प्रयोग होता है इसका अर्थ बाहर होता है।

Read the following sentences:

The **outside** of a pineapple is rough but the inside is sweet and juicy.
She parks her car **outside** her house.
Farmers are **outside** in the hot sun.

Within

We use 'Within' when we talk about someone/something that is inside something.

Read the following sentences:

Limit of something:

There is a new mobile **within** the box.

There are fruits **within** the basket.

ध्यान दें: **within = inside.**

From

We use 'From' when somebody comes or returns from any place.

जब व्यक्ति किसी जगह से आता है या उसके 'birthplace' की बात हो, तो from का प्रयोग होता है।

Read the following sentences:

We are coming **from** Punjab.

She is **from** India.

Exercise-2

(A) Fill in the blanks with on, in or under.

1. The tree is __________the garden.
2. A parrot is __________ the tree.
3. Boy is sitting __________ the tree.

(B) Look at the pictures and pick the correct words from the box to complete the sentences.

on, in, in, under

1. Students are sitting ______ the chairs.

2. The cat is ______ the table.

3. The papers are ______ the dustbin.

4. The pencil is ______ the box.

(C) Tick (✓) the correct word to complete the sentences.

1. The eggs are (in, out) the basket.
2. The bread is (on, under) the plate.
3. The boy jumped (over, into) the wall.
4. The watch is (on, in) the wall.
5. The animals are(on, in) the zoo.
6. The teacher is (near, in) the blackboard.

(D) Underline the prepositions in these sentences.

1. The girl is sitting in the park.
2. The birds are flying over the tree.
3. Meena is sitting between Rohan and Mohan.
4. Listen to me, please.
5. The watch is on the wall.
6. School is near my house.
7. The car is parked in front of the gate.
8. Sheetal writes with a pencil.
9. I purchased the fruits from the market.
10. The medicine is for you.

Exercise-3

(A) Fill in the blanks with the prepositions of place.

in, on, at

1. She liked to live ________ a city.
2. His brother was born ________ a farm.
3. We were ________ England at that time.
4. She kept her clothes ________ the almirah.
5. He put the cup ________ the table.
6. Her elder sister lives ________ 8 Mission Road.
7. I prefer to work ________ a bank.
8. They saw some marks ________ the ceiling.
9. People love bull fight ________ Spain.
10. She lives ________ a little house ________ the mainstreet.

Exercise-4

(A) Fill in the blanks with the correct prepositions of position.

between, underneath, in front of, above
over, under, among, under, behind, above

1. We have hung the calender ________ the fire place.
2. He put his sign ________ mine.
3. They could see the valley ________ them.
4. There were clouds ________ us.
5. Dog buried the bone ________ the ground.
6. The water was ________ his knees.
7. The hat fell ________ the table.
8. We stood ________ the crowd.
9. The child hid himself ________ a quilt.
10. He stood ________ his brother and his sister.

Prepostions of time.

Prepositions of time refer to time or duration like:- **at, on, in, by, until, for, during, between, within, since, after and before, around, till.**

Examples:-

I reached there **at** 9 : 00 am.

She has been working **for** 8 hours.

Lets' understand the prepositions of time with examples.

In

We use 'in' for year, month, and parts of the day besides night.

Read the following sentences:

For season, parts of the day, month, year:

Rainy season is **in** August.

Cold wind blows **in** winter.

I will reach there **in** two hours.

ध्यान दें: 'In' का प्रयोग month, year, parts of the day के साथ प्रयोग होता है, लेकिन night शब्द के साथ 'at' का प्रयोग होता है।

Example: I was ill **in** the morning.

On

It is used for day and date.

'On' शब्द का प्रयोग Date or Day के साथ होता है।

Read the following sentences:

Mohit is coming **on** Monday.

My exam is **on** 23rd June.

ध्यान दें: 'On' sense में 'upon' के बराबर होता है और upon शब्द ज़्यादा formal होता है 'on' शब्द से।

Examples:-

A glass of water fell **on** the floor.
A glass of water fell **upon** the floor.

ध्यान दें: On = upon.

Note: We use 'on' with the word time.

Examples:-

Be **on** time.

Train is **on** time.

At

It is used with exact time, the word night and weekend.

जब 'at' का प्रयोग time preposition में होता है, तो exact time, night और weekend शब्दों के साथ होता है।

Read the following sentences:

Stars shine **at** night.

We complete our personal work **at** weekends.

Class starts **at** 7 : 30 am.

'Before' शब्द का प्रयोग तब किया जाता है जब कोई काम किसी दिये हुए time से पहले हो जाता है।

Read the following sentences:

The train is coming **before** 6 pm.

I will reach there **before** 9 pm.

After

It is used for later time than a particular time.

'After' का प्रयोग तब किया जाता है जब कोई काम किसी दिये गये **time** के बाद होता है।

Read the following sentences:

My class started **after** 7 : 30 am.

The movie started **after** 4 o' clock.

By

It is used for near time of any action.

'By' का प्रयोग समय के साथ जब किया जाता है, तो **'Near time'** का **sense** होता है।

Read the following sentences:

(A) For timing:

My father will reach there **by** 6 o'clock.

I need to reach office **by** 9 : 30.

Note: 'By' means before the given time but not later than given time.

During

It is used for the same time on which two actions occur.

जब किसी काम के चलते एक और काम शुरू हो जाए तब **during** का प्रयोग किया जाता है।

Read the following sentences:

Monika works in a school **during** the day.

We should not talk **during** a movie.

From

It is used for starting point of something.

'From' शब्द का प्रयोग किसी **action** के शुरू होने का बोध कराता है।

Read the following sentences:

(A) For starting point:

Tickets are available **from** Monday.

Class will start **from** June.

Until

It is used for time limit but action goes on or up to a particular point of time.

Until का प्रयोग तब होता जब कोई कार्य अपने अंतिम समय में खत्म होता है, जब वह **action** शुरू हो और उसके अंत तक के लिए **until** का प्रयोग होता है, इसका अर्थ 'तक' होता है।

Read the following sentences:

Something continues till its end:

She will leave her office **until** 7 pm.

We played ludo **until** midnight.

ध्यान दें: **'By' means before the time or on time.**

Example: I will be **in** the office **by** 6 pm.

मैं दफ्तर में पहुँचूँगा छह बजे लेकिन पहुँचा नहीं हूँ।

Until: up to finishing time:

Example: I will be **in** the office **until** 6 pm.

मैं दफ्तर में छह बजे तक रहूँगा। (**मतलब मैं office में ही हूँ।**)

Note: Until = till but until is more formal than till.

Within

It is used for ending an action before the given time or less than an amount of time.

कोई काम दिये हुये समय के अंदर हो, तो **within** शब्द का प्रयोग होता है।

Read the following sentences:

My grandfather gets tired **within** 10 minutes.

We need to finish this project **within** 7 weeks.

For

When we talk about period of time, length of action or how long an action goes on.

जब हम **action** के **period** या **length** की बात करते हैं कि कब तक चला, तो **for** का प्रयोग करते हैं।

Read the following sentences:

Reena watched a movie **for** two hours.

They played cricket **for** five hours.

Since

It is used for starting time of an action or point of time of starting action.

Since का प्रयोग किसी **action** के **starting time** को दर्शाता है।

Read the following sentences:

She has been cooking food **since** 6 o'clock.

Children have been playing **since** morning.

Between

When we talk about duration between two points of time then we use between.

'Between' का प्रयोग दो समय हो और उनके बीच के दौरान की बात हो, तब किया जाता है।

Read the following sentences:

I was at my home **between** 9 am and 12 pm.

He was lying on the road in a pool of blood **between** 5 pm and 9 pm.

About

When we talk about an expected time of an action then we use about.

जब हम समय का अनुमान लगाते हैं किसी कार्य का, तो **about** का प्रयोग करते हैं।

Read the following sentences:

The two trains hit each other **about** 5 o'clock.
The train came at the station **about** 6 o'clock.

Exercise-5

Complete the sentences about holidays and festivals in India, with in, at, on preposition.

1. Teacher's Day is _________ 5th September.
2. Flag Day is _________ December.
3. Indians celebrate Gandhi Jayanti _________ 2nd October.
4. National Youth Day is celebrated _________ 12th January.
5. Children's Day is celebrated _________ 14th November.
6. Some people go to church _________ midnight _____ Christmas Day.
7. There is usually a ten day holiday in schools _________ Dussehra.
8. Most of the people don't work _________ the weekends.

Exercise-6

Fill in the blanks with the suitable prepositions.

Mohan played 1. ________ (for, about) two hours in the evening. He was tired 2. ________ (by, in) the time, the match was over. He reached home 3. ________ (in, at) 7 p.m then he studied 4. ________ (between, in) 8 pm and 9 pm. He had to complete his assignment 5. ________ (within, during) two days. He worked on the project 6. ________ (by, until) he completed it.

Exercise-7

Fill in the blanks with the correct prepositions:

1. He drove the car ________ the road.
2. He tried to swim ________ the river.
3. She took the picture ________ the wall.
4. The crowd came ________ the city from the nearby villages.
5. The child ran ________ the house.
6. He came ________ the water.
7. They sailed ________ England ________ France.
8. The girls walked ________ the street.
9. He threw the bundle ________ the window.
10. The thief entered the house ________ the window.

Prepositions of Direction

Prepositions of direction are those prepositions which indicate the direction or movement of a noun or a pronoun like, **towards, through, around, over, to, into, up, down, along and so on.**

Examples:-

Mohan jumped **into** the river.
He came **to** me.

Around

We use around for various places or directions.

जब कोई व्यक्ति या वस्तु विभिन्न दिशाओं में चारों और हो, तो **around** का प्रयोग किया जाता है।

Read the following sentences:

(A) Someone or something in different directions:

You will become famous **around** the world.

I have my house **around** the corner of street.

(B) For approximately:

The time was **around** 5 o' clock.

There are **around** two hundred people.

Beyond

When we talk about someone or something it is to the other side of something.

जब हम बात करते हैं कोई व्यक्ति या वस्तु का होना जिसे दूसरी ओर या किसी चीज़ के परे, तो **'beyond'** का प्रयोग होता है।

Read the following sentences:

(A) Someone or something to the other side:

There is a village **beyond** this hill.

Life exists **beyond** our world.

(B) Out of limit:

We should not stop our cars **beyond** the zebra crossing.

People don't work **beyond** the age of 60.

Note: out of = beyond

Into

When we talk about somebody or something moving from outside to inside then we use into.

जब कोई चीज़ या वस्तु बाहर से अंदर की ओर आती है, तो **into** का प्रयोग किया जाता है।

Read the following sentences:

She jumps **into** the swimming pool.

He is looking **into** the well.

By

When we talk about the other uses of 'By' which are as follows.

जब हम **by** के प्रयोग की बात करते हैं, तो इसको यातायात के लिए या किसी चीज़ की कीमत या माप में बढ़ना या घटने के लिए **'by'** का प्रयोग होता है।

Read the following sentences:

(A) Mode of action (method or way):

We can learn English **by** using this Grammar book.

We cut vegetables **by** knife.

I will pay **by** cash.

(B) For transportation:

I come **by** bus.

He went to Mumbai **by** train.

(C) Rise or fall of something or measurement:

The price of petrol has increased **by** 10%.

The temperature decreases **by** 5 degrees.

(D) For showing something that happens due to something:

I got good job **by** chance.

Mohan's father died **by** heart attack.

With

When we talk about an action done by using something then we use 'With'.

जब कोई काम किसी instrument की मदद से होता है तो 'With' का प्रयोग किया जाता है।

Read the following sentences:

(A) For company:

The king lives in his palace **with** his Queen.

I was **with** my father in the party.

(B) Action done by something:

Mother cuts vegetable **with** knife.

We eat rice **with** spoon.

for done action by an instrument.
By = with

Up to

When we talk about a limit or a boundary less or equal but not more than the mentioned value.

जब हम बात करते हैं कोई चीज़ किसी limit से कम है या बराबर, तो 'Up to' का प्रयोग होता है।

Read the following sentences:

(A) For limit of something:

There are **up to** 500 people in the flight.

The water level reached **up to** knee.

(B) For number/amount to show approx or guess:

During Christmas, the discount **went up to** 70%.

I've read **up to** 5th chapter.

(C) For willing/option

It is **up to** her to play or not.

It is **up to** her whether to buy a pen or a pencil.

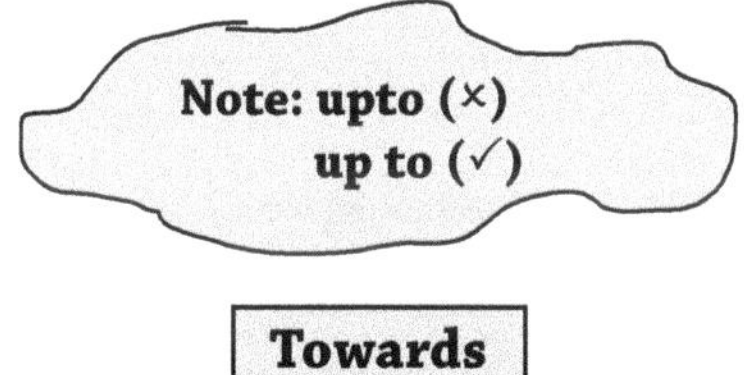

Towards

It is used with directions to someone/something.

जब हम किसी व्यक्ति या वस्तु की ओर इशारा करते हैं किसी की तरफ "point out" करते हैं या किसी व्यक्ति या वस्तु के direction की बात हो, तो towards का प्रयोग किया जाता है।

Read the following sentences:

Mohan and Monika were going **towards** the swimming pool.

Look **towards** the camera.

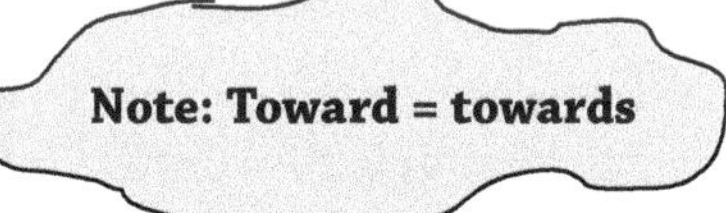

TO

It is used when somebody or something reaching to a particular destination.

जब किसी व्यक्ति या वस्तु की destination की बात हो उसके मंज़िल की बात हो तो 'to' का प्रयोग होता है।

Read the following sentences:

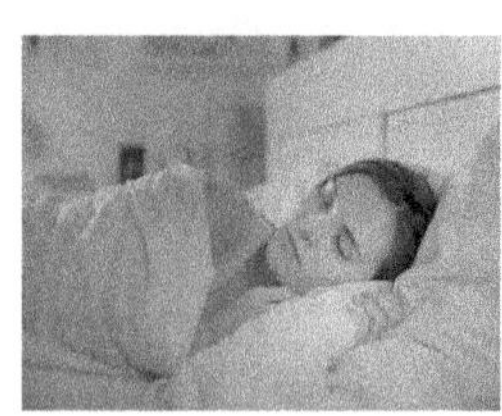

(A) For destination:

Mother goes **to** bed at 10 p.m.

We will go **to** the institute **to** learn English.

(B) In case of receiving something:

My father gave ₹ 100 **to** me.

We paid money **to** you.

(C) In case of reaching to a particular state/limit/end point.

The thief beat the innocent man **to** death.

Mother swings the child **to** sleep.

Smoking is dangerous **to** health.

Through

It is used for movement from one end or side of something to the other.

जब हम किसी चीज़ की शुरूआत से अंत तक की बात करते हैं या एक 'side' से दूसरी 'side' की बात हो तो 'through' आता है।

Read the following sentences:

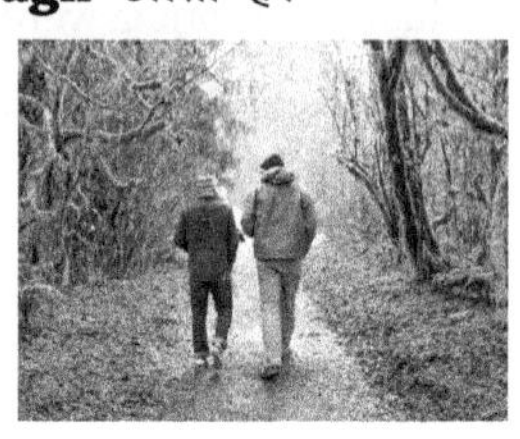

(A) Movement into one side to outside:

Mohan and Sohan walked slowly **through** the forest.
I rode my bicycle every day **through** the tunnel.
The cat jumped **through** the ring.

(B) From the beginning to the end of something:

We sat in front of T.V. **through** the movie.
Kedarnath temple stood **through** the tsunami.
I work in school Monday **through** Saturday.

Onto

It is used for movement of somebody or something into or on a particular place.

जब हम किसी जगह पर या उसके ऊपर किसी व्यक्ति या वस्तु की आने की या लगने की बात करते है तो **'onto'** आता है।

Read the following sentences:

(A) Movement on a particular place.

I am applying cream **onto** my face.
The dog jumped **onto** the roof of the house.

(B) Action is going to:

Mohan is **onto** preparation of his exam.
I am **onto** writing of my next book.

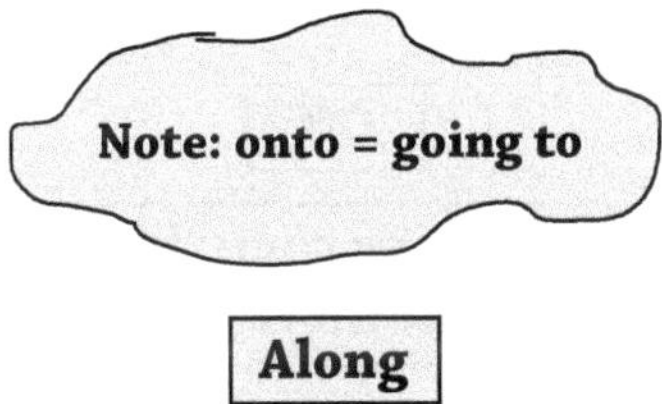

Note: onto = going to

Along

When we talk about someone/something that is by the side of someone/something.

जब बात होती है कोई व्यक्ति या वस्तु के बराबर में होने की तब **along** शब्द प्रयोग होता है।

Read the following sentences:

(A) One side of something:

The signboard is **along** the road.
Beautiful buildings are **along** the river.
I was walking **along** the pavement.

Note: It shows parallel movement or a side by side movement.
Example: I was riding a bicycle along the river.

From

When someone receives something from somebody or somewhere.

जब कोई व्यक्ति कुछ प्राप्त करता है किसी से या कहीं से:

Read the following sentences:

(A) Receiving from someone:

We get energy **from** the Sun.
Mohan takes money **from** father.

(B) Making something from something:

We make chapatti **from** flour.
Mohan makes broom **from** twig.

Off

When we talk about someone or something that is away from the place or fall down from the place.

जब कोई व्यक्ति या वस्तु अपनी जगह से नीचे आए या गिर जाए तो 'off' का प्रयोग होता है।

Read the following sentences:

The boy fell **off** the ladder.
The man fell **off** the hill.
The baby fell **off** the walker.

Out of

It is used for something/someone out of somewhere.

किसी व्यक्ति या वस्तु की किसी जगह से बाहर आना या निकलने के लिए 'out of' का प्रयोग करते हैं।

Read the following sentences:

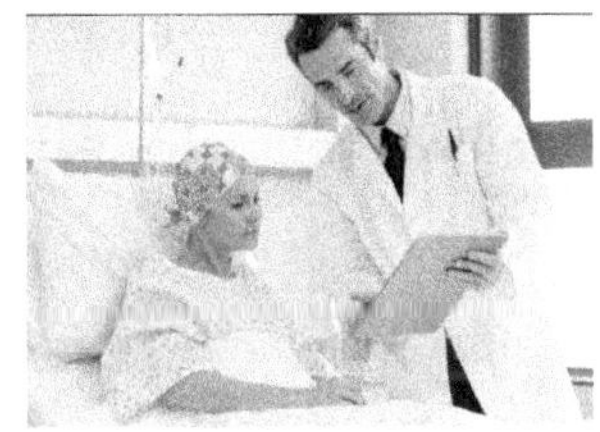

The patient is **out of** danger now.

Mother is **out of** the village for two days.

He looked **out of** the window.

Sheetal took the apples **out of** the fridge.

Up

When something/someone goes up somewhere.

जब कोई व्यक्ति या वस्तु किसी जगह पर ऊपर की ओर जाती हो तो 'Up' का प्रयोग होता है।

Read the following sentences:

The ice-cream cart went **up** the slope.

The child ran **up** the stairs.

Down

When someone/something comes down from somewhere.

जब कोई व्यक्ति या वस्तु किसी जगह से निचले पायदान पर आती है, तो 'Down' शब्द का प्रयोग होता है।

Read the following sentences:

The children ran **down** the stairs.

The man came **down** the hill.

Round

It is used for someone or something that goes round someone or something.

जब कोई व्यक्ति या वस्तु किसी व्यक्ति या वस्तु के चारों ओर चक्कर लगाती है, तो 'Round' शब्द का प्रयोग होता है।

Read the following sentences:

The baby walked **round** the mother.

The Earth revolves **round** the Sun.

Past

It is used for someone or something that goes forward beyond somewhere or a particular place.

Read the following sentences:

She has run **past** the river.

She walked **past** the hospital and reached the chemist.

Exercise-8

(A) Fill in the blanks and choose the correct prepositions from the brackets.

1. The boy gave the book ____________ the girl. (of, to)
2. Renu in hiding ____________ the tree. (behind/on)
3. The dog is ____________ the puppies. (between/on)
4. Mother is cutting the vegetables ____________ a knife. (with/on)
5. Mohan is sitting ____________ the television. (in front of/on)

(B) Fill in the blanks with suitable prepositions from the box.

for, to, of , on , after, in, with, under

1. They are talking __________ the teacher.
2. They are talking __________ the class.
3. I go to school __________ my sister.
4. The table is made __________ wood.
5. It's raining, come __________ my umbrella.
6. The book is __________ the table.
7. Morning comes __________ night.
8. My father has brought a gift __________ me.

(C) Look at the picture and fill in the blanks with prepositions to complete the paragraph.

near, on, in front of, on, to

1. The students are sitting __________ the benches.
2. The teacher is standing __________ the blackboard.
3. There is a watch __________ on the wall.
4. The teacher is standing __________the students.
5. The teacher is explaining a sum __________ the students.

Exercise-9

(A) Fill in the blanks with at, on or in.

1. They are arriving __________ Monday.
2. He has a meeting __________ 8 pm.
3. I arrived __________ the morning.
4. He met us __________ night.
5. She came to pick me __________ noon.
6. The wedding is __________ April.
7. The wedding is __________ 20th April this year.

(B) Fill in the blanks with behind, in front of or near.

1. The boy is __________ the pillar.
2. His mother is standing __________ the window.
3. The cycle is kept __________ the window.
4. The girl is hiding __________ the curtain.

(C) Fill in the blanks with among or between.

1. She distributed chocolates __________ her friends.
2. The cat is sitting __________ two kittens.
3. Shweta is standing __________ Sunita and Sonia.
4. I kept the pen __________ your books on the table.

(D) Fill in the blanks with to, from or for.

We stayed in Delhi 1. __________ eight years. We stayed there 2. __________ 2010 3. __________ 2019 4. __________ there we later shifted 5. __________ Jaipur. There, I went 6. __________ St. Johnson School. My school timings were 7. __________ 8 am. 8. __________ 2 pm. Our summer vacation was 9. __________ almost two months and during that period, we visited Delhi. After the vacation, we returned 10. __________ Jaipur in July.

(E) Fill in the blanks with in, into, or out of.

1. Raman jumped __________ the swimming pool.
2. He did not like to swim so he came __________ the water.
3. __________ our country we celebrate many festivals.
4. Mother keeps her ornaments __________ her locker.
5. The dog went __________ the kitchen but my mother sent it out.

The other uses of prepositions

1. 'About' can be used:

- **For approximately:**

Examples:-

There are about ten books in my bag.
There are about two hundred fifty people in this flight.

- **For guessing numbers or amount:**

Examples:-

There are about ten students in the class.
She is about 18-years-old.

2. 'Around' can be used:

- **For turning the face in the opposite direction:**

He turned around and went from there.
The situation turned around.

3. 'Through' can be used:

- **For using by:**

Examples:-

The protesters told the story of Independence through song.
I purchased my new car through finance.
I got this toy through father.

4. 'To' can be used:

- **'To' comes after adjective to show behaviour or feeling:**

Examples:-

The boy was cruel to animals.
My mother is kind to me.

Let us help you:

Use of 'To' and For:

(A) 'To': It is used for reason/motive/objective:
Example:- We learn English **to** get a job.

'For': It is used for reason/motive/objective:
Example:- We learn English **for** a job.

Note: 'To' for action whereas 'For' stands for noun but the sense is same.

(B) 'To': For destination:

Examples:-

What did you do **to** my brother?
He brought my bicycle **to** me.

We use 'for', doing something good or nice:

Examples:-

What did you do **for** my brother?
He brought my bicycle **for** me.

Note: Here is 'To' for destination but 'For' is used for something good or nice.

5. 'Off' can be used:

(A) For leaving transport:

Examples:-

We need to get **off** the train to the next station.
He got **off** the moving bus.

(B) For removing:

Mother was taking **off** her sandal.
Mother was taking **off** the lid of jar.

(C) For switching off:

The bulb is **off**.
The wheel of the bus is **off**.

6. 'Of' can be used:

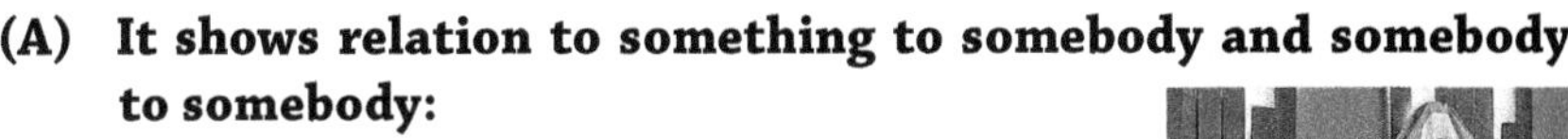

(A) It shows relation to something to somebody and somebody to somebody:

Examples:-

There are bottles **of** milk in fridge.
This is the coat **of** your father.
Monika is the daughter **of** Mr. Kapoor.

(B) It shows relation to somebody to something and something to something.

Examples:-

Salman Khan is the son **of** Mr. Salim Khan.
It is the tyre **of** a bus.
It is the pizza **of** Domino's.

7. 'Because of' can be used:

- **It is used for reason:**

Examples:-

Mohan is a doctor **because of** his father.
No one likes bitter gourd **because of** its taste.

ध्यान दें: **'Because of'** हम **noun** या **verb + ing** से पहले प्रयोग करते हैं, लेकिन **because** के बाद **subject** और **verb** आता है।

8. Use of 'In and 'Into'

'In' is used for something that is inside a limited area:

Examples:-

Students were **<u>in</u>** the classroom.
The pen is **<u>in</u>** the box.

Note: The position of students and the pen inside a limited area.

'Into' is used for the movement of something or somebody that goes inside from outside.

Examples:-

She walked **<u>into</u>** the room.
He jumped **<u>into</u>** the river.

Group Prepositions

There are some groups of words which function as prepositions.

1. Owing to: because of something. (के कारण)

owing + to + reason

Examples:-

<u>Owing to</u> poor financial conditions, I could not study.

<u>Owing to</u> lack of funds, he didn't take his mother to a private hospital.

Many accidents took place yesterday **<u>owing to</u>** fog.

2. In spite of: despite-even though (के बावजूद)

in spite of + noun (fact that makes something)
in spite of + v_1 + ing (else surprising)

Examples:-

He has earned a good amount of money **<u>in spite of</u>** recession.

We won the match **<u>in spite of</u>** that many players got out.

We entered on time in the cinema hall **<u>in spite of</u>** the long queue.

They arrived late **in spite of** leaving the house a long time ago.
He failed his exam **in spite of** the fact that he studied too much.
You went to market **in spite of** the rain.

Note: **In spite of** that it was raining. (×)
In spite of the fact that it was raining. (✓)

3. On account of: because of something (के कारण)

on account of + noun | reason |
for problem | difficulty

Examples:-

IPL game was cancelled **on account of** coronavirus.

On account of my injury, I didn't play.

She couldn't attend the wedding **on account of** the children.

owing to = on account of = due to = because of having the same sense.

4. For the sake of: for advantage | benefit (के खातिर)

(For the sake of + noun)

Examples:-

For the sake of you, I have brought it.

We shouldn't fight **for the sake of** unity of our family.

I left my job **for the sake of** my study.

ध्यान दें: For the sake of it कुछ करना बिना कारण के

He was talking **for the sake of** it.
For the sake of it, I was helping you (ऐसे ही/ऐवाई)

5. With reference to: about, concerning के सदंर्भ में/हवाला देते हुए।
with reference to + noun.

Examples:-
I have something to add **with reference to** what was said earlier.
She was writing to her boss **with reference to** the salary.

Note: In reference to = with reference to

6. With regard to: concerning, regarding (के बारे में) with regard to + somebody/something

(The subject that is being talked or written about)

Examples:-
With regard to breakfast, I will eat bread and butter.
With regard to population, our country is making new schemes.
I am calling **with regard to** your son's performance.
This book is **with regard to** English Grammar.

with regard to = in regard to = in respect to, with respect to = in view of = as regards = in relation to having same sense concerning, regarding, respecting, about

ध्यान दें: **with regards to (×)**
with regard to (✓)

7. By means of: method, process, system (के ज़रिये)

by means of + noun

I get knowledge **by means of** books.
I stood first in my class **by means of** hardwork.
We fill the tank **by means of** water pump.
I bought a new bike **by means of** loan.

Note: by means of = by dint of

8. As a result of: because of, from (नतीजे में/परिणामस्वरूप) as a result of + reason

Examples:-

As a result of coronavirus, every one has been jobless.
Her performance has declined **as a result of** her friend circle.
My flight has been cancelled **as a result of** fog.
Mohan's father died **as a result of** an accident.
He took so many loans and **as a result**, he went bankrupt.
Mohan's teacher twisted his arm and **as a result**, the teacher was expelled from the school.

9. Make use of: utilize, use (उपयोग करना)

Make use of + noun

Examples:-

Can you **make use of** these waste papers?
I will **make good use of** this book.
You **made use of** that information.
We **made use of** a digital camera to photograph you.

10. In case of: if, when something happens what to, in situation (यदि/स्थिति में)

(A) In case of + noun:

Examples:-

In case of breakdown, please call me.
In case of fire, break the glass and push the alarm button.
She carries an umbrella **in case of** sudden rain.

(B) In case + subject + verb:

Examples:-

Here is number **in case** we separate from each other.
In case I forget, please help me in my exam.
Shall I keep some food for your brother **in case** he comes, so he can eat?
We have kept some extra clothes **in case** we may stay there longer.

11. Accompanied by: to happen/exist at the same time as something else (के साथ)

accompanied + by + somebody/something

Examples:-

The Prime Minister of India was **accompanied by** all members.
The kids under 10-years-old must be **accompanied by** their parents.
She used to **accompany** her husband wherever he went.
Shall I **accompany** you on the stage?

Note: Accompany to travel to go somewhere with somebody.

Headache due to viral infection may be **accompanied by** fever.
Passport application form should be **accompanied by** two passport photographs.
The celebrity is always **accompanied by** bodygaurds.

ध्यान दें: Booklet जिसमें instructions होती है जो समान के साथ आती है। उसके लिए:

Please read the **accompanying** information before use.
Please see the **accompanying** booklet for instructions.
My book is **accompanied by** a workbook.

Note: Subject + be + accompanied + by + someone or something.

12. Prefer: like one thing more than another. (चुनना)

(A) Prefer + one thing + to + another thing

Examples:-

I prefer veg **to** non-veg.

We prefer newspaper **to** online news.

I prefer having cold drink **to** tea.

I prefer **to** die to live/I prefer dying **to** living.

We use 'to' with the word prefer in comparison of two things.

(B) Subject + would prefer + to + V_1

Examples:-

I would **prefer to** dance alone.
My father **would prefer** not **to** drive at night.

(C) Subject + would prefer + object pronoun + to V_1

Examples:-

She **would prefer** me **to** sing first.
Would you **prefer** me **to** drive?

Note:

(a) I **prefer** not **to** drive at night. (✓)
I **prefer** not drive at night. (×)

(b) People **prefer** cricket **to** football. (✓)
People **prefer** cricket **rather than** football. (✓)
People **prefer** cricket **than** football. (×)

13. Taste for: having interest, knowledge
(किसी चीज़ के लिए दिलचस्पी या knowledge होना)

Taste + for + noun

Examples:-

She has no **taste for** music.
I have no **taste for** cricket.

14. Be + married + to + someone: married (शादीशुदा होना)

be + married + to +somebody

Examples:-

He is **married to** Pooja Gupta.
Monika got **married to** Mohan.

ध्यान दें: Married शब्द के साथ with नहीं आता है।

Example:

He is **married with** Pooja Gupta. (×)

(B) Be + married + with + someone

Examples:-

Monika is now **married with** two children.
I am **married with** one child. (means having kids)

15. Laugh'at: make fun of (किसी पर हँसना) laugh + at + noun

Examples:-

They **laughed at** me.
We should not **laugh at** the mistakes of others.

16. Worthy of: good enough (के लायक)

be + worthy + of + noun

Examples:-

This mobile is **worthy of** praise.
No one among them was **worthy of** trust.

17. Thankful to: grateful (शुक्रगुज़ार)

(A) In case of somebody:

thankful + to + noun

Examples:-

She is very **thankful to** me.
Students were **thankful to** the teacher.

(B) In case of something:

thankful + for + noun

I am very **thankful for** the support/help.
We should be **thankful for** good things.

18. Good at (किसी चीज़ में अच्छा होना)

good + at + activity

Examples:-

My mother is **good at** cooking.
She is **good at** singing.

19. Good to: (किसी के प्रति अच्छा होना)

Good + to + someone

Examples:-

The man was **good to** children.
She is **good to** me.

20. Listen to: to hear (सुनना)

Listen + to + someone/something

Examples:-

She **listens to** me.
I will **listen to** the songs on radio.

Note: We use 'To' with the word 'Listen' example 'Listen to'.

21. Sure: confident (पक्का)

(A) Sure that + subject + v_1

Examples:-

He is **sure that** she will not help.
Are you **sure that** you know how to reach there?

(B) Be not + sure + how/if/weather/what

Examples:-

He wasn't **sure whether** he was right or wrong.
I wasn't **sure what** to say.

(C) be + sure of + noun

Examples:-

I wasn't **sure of** my car's number.
They were **sure of** their piece of information.

22. Reply to: answer (जवाब देना)

reply + to + object

Note: 'Reply' without 'To' is more common.

Examples:-

I will **reply to** you soon.
She hasn't **replied to** my question.
The teachers refused to **reply to** the students' questions about holiday homework.

23. Pray to: prayer (प्रार्थना करना)

(A) Pray + to + God + that + subject + verb

Examples:-

I **pray to God that** you will get the job.
I **pray to God that** it may rain today.

(B) Pray + to + God + to + verb

Examples:-

I **pray to God to** help everyone.
My mother **prays to God to** take me out of the loans.

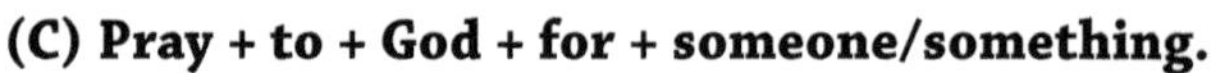

(C) Pray + to + God + for + someone/something.

Examples:-

I **pray to God for** good weather.
My teacher **prays to God for** us.

Note: I **pray to God** everyday.
We **pray for** rain.

24. Tired of: to be bored of something. (थक जाना)

(A) be + tired + of + v_1 + ing

Examples:-

I am **tired of** telling you to study.

She is **tired of** living at home during lockdown.

My father is **tired of** earning money for us.

(B) get + tired = of + v_1 + ing

Examples:-

I don't want to **get tired of** eating pizza.

He has **got tired of** doing the same work daily.

25. Afraid of: feeling fear or worry about (किसी का डर)

(A) be + afraid of + noun

Examples:-

I am **afraid of** my father.

She is **afraid of** spiders.

(B) be + afraid for + noun.

(किसी के लिए चिंतित होना)

I am **afraid for** my father.

She is **afraid for** her job.

(C) be + afraid + to + verb

Examples:-

I am **afraid to** open the door.

Sheetal is **afraid to** speak anything.

She is **afraid of** going out alone at night.

26. Accuse of: to blame (दोष लगाना)

Accuse + of + noun/v_1 + ing

Examples:-

Is she **accusing** you **of** beating her.

Mohan and his sister were **accused of** murder.

My father has **accused** my mother **of** having an affair with another man.

27. Apply to: written request for something (लागू होना/लगाना)

Apply + to + noun

Examples:-

I am **applying** cream **to** my face.
The new technology was **applied to** farming.
What government says that **applies to** all of us.

28. Key to: solution/key (कुंजी)

Examples:-

Hardwork is the **key to** success.
Satisfaction is the **key to** happiness.

Note: the + key + of + something. (×)
the + key + to + something. (✓)

29. Annoyed with: angry (नाराज़ होना)

be + annoyed + with + noun

Examples:-

I am **annoyed with** the government.

She is **annoyed with** her husband at his mistakes.

30. Died of: to die due to something (के कारण मरना)

died + of + noun

Examples:-

He **died of** hunger.
Mohan **died of** cancer.

Note: Here, we can use from and as a result of:

Examples:-

Mohan's father **died of** cancer. (✓)
Mohan's father **died from** cancer. (✓)
Mohan's father died **as a result of** cancer. (✓)

31. Care for: take care of (परवाह करना)

Care for + noun

Examples:-

You must **care for** your health.
A father **cares for** his child.

Note: Use 'Of' with the word 'Care' in case of using 'Take'.

Examples:-

I take **care of** trees.

She takes **care of** her children.

32. Boast of: to praise of someone/something (डींग मारना)

boast + of + noun

Examples:-

She always **boasts of** her daughter's beauty.

He keeps **boasting of** his rich relations.

Mohan is **boasting of** his promotion these days.

33. Congratulation on: wishing someone (बधाई देना)

(A) Congratulate + on + something

Examples:-

I was **congratulated on** my marriage.

She was **congratulated on** having a baby.

I want to **congratulate** you **on** purchasing a new car.

(B) Congratulate + for + something

Note: To praise someone for achievements.

Examples:-

Everyone is **congratulating** me **for** completing 5 years in the company.

I **congratulated** my brother **for** supporting me in business.

Note:

(a) In case of contribution of someone for making something successful then use 'for':

Example:- I would like to congratulate the organisers for doing the best to make the programme enjoyable.

(b) For action of someone:

Example:- I congratulated the CM of Delhi for his prompt action.

34. Sympathise with: understand and care about someone's problem (हमदर्दी करना)

Sympathise + with + noun

Examples:-

She sympathised with those who have lost their jobs.

He sympathised with me in my hard times.

I sympathise with you for your loss.

35. Insist on: (ज़ोर डालना)

(A) Insist on + noun/verb + ing

Examples:-

The shopkeeper was **insisting on** purchasing the black dress.
She **insisted on** taking decision fast.
The children **insisted on** going out with their parents.
She **insists on** eating food with me.

Subject + insist + that + sub + v_1

Examples:-

Mohan **insisted that** she was right.
Sonu **insisted that** his friend went there himself.

36. Complain of: to say about problem. (शिकायत करना)

(A) Complain + of + noun

I will **complain of** the condition of hotel.
She **complained of** garbage lying here and there.

(B) Complain + to + someone

She **complained to** the police about stealing.
I will **complain to** the forest officer regarding animal hunting.

Let us help you:

1. Prepositions of place tells us about the place, position or location of a noun or a pronoun.
2. Prepositions of time tells us about time or duration.
3. Propositions of direction tells us about the direction or movement of persons and things.

End...

Test Paper-3

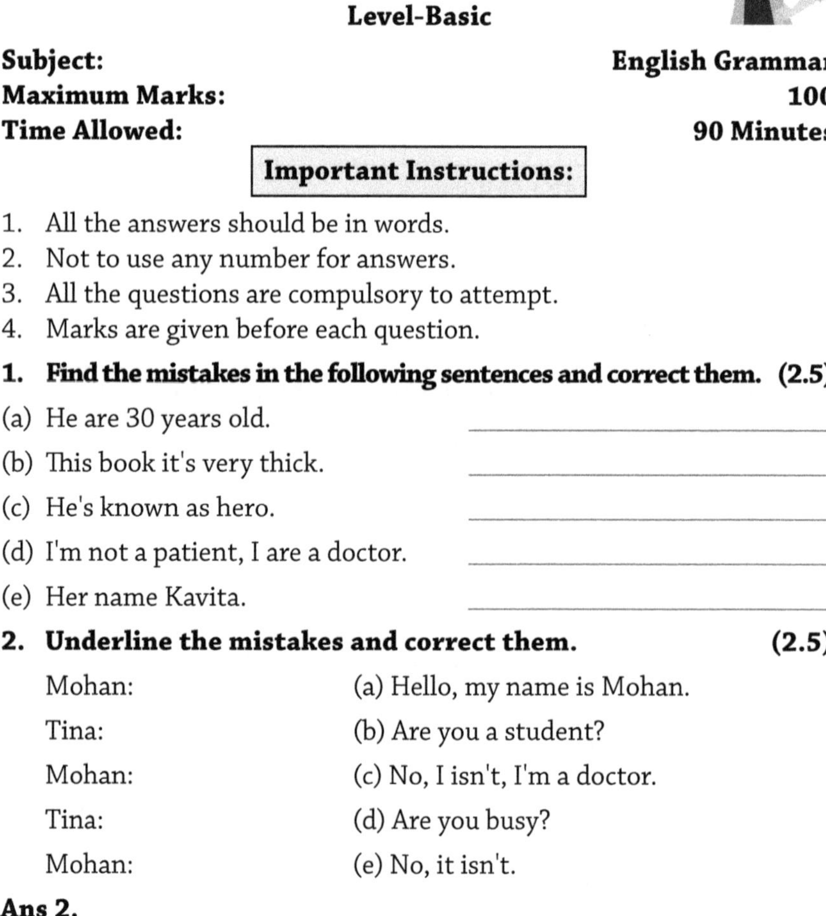

"Test of your honesty"

पूरा टेस्ट करने के बाद ही अपने 'Answers' को Match करें।

Level-Basic

Subject:	**English Grammar**
Maximum Marks:	**100**
Time Allowed:	**90 Minutes**

Important Instructions:

1. All the answers should be in words.
2. Not to use any number for answers.
3. All the questions are compulsory to attempt.
4. Marks are given before each question.

1. Find the mistakes in the following sentences and correct them. (2.5)

(a) He are 30 years old. ____________

(b) This book it's very thick. ____________

(c) He's known as hero. ____________

(d) I'm not a patient, I are a doctor. ____________

(e) Her name Kavita. ____________

2. Underline the mistakes and correct them. (2.5)

Mohan: (a) Hello, my name is Mohan.

Tina: (b) Are you a student?

Mohan: (c) No, I isn't, I'm a doctor.

Tina: (d) Are you busy?

Mohan: (e) No, it isn't.

Ans 2.

(a) ____________ (b) ____________ (c) ____________

(d) ____________ (e) ____________

3. Fill in the blanks using with this, that, these, those. (2.5)

(a) Is ________ your bag? (far)

(b) ________ is your car. (near)

(c) ________ is my husband, Mohan. (near)

(d) Who are ________ people? (far)

(e) Are ________ your children? (near)

4. Fill in the blanks with is or are. (2)

(a) There ________ two books on the table.

(b) There ________ five students in the class.

(c) There ________ a tub in the bathroom.

(d) There ________ money in my hand.

5. Read the following sentences and correct the mistakes. (8)

(a) There is ten thousand women in the function. ________________

(b) There is a water in the tank. ________________

(c) In Mumbai the bus are red. ________________

(d) There is an old women in the street. ________________

(e) This is my boxes. ________________

(f) Are the childs in the room? ________________

(g) The fishes are in the river. ________________

(h) The sandwichs are fresh. ________________

6. Read the following sentences and correct the mistakes. (8)

(a) Whos Ahmed's brother? ________________

(b) Rosy, Rehana and Sohana house. ________________

(c) Kavita lives with his brother. ________________

(d) My father's name's Bhupendra. ________________

(e) Your phone is better then my. ______________________

(f) This is not your. ______________________

(g) They know my name but I don't know their. ______________________

(h) Mine health is not fine today. ______________________

7. Write a/an or nothing (0) before the nouns. (3)

(a) __________ honesty, (b) __________ tomato (c) __________ sugar
(d) __________ owl (e) __________ apple juice, (f) __________ mobile.

8. Make plural forms of the following singular forms. (5)

Singular form	**Plural form**
(a) Wheat	__________
(b) Umbrella	__________
(c) Orange	__________
(d) Milk	__________
(e) Potato	__________
(f) Money	__________
(g) Orange juice	__________
(h) Flour	__________
(i) Rupee	__________
(j) Sugar	__________

9. Complete the questions using How much/How many. (2)

(a) __________ time will it take to go there?

(b) __________ pens have you purchased?

(c) __________ books are there in your bag?

(d) __________ money does she have in her account?

10. Circle the mistakes and rewrite the sentences. (3)

(a) There aren't much books. ______________________

(b) How many books is in the bag? ______________________

(c) The dog is bitting me. ______________________

(d) Mohan is eating an aple. ______________________

(e) She is runing very fast. ______________________

(f) They is swiming really well. ______________________

11. Fill in the blanks using in, at, on or no. (3)

(a) Valentine's Day is celebrated __________ 14th February.

(b) Gandhi Jayanti is celebrated __________ 2nd October.

(c) Children's Day is celebrated __________ November.

(d) People go to church __________ midnight __________ Christmas Eve.

(e) I do pending work __________ the weekends.

(f) There is usually a ten-day holiday in schools __________ Dussehara.

12. Correct any mistakes in the following sentences and correct them. (4)

(a) My father was born on the 1952. ______________________

(b) I cannot sleep in the night. ______________________

(c) Will you pay on the future? ______________________

(d) She sang on Christmas. ______________________

(e) Mohan was ill in past. ______________________

(f) It snow falls in Shimla at winter. ______________________

(g) She came at midnight. ______________________

(h) She shocked in moment. ______________________

12. (a) __________ (b) __________

(c) __________ (d) __________

(e) __________ (f) __________

(g) __________ (h) __________

13. Complete the blanks using to/from/over/on/off/out of/along (3.5)

Mohan: (a) How do I get __________ the college __________ the hospital?

Anil: (b) Go __________ the college __________ the road __________ then turn right, go __________ the bridge and there will be a building.

Mohan: (c) Is it a long way?

Anil: (d) No, it's not. If you get __________ the number 347 bus outside the college and get __________ next to the bridge.

14. Tick the correct options of the following sentences. (3)

(a) He (was/were) a doctor.

(b) We (was/were) students at that time.

(c) (Was/were) you angry yesterday?

(d) It (was not/were not) mine.

(e) They (was not/were not) happy.

(f) I (was not/were not) ill yesterday.

14. (a) __________ (b) __________

(c) __________ (d) __________

(e) __________ (f) __________

15. Complete the blanks with was or were: (6.5)

A: (i) How (a) _________ the time during lockdown?

B: It (b) _________ a horrifing time. I (c) _________ totally fed-up so I (d) _________ under depression. We (e) _________ at home.

A: (ii) Where (a) _______ your wife and children?

B: (iii) They (a) _______ with me locked in the house. They (b) _______ upset too due to corona That (c) _______ dangerous. There (d) _______ many problems and there (e) _______ not a lot of ration. The children (f) _______ getting bored and they (g) _______ very frightened.

16. Make questions of the following sentences. **(4)**

(a) How long | lockdown | during Corona?

(b) You | getting | bored sitting at home?

(c) Your friend | infected | from Corona | ?

(d) People | in the | houses | during | lockdown?

Ans. 16. (a) ______________ (b) ______________?

(c) ______________ (d) ______________?

17. Write the opposite words of the following adjectives: **(5)**

(a) Short ______________ (b) Happy ______________

(c) Slow ______________ (d) Cold ______________

(e) Quiet ______________ (f) Expensive ______________

(g) Boring ______________ (h) Old (person) ______________

(i) Old (thing) ______________ (j) Rich ______________

18. Write the superlative forms of the following adjectives. **(4)**

(a) Safe ______________ (b) Dangerous ______________

(c) Cheap ______________ (d) Delicious ______________

(e) Boring ______________ (f) Good ______________

(g) Relaxing ______________ (h) Clean ______________

19. Correct the mistakes of the following sentences: **(4)**

(a) Taj Mahal is the interestingest building in Agra.

____

(b) Chennai is the most far place from Delhi.

____

(c) This is goodest book in the world.

____

(d) Is she the most old lady in her family.

____

20. Make these sentences into questions. **(2)**

(a) Sheetal and Rahul were late. ______________________?

(b) Her anger was dangerous. ______________________?

(c) He is a doctor. ______________________?

(d) We are happy. ______________________?

21. Put the words in the correct order to make questions. **(4)**

(a) she | fatima | was? ______________________?

(b) you | will | go | where? ______________________?

(c) the film | how long | was? ______________________?

(d) his | bag | is | where? ______________________?

22. Write much or many to make questions. **(3)**

(a) How __________ times a day does she eat?

(b) How __________ does it cost me?

(c) How __________ pens are in your bag?

(d) How __________ cake did he eat?

(e) How __________ people were there?

(f) How __________ water is in the glass?

23. Write true (T) or false (f). **(3)**

(a) I hear with my ears. ( )

(b) I walk with my hands. ( )

(c) I see with my eyes. ( )

(d) I smell with my nose. ( )

(e) Banana is a vegetable. ( )

(f) Potato is a fruit. ( )

24. Match the animals with their sounds. **(2.5)**

(i) A tiger	(a) Mews
(ii) A dog	(b) Trumpets
(iii) A wolf	(c) Barks
(iv) An elephant	(d) Howls
(v) A cat	(e) Roars
(vi) A lion	(f) Growls

25. Add suitable question tags to the following sentences. **(6)**

(a) It is very cold today, ...

(b) It is not cold today, ...

(c) He has plenty of money, ...

(d) None of these pens worked, ...

(e) I saw nobody whom I knew, ...

(f) She goes nowhere these days, ...

(g) I could hardly hear what she said, ...

(h) Few boys were present, ...

(i) Mohan has a car, ...

(j) I'm more intelligent than you, ...

(k) Pass me the book, ...

(l) Let's go out for a walk, ...

26. Write the following times into words. **(4)**

(a) 9 : 50, ______________________

(b) 11 : 45, ______________________

(c) 10 : 45, ______________________

(d) 10 : 30, ______________________

Appendix (A)

(Reading Materials)

Revision of 'A'

Cat (बिल्ली) **Read aloud:** **Van** (गाड़ी)

1.	At (पर)	2.	An (एक)
3.	Ban (मनाही)	4.	Bad (बुरा)
5.	Bar (लोहे का सरिया)	6.	Bag (बोरा, थैला, झोला)
7.	Bat (बल्ला)	8.	Cab (गाड़ी)
9.	Can (डिब्बा टीन का)	10.	Cat (बिल्ली)
11.	Cap (टोपी)	12.	Dam (बांध)
13.	Chat (गपशप)	14.	Fan (पंखा)
15.	Dad (पिता)	16.	Gab (गपशप, बकबक)
17.	Fad (सनक, झक)	18.	Had (पास होना)
19.	Fat (मोटा)	20.	Ham (सूअर का माँस)
21.	Gap (दरार, फासला)	22.	Hat (टोपी)
23.	Hang (लटकाना, फंसा देना)	24.	Lap (गोद)
25.	Jab (गढ़ाना, घुसाना)	26.	Mad (पागल)
27.	Lab (प्रयोगशाला)	28.	Nab (दबोचना, पकड़ना)
29.	Lad (बालक, लड़का)	30.	Nap (झपकी)
31.	Man (पुरूष)	32.	Pad (गद्दा)
33.	Map (नक्शा)	34.	Pan (बर्तन)
35.	Mat (चटाई)	36.	Pat (थपकी थपथपाना)
37.	Nag (टोकना)	38.	Rag (फटे पुराने कपड़े)
39.	Ran (दौड़)	40.	Ram (भेड़ा)
41.	Rat (चूहा)	42.	Sap (पौधो का रस, खत्म करना)
43.	Sad (दु:खी)	44.	Sat (बैठा)
45.	Tab (फीता)	46.	Than (की जगह, से)
47.	Tan (धूप से झुलसना)	48.	That (कि, ताकि)
49.	Vat (टब, कुण्ड)	50.	Van (बंद गाड़ी)

Revision of 'E'

Hen (मुर्गी) **Read aloud:** **Bell (घंटी)**

1.	Beg (भीख मांगना)	2.	Bed (खाट)
3.	Bend (झुकना)	4.	Bet (शर्त)
5.	Best (सबसे अच्छा)	6.	Cent (सैकड़ा)
7.	Cell (कोठरी)	8.	Egg (अण्डा)
9.	Den (बिल)	10.	End (अंत)
11.	Fell (गिरा)	12.	Gem (रत्न, मोती)
13.	Get (पाना)	14.	Jet (विमान)
15.	Hell (नरक)	16.	Led (सीसा)
17.	Hen (मुर्गी)	18.	Leg (टाँग)
19.	Jelly (मुरब्बा)	20.	Lend (उधार देना)
21.	Left (उल्टा)	22.	Men (पुरुष)(दो या दो से ज़्यादा पुरुषों के लिए)
23.	Let (आज्ञा देना)	24.	Met (मिला)
25.	Melt (गलना)	26.	Neck (गर्दन)
27.	Net (जाली)	28.	Nest (घोंसला)
29.	Peg (खूंटा)	30.	Pen (कलम)
31.	Pet (पालतू)	32.	Red (लाल)
33.	Rent (किराया)	34.	Sell (बेचना)
35.	Send (भेजना)	36.	Set (जमना)
37.	Smell (सूघँना)	38.	Tell (बताना)
39.	Test (इम्तेहान)	40.	Ten (दस)
41.	Then (तब, कब)	42.	Vet (पशु चिकित्सक)
43.	Vest (बनियान)	44.	Well (कुँआ)
45.	Web (मकड़ी का जाला)	46.	When (कब)
47.	Wet (गीला)	48.	Yes (हाँ)
49.	Zest (जोश)	50.	Yet (फिर भी)

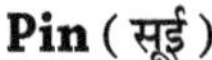

Pin (सूई)

Revision of 'I'

Pip (बीज)

Read aloud:

1.	Big (बड़ा)	2.	Bib (छोटा कपड़ा जो बच्चे की छाती पर लगता है)
3.	Chin (ठोड़ी)	4.	Bid (बोली)
5.	Dig (खोदना)	6.	Big (बड़ा)
7.	Fit (ठिक)	8.	Bit (थोड़ा)
9.	Hill (पहाड़ी)	10.	Chip (किनारा)
11.	Igloo (इग्लू)	12.	Dim (धुधंला)
13.	His (उसका, उसकी)	14.	Dip (डुबाना)
15.	In (अंदर)	16.	Fig (अंजीर)
17.	It (वह)	18.	Fill (भरना)
19.	Kid (बच्चा)	20.	Fix (जमाना)
21.	Kit (सामान का डिब्बा)	22.	Him (उसे)
23.	Lid (ढक्कन)	24.	Hip (कुल्हा)
25.	Lip (होंठ)	26.	If (अगर)
27.	Lit (चमकीला)	28.	Is (है)
29.	Mix (मिलाना)	30.	Kiss (चूमना)
31.	Nib (नोक)	32.	Pig (सूअर)
33.	Nil (शून्य)	34.	Pit (गड्ढ़ा)
35.	Pin (सूई)	36.	Rib (पसली)
37.	Sin (पाप)	38.	Sit (बैठना)
39.	Sip (घूंट)	40.	Skin (खाल)
41.	Skid (फिसलना)	42.	Thick (मोटा)
43.	Slim (पतला)	44.	Tin (टीन का डिब्बा)
45.	Twin (जुड़वा)	46.	Tip (नोक)
47.	Will (इच्छा)	48.	Trim (काट-छाँट)
49.	Zip (चेन)	50.	Win (जीत)

Dog (कुत्ता)

Revision of 'O'

Lock (ताला)

Read aloud:

1.	Block (खंड, कुन्दा)	2.	Blog (चिट्ठा)
3.	Boss (नेता)	4.	Bob (झांसा)
5.	Cot (खाट)	6.	Bog (दलदल)
7.	Dock (बदंरगाह)	8.	Box (डिब्बा)
9.	Dot (नुक्ता)	10.	Cob (ढेला)
11.	Glow (चमक)	12.	Cod (फली)
13.	Got (पाना)	14.	Cog (पहिये के दाँत)
15.	Hog (सूअर)	16.	Flow (बहना)
17.	Job (नौकरी)	18.	God (भगवान)
19.	Log (लट्ठा)	20.	Hollow (छेद)
21.	Loss (नुकसान)	22.	Hot (गर्म)
23.	Lot (बड़ी मात्रा)	24.	Jog (धक्का)
25.	Mob (गिरोह)	26.	Lock (ताला)
27.	Mom (माँ)	28.	Lop (काटना)
29.	Nod (आज्ञा)	30.	Mop (पोछा)
31.	Own (अपना)	32.	Moss (काई)
33.	Frog (मेढक)	34.	Not (नहीं)
35.	Pod (फली)	36.	Odd (अनोखा)
37.	Pop (पॉप संगीत, पिता)	38.	Pot (बर्तन)
39.	Hop (छलाँग)	40.	Rod (लाठी)
41.	Rot (सड़ना)	42.	Row (धीमे)
43.	Row (कतार)	44.	Show (दिखाना)
45.	Slob (कामचोर)	46.	Snow (बर्फ)
47.	Slow (धीरे)	48.	Sob (सिसकी)
49.	Top (चोटी)	50.	Toss (उछलना)

Bus (बस) **Cup (प्याला)**

Revision of 'U'

Read aloud:

1.	Sun (सूरज)	2.	Fun (मज़ा)
3.	Run (दौड़ना)	4.	Bun (मोटी रोटी)
5.	Cut (काटना)	6.	Hut (झोपड़ी)
7.	Jug (जग)	8.	Cup (प्याला)
9.	Nut (अखरोट)	10.	Mug (प्याला)
11.	Bus (बस)	12.	Tub (टब)
13.	Gun (बदूंक)	14.	Hub (केंद्र)
15.	Gum (गोंद)	16.	Slug (सुस्त)
17.	Fuss (झमेला)	18.	Rug (कम्बल)
19.	Buck (नर खरगोश)	20.	Duck (बतख)
21.	Tuck (दबाना, सिकुड़ना)	22.	Sum (जोड़)
23.	Drum (ढोल)	24.	Shut (बंद करना)
25.	Thumb (अगूँठा)	25.	Rub (रगड़ना)

Revision of Sounds 'a', 'e', 'i', 'o', 'u':

'a'	'e'	'i'	'o'	'u'
Man	Hen	Sin	Top	Cup
Fan	Bell	Sip	God	Tub
Van	Beg	Chip	Lot	Sun
Sad	Ten	Dig	Hot	Fun
Map	Wet	Pit	Box	Bus

Sound of Sh : And : Doing Actions:

Fish (मछली) **Read aloud:** **Ship** (जहाज़)

1.	Bush (झाड़ी)	2.	Dish (बर्तन)
3.	Brush (ब्रश)	4.	Shirt (कमीज़)
5.	Shoe (जूता)	6.	Push (धक्का)
7.	Ship (जहाज़)	8.	Fish (मछली)
9.	Cash (नकद)	10.	Shadow (छाया)
11.	Shoot (मारना)	12.	Shut (बंद करना)
13.	Shop (दूकान)	14.	Wash (धोना)
15.	Shy (शर्मीला)	16.	Seashore (समुद्र तट)
17.	Fresh (ताज़ा)	18.	Shave (हजामत करना)
19.	Polish (चमकाना)	20.	Show (दिखाना)
21.	Shake (हिलाना)	22.	Sharp (तेज़)
23.	Wish (इच्छा)	24.	Short (छोटा)
25.	Crash (दुर्घटना)	25.	Shrink (सिकोड़ना)

Read the following sentences:

A mobile **and** a computer.
A cat **and** a dog.
A bear **and** an elephant.
This is a book **and** that is a top.
This is a ball **and** that is a tap.

Doing Actions:

The cow **and** the goat are sitting.
The black horse **and** the white horse are running together.
Anil **and** Sunil are studying.
Mother is cooking food **and** father is reading a newspaper.

Sound of Ch : But : Doing Actions:

Watch (च sound) **Chemist shop (क sound)**

Read aloud: **(Ch- च, क)**

1.	Chain (माला)	11.	Church (चर्च)
2.	Chair (कुर्सी)	12.	Choose (चुनना)
3.	Cheat (धोखा)	13.	Watch (देखना)
4.	Chase (पीछा)	14.	Fetch (जाकर लाना)
5.	Chat (बातचीत)	15.	Kitchen (रसोई घर)
6.	Chew (चबाना)	16.	Match (बाज़ी, वर)
7.	Cheese (पनीर)	17.	Itch (खुजाना)
8.	Chop (टुकड़े करना)	18.	Catch (पकड़ना)
9.	Chill (ठंड)	19.	Watch (देखना)
10.	Charm (जादू)	20.	Chin (ठूडी)

English Grammar समझ तो आती है।

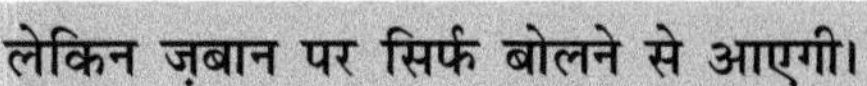

Read the following sentences:

My cat is white **but** your cat is black.

This tree is big **but** that plant is small.

My father is old **but** my uncle is young.

Doing Actions:

I am doing mathematics **but** you are learning English.
I am working in a printing press **but** my sister is working in a hospital.
He is exercising **but** they are sitting.

Let us help you:-

Am	Only with 'I'	I + am + V_1 + ing	I am reading a newspaper.
is	He, She, It, Name	He, She, It, Name + is + V_1 + ing	She is cooking food.
are	You, They, We or plural subjects	You, they, We + Mohan and Rahul + V_1 + ing	Mohan and Rahul are studying.

Sound of 'th': or' Doing Actions:

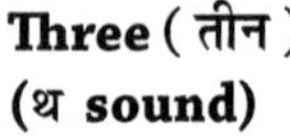

Three (तीन)
(थ sound)

Feather (पंख) (द sound)
(Th- थ, द)

Read aloud:

1.	Thief (चोर)	2.	Thorn (काँटा)
3.	Think (विचार)	4.	The (वह, वही)
5.	Cloth (कपड़ा)	6.	That (की, जोकि)
7.	Then (तब, फिर)	8.	Their (उनका, उनकी)
9.	Them (उन्हें)	10.	They (वह लोग)
11.	That (वह)	12.	This (यह)
13.	These (ये)	14.	Those (वे)
15.	There (वहाँ)	16.	Than (से)
17.	With (साथ)	18.	Path (रास्ता)
19.	Thunder (बिजली)	20.	Thank (धन्यवाद)

Read the following sentences:

A laptop **or** a computer.

A cold drink **or** a tea.

Doing Actions:

What are you drinking, tea **or** cold drink?

Where is Meena visiting, Shimla **or** Manali?

What are Mohan and Pooja doing, job **or** studying?

What will you purchase, a laptop **or** a computer?

Sound of "Wh": because: Doing Actions:

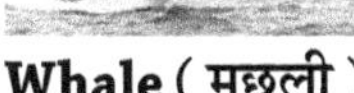

Whale (मछली)

Wheel (पहिया)

(Wh-वेह)

Read aloud:

1.	Who (कौन)	2.	Why (क्यों)
3.	What (क्या)	4.	When (कब)
5.	Which (कौन-सा)	6.	Where (कहाँ)
7.	Whose (किसका)	8.	Whom (किसको)
9.	Whatever (जो भी)	10.	Whoever (जो कोई)
11.	Wherever (कहीं भी)	12.	Whether (कि, या, यदि)
13.	While (जिस समय)	14.	Wheat (गेंहू)
15.	Whirlpool (भंवर)	16.	While (जब तक)
17.	Whole (पूरा, सारा)	18.	White (सफेद)
19.	Whale (मछली)	20.	Wheel (पहिया)

Read the following sentences:

Alexander was the King of the world **because** he was very strong.

Manisha was taking medicine **because** she was ill yesterday.

They were drinking hot soup **because** it was cold last month.

Ram and Rahim missed the bus **because** they reached late.

 **Let us help you:-**

Was	He, She, It, Name, I	He was dancing.	I was reading.
Were	You, They, We, Reena and Seema	You were sleeping.	Naina and Meena were playing.

Sound of 'Ck': When" Doing Actions:

Duck (बतख)

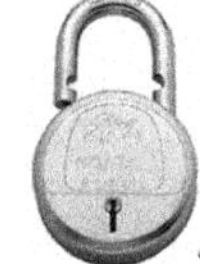

Lock (ताला)
(Ck- क)

Read aloud:

1.	Back (पीछे)	2.	Lick (चाटना)
3.	Sick (बीमार)	4.	Brick (ईंट)
5.	Neck (गर्दन)	6.	Chick (चूज़ा)
7.	Sock (मौज़ा)	8.	Truck (ट्रक)
9.	Kick (लात)	10.	Luck (भाग्य)
11.	Block (बंद करना)	12.	Stick (छड़ी)
13.	Check (जाँचना)	14.	Click (दबाना)
15.	Black (काला)	16.	Pick (चुनना)
17.	Attack (हमला करना)	18.	Thick (मोटा)
19.	Duck (बत्तख)	20.	Lock (ताला)

Read the following sentences:

Anil was sleeping, **when** his father called him.
It was raining, **when** I was going to the temple.
Madan and his wife fell down from the scooter **when** they were going to market.
Thief was stealing **when** police came.
Sunita and Aarti were dancing **when** guests came.

 **Let us help you:-**

We use when (जब) to indicate two things that happen at the same time. जब दो (Actions) एक time पर होते हैं।

Sound of Gh: If: Doing Actions:

Cough (खाँसी) **Read aloud:** **Laugh (हंसी)**

1.	Through (के ज़रिये)	2.	Enough (काफी)
3.	Tough (कठोर)	4.	Dough (गुंधा हुआ आटा)
5.	Though (हालांकि)	6.	Although (हालांकि)
7.	Bough (डाली)	8.	Bought (खरीदा)
9.	Daughter (बेटी)	10.	Slaughter (कसाई)
11.	Laugh (हसँना)	12.	High (ऊँचा)
13.	Sigh (गहरी साँस)	14.	Thigh (रान)
15.	Light (प्रकाश)	16.	Right (ठीक)
17.	Tight (कसके)	18.	Flight (उड़ान)
19.	Night (रात)	20.	Rough (पथरीला)

Read the following sentences:

You will get good marks **<u>if</u>** you work hard.
We will go to watch a movie **<u>if</u>** we get tickets.

Doing Actions:

Present	**Past**
I am singing a song. मैं गाना गा रहा हूँ।	He was running. यह दौड़ रहा था।
He is writing a book. वह एक किताब लिख रहा है।	They were selling fruits. वे फल बेच रहे थे।
Man is reading a newspaper. एक आदमी अख़बार पढ़ रहा है।	I was dancing. मैं नाच रहा था।
They are sitting silently. वे चुप-चाप बैठे हैं।	You were learning English. तुम अंग्रेजी सीख रहे थे।
We are swimming in the river. हम नदी में तैर रहे हैं।	She was cooking food. यह खाना पका रही थी।

Sound of ph : So : Doing Actions:

Elephant (हाथी)

Dolphin (मछली)

(ph = F)

Read aloud:

1.	Phone (फोन)	2.	Nephew (भांजा)
3.	Dolphin (मछली)	4.	Orphan (अनाथ)
5.	Graph (ग्राफ)	6.	Autograph (हस्ताक्षर)
7.	Photograph (फोटोग्राफ)	8.	Photo (फोटो)
9.	Phobia (डर)	10.	Emphasis (ज़ोर)
11.	Telephone (टेलीफोन)	12.	Joseph (जोसेफ)
13.	Prophet (प्रोफेट)	14.	Triumph (विजय)
15.	Pamphlet (पुस्तिका)	16.	Phenomenon (घटना)
17.	Physical (शारीरिक)	18.	Phrase (वचन)
19.	Hyphen (चिह्न)	20.	Alphabet (ABCD)

Read the following sentences:

I was exercising **so** I was losing weight.

He was taking bath with cold water **so** he was getting ill.

Tarun was watering the plants daily **so** they were growing.

Doing Actions:

Present

I am going to Delhi.
मैं दिल्ली जा रहा हूँ।

The boys are swimming in the river.
लड़के नदी में तैर रहे हैं।

It is raining.
वर्षा हो रही है।

Past

I was going to my house.
मैं अपने घर जा रहा था।

They were shivering with cold.
वे सर्दी से काँप रहे थे।

It was drizzling.
बूदां-बांदी हो रही थी।

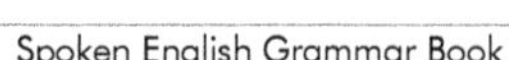

Reading-1

Mohan: Is this a duck?
Rohan: No, it is not.
Rohan: It is a hen.
Mohan: Ok.

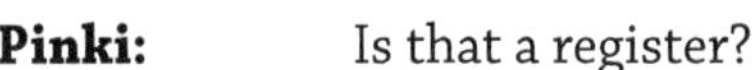

Pinki: Is that a register?
Shopkeeper: No, that is not.
Shopkeeper: That is a book.
Pinki: Ok.

Varun: Are these oxen?
Mohan: No, these are not.
Mohan: These are cows.
Varun: Ok.

Duck (बत्तख)	Peacock (मोर)	Hen (मुर्गी)
Not (नहीं)	This (यह)	These (ये)
Horse (घोड़ा)	Elephant (हाथी)	Cow (गाय)

Vocabulary is the petrol of English.

Without words we can't speak English.

Learn words and their forms.

Reading-2

This is Anil.

He has a black and white ball.

This is his favourite ball.

The ball is big.

This is Meenakshi.

She has a blue pen.

The pen is blue.

The pen is gifted.

Those are flowers.

Those are Mohan's flowers.

The flowers are different and beautiful.

Mohan likes red rose.

Favourite (प्रिय)	His (उसका, उसकी)	Big (बड़ा)
Has (पास होना)	Gift (उपहार)	Those (वे)
Different (अलग)	Like (पसंद करना)	Beautiful (सुन्दर)

Reading-3

This is Mohan's room.

He has an expensive laptop.

The laptop and the book are on the table.

His bat and ball are under the table.

His chair is upside down.

He has a big sofa. The sofa is very nice.

The sofa and the telephone are by the window.

The window is open. His watch is on the wall.

Has (पास होना)	Expensive (महँगा)	On (ऊपर)
Under (नीचे)	Upside down (उल्टा)	Big (बड़ा)
Nice (अच्छा)	By (पास में होना)	Open (खुला)
His (उसका)	Wall (दिवार)	Window (खिड़की)

Reading-4

This is a classroom.
This is a very big and beautiful classroom.
There are many students in this classroom.
Students are in the school uniform.
They are writing in their classroom.
They are looking very happy.

She is Mrs. Pooja Gupta, she is a teacher.
She is in a top and a skirt.
She is teaching in the classroom.
She has a marker in her hand.
The board and the watch are on the wall.

Many (बहुत सारे)	Writing (लिखना)	Their (उनका, उनके)
Looking (दिखना)	Very (बहुत)	Happy (खुश)
Teaching (पढ़ाना)	His (उसका, उसके)	Beautiful (सुंदर)

Reading-5

This is a beautiful garden. There are trees and flowers in this garden. This garden is beside a river. There are many people in the garden. Some children are playing in the garden. One boy is under a tree. He is playing with his friends. One girl is skipping in the garden. She is skipping very fast. Some old men are sitting on the bench. They are talking together. They are all enjoying in the sunshine. There is plenty of natural beauty and fresh air in the garden.

Beside (बराबर में)	Many (बहुत सारे)	Play (खेलना)
Some (कुछ)	Under (नीचे)	With (साथ)
Skip (रस्सा कुदना)	Sit (बैठना)	Enjoy (मज़े करना)
Together (साथ में, मिलकर)	Sunshine (धूप)	Talk (बात करना)

Reading-6

The Lion and the mouse

A lion and a mouse lived in a jungle. One day the lion was sleeping in the jungle. This mouse started running up and down his body for fun. The mouse disturbed the lion when he was sleeping. He got up angrily and was about to eat the mouse when the mouse requested the lion to spare his life. "I promise you, I will help you whenever you are in danger. The lion thought and laughed at the mouse's confidence and let him go.

One day some hunters came into the forest and trapped the lion in the net. The lion struggled to get out of the net but could not. Thus he roared angrily. The mouse heard the lion's roaring and came out to help the lion to come out of the net. The mouse gnawed the net and the lion came out of the net quickly and roared at the hunters. The hunters ran away from the jungle. Both lived in the jungle happily.

Moral of the story: "A small act of kindness can pay much in return."

Once upon a time (एक समय की बात है)	Get up (जागना)
Beside (बराबर में)	Spare somebody's life (जान बक्शना)
Angrily (गुस्से में)	Detain (बंद करना)
Hunter (शिकारी)	Struggle (परिश्रम)
Net (जाल)	Come out (बाहर आना)
Roar (दहाड़ मारना)	Gnaw (कुतरना)

Reading-7

The Boy and the Wolf

A boy and an old father lived in a village. The old man told his son that he was old enough to watch the sheep while they grazed in the fields. Every day the boy had to take the sheep to the grassy fields and watch them while they grazed. One day the boy decided to have fun with the villagers so that he could enjoy and make his day a funny day. The boy shouted Wolf! Wolf. All the villagers came running with sticks and stones to kill the wolf.

When the villagers came and saw that there was no wolf, they went away whispering and muttering about how the boy had wasted their time. The next day the boy once again cried Wolf! Wolf. And again the villagers came there to chase the wolf away.

The boy laughed at the fear or the foolishness of the villagers. He thought that he had befooled the villagers. The villagers went away angrily. The third day, as the boy came to the grassy field with his sheep, suddenly the wolf attacked the sheep and the boy cried Wolf! Wolf! Wolf. But not a single villager came to help him. The villagers thought that he was trying to make them fool again. As a result, the wolf killed many of his sheep. The boy thought that he lost many of his sheep because of his foolishness.

Moral of the story: "We must not lie".

Suddenly (अचानक)	Graze (चरना)	Grassy (हरी-भरी)
Watch (नज़र रखना)	Have fun (मज़ा करना)	So-that (ताकि)
Whisper/mutter (बड़बड़ाना)	Shout (चिल्लाना)	Attack (हमला करना)

Reading-8

The Fox and the Stork

One day, a selfish fox invited a stork for dinner. The stork was very happy with the invitation. The stork reached the fox's home on time and knocked at the door with its long beak.

The fox set the dining table and served soup in shallow bowls for both of them. As the bowl was too shallow for the stork, the stork was not able to have soup at all. However, the fox licked up his soup as well as the soup of the stork.

The stork was sad and angry. But the stork behaved well and showed that it was normal and polite. To teach a lesson to the fox, the stork invited the fox for dinner the next day. The stork served soup in narrow vases. The stork tasted the soup easily but the fox was not able to taste the soup at all because of the narrow vase. The fox realised his mistake and went home hungry.

Moral of the story: "As you sow, so shall you reap".

Selfish (मतलबी)	Invite (दावत देना)	Stork (सारस)
Beak (चोंच)	Shallow (फैला)	Narrow (पतला)
Lick (चाटना)	Behave (बर्ताव)	Vase (कलश)
Serve (भोजन परोसना)	Realise (अहसास करना)	Knock (खटखटाना)

Reading-9

Greedy wish for Gold

Once upon a time there lived a greedy man in a small village. He was a rich man and he loved gold and all expensive things. He had a daughter whom he loved more than anything. One day, he got a chance to help a fairy who was in a problem. The rich man helped the fairy to come out of her problem. The fairy granted him a wish. The greedy man said, "All that I touch should turn to gold. The greedy man thought that he would become richer by asking such a wish and his wish was granted by the grateful fairy.

The greedy man came and told his wife and daughter about his wish. The stones and pebbles turned into gold as the man touched them. He was very happy. One day, his daughter came to him. As soon as the man touched his daughter. She turned into a gold statue. The man cried and tried to bring his daughter back to life. The greedy man looked for the fairy in order to take back her wish. The greedy man was upset and disappointed for the rest of his life.

Moral of the story: "We shouldn't be greedy".

Greedy man (लालची व्यक्ति)	Expensive (कीमती)	Fairy (जादूगरनी)
Grant (उपहार)	Wish (इच्छा)	Pebbles (कंकड़)
Convert (रूप बदलना)	Basing (आधारित)	Statue (मूर्ति)
In order to (के लिए)	Upset (चिंतित)	Disappointed (निराश)

Reading-10

The Milkmaid and her Bucket

Pinky, a milkmaid, milked her cow and filled two buckets of milk. She carried the two buckets to the market to sell the milk. As she entered the market, she started thinking about the money which she would make from selling the milk. Later she thought what she would do with that money. She was talking to herself and thinking once I get the money, I will buy a hen, the hen will lay eggs and I will get more chickens, they will all lay eggs and I'll sell them for more money. Then I'll buy a house on the hill. She was very happy that she would be very rich. She kept on walking ahead with these happy thoughts.

Suddenly, she fell down. Both the buckets of the milk fell and all her dreams were shattered. Pinky was very sad and started weeping. No more dreams she cried angrily.

Moral of the story: "Don't count your chickens before they are hatched."

Milkmaid (दूधवाली)	Wealth (दौलत)	Lay (अंडा देना)
Sell (बेच देना)	Buy (खरीदना)	Fell (गिरा)
Suddenly (अचानक)	Shatter (चकनाचूर करना)	Weeping (रोना)

Reading-11

The Proud Rose

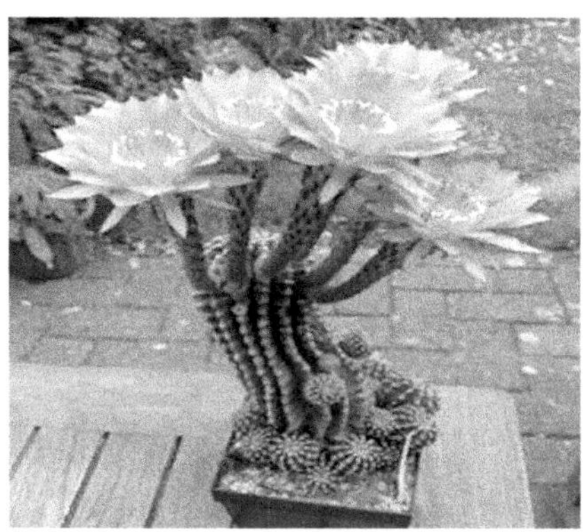

Once upon a time, there was a beautiful rose plant in a garden. One of the rose flowers on the plant was proud of its beauty. However, it was disappointed that it was growing next to an ugly cactus. Every day, the rose would insult the cactus about its looks. But the cactus stayed quiet. All the other plants in the garden tried to stop the rose from bullying the cactus, but the rose was too swayed by its own beauty to listen to anyone.

One summer, a well in the garden dried up and there was no water for the plants. The rose slowly began to wilt. The rose saw a sparrow dipping its beak into the cactus for some water. The rose felt ashamed for making fun of the cactus. It went to ask the cactus if it could have some water. The kind cactus agreed, and they both got through summer as friends.

Moral of the story: "Never judge someone by the way they look".

Proud (गर्व)	Ugly (बुरा)	Sway (बोल-बाला)
Dried up (सूखना)	Wilt (मुरझाना)	Make fun (मजाक बनाना)
Disappoint (दु:खी)	Quiet (शांत)	Ashamed (शर्मीदा)

Reading-12

The Bear and Two Friends

One day two best friends were walking on a lonely and dangerous path through a jungle. As the sun began to set, they grew afraid but held on to each other. Suddenly, they saw a bear in their path. One of the boys ran to the nearest tree and climbed it up in a jiffy. The other boy did not know how to climb the tree by himself, so he lay on the ground, pretending to be dead. The bear approached the boy on the ground and sniffed around his head.

After appearing to whisper something in the boy's ear, the bear went on its way. The boy on the tree climbed down and asked his friend what the bear had whispered in his ear. He replied, "Do not trust friends who do not care for you".

Moral of the story: "A friend in need is a friend indeed."

Lonely (अकेला)	Dangerous (खतरा)	Afraid (डरा हुआ)
Climb (चढ़ना)	Jiffy (पल, जल्दी में)	Pretend (बहाना करना)
Whisper (काना-फूंसी)	Approach (लगभग)	Sniff (सूघँना)
Trust (यकीन)	Indeed (सचमुच)	Suddenly (अचानक ही)

Reading-13

The Little Mermaid

In the underwater kingdom of Atlantica, lived the mer-people. Here lived a little mermaid who loved nothing more than to look at things on the surface and observe how humans lived. She longed to be human, and when she ended up rescuing a handsome prince from drowning, she decided that she must become human at any cost, as she wanted to be with him. This led her to visit a sea and asked the mermaid to sacrifice her voice, in exchange for human legs, on the condition that the mermaid would return as a slave if the prince did not marry her. The mermaid then went to her prince, but faced a series of challenges, separating from the prince not recognizing her and other suitors coming forward to marry him. However, at the end, both the mermaid and the prince reunite, defeating the witch and living happily ever after.

Mermaid (जलपरी)	Slave (गुलामी करना)	Defeat (हार)
Rescue (बचाव करना)	Recognise (सम्मान करना)	Brave (बहादुर)
Sacrifice (कुरबानी)	Reunite (फिर से एक होना)	Suitors (विवाह प्रस्तावक)

Reading-14

Cinderella

The story of Cinderella tells the story of a kind-hearted young woman who was treated cruelly by her step-mother and step-sisters nevertheless, kept a humble attitude.

One day, the king decided to throw a ball and invited all the young maidens in the kingdom. While Cinderella made her sisters help them to get ready for the ball, not once did they ask her if she would like to go with them.

Once they left her, a fairy Godmother appeared and helped Cinderella go to the ball with a bit of magic that would last only until midnight. At the ball, Cinderella caught the eye of the prince, as she was the most beautiful girl there, and they danced all night.

When midnight came, Cinderella had to leave the ball, and in her hurry, one of her glass slippers fell off her feet. The prince found this slipper and vowed to marry the girl who the slipper belonged to. The prince went from house to house, looking for the girl who's foot fit the slipper and he reached Cinderella's house. Though Cinderella's step-sisters and step-mother tried to prevent her from trying it on, the glass slipper perfectly fit her and she was soon married to the prince and lived happily ever after.

Moral of the story: "This is a wonderful story that captures how keeping a humble attitude will reap its rewards."

Kind-hearted (दरिया दिल)	Midnight (आधी रात)	Vow (शपथ खाना)
Step-mother (सौतेली माँ)	Ball (अंग्रेज़ी नाच)	Looking for (ढूढ़ना)
Humble (नम्र)	Slipper (चप्पल)	Maiden (कुमारी, कन्या)

Reading-15

The Tale of the Pencil

A boy named Rahul was upset because he had done poorly in his English test. He was sitting in his room when his grandmother came and comforted him. His grandmother sat beside him and gave him a pencil. Rahul looked at his grandmother puzzled, and said he didn't deserve a pencil after his performance in the test.

His grandmother explained, "You can learn many things from this pencil because it is just like you. It experiences a painful sharpening, just the way you have experienced the pain of not doing well in your test. However, it will help you become a better student. Just as all the good that comes from the pencil is within itself, so you will also find the strength to overcome this hurdle and finally just as this pencil will make its mark on any surface, you too shall leave your mark on anything you choose to. Rahul was immediately consoled and promised himself that he would do better.

Moral of the story: 'We all have the strength to be who we wish to be'.

Upset (दु:खी)	Experience (अनुभव)	Console (दिलासा देना)
Deserve (लायक होना)	However (मगर)	Overcome (जीतना)
Learn (सीखना)	Strength (ताकत)	Immediately (तुरंत)

Reading-16

A Bundle of Sticks

Once upon a time, three neighbours living in a village were having trouble with their crops. Each of the neighbours had one field, but the crops on their fields were infested with pests and were wilting. Every day, they would come up with different ideas to help their crops. The first one tried using a scarecrow in his field, the second one used pesticides, and the third one built a fence on his field, but all to no avail.

One day, the village head came by and called the three farmers. He gave them each a stick and asked them to break it. The farmers could break them easily. He gave them a bundle of sticks, and again, asked them to break it. This time, the farmers struggled to break the sticks. The village head said, "Together you are stronger and work better than you do it alone." The farmers understood what the village head was saying. They pooled in their resources and got rid of the pests from their fields.

Moral of the story: "Unity is strength."

Neighbour (पड़ोसी)	Infest (फैलजाना)	Pesticide (किटनाशक)
Trouble (तकलीफ)	Fence (घेरा)	Break (तोड़ना)
Crop (फसल)	Avail (उपयो/लाभ)	Field (खेत)

Reading-17

The Ant and the Dove

On a hot scorching day, an ant was moving around in search of water. After moving around for some time, she saw a river and was delighted to see it. She climbed up on a small rock to drink the water, but she slipped and fell into the river. She was drowning when a dove who was sitting on a nearby tree helped her. Seeing the ant in trouble, the dove quickly dropped a leaf into the water. The ant moved towards the leaf and climbed up on it. The dove then carefully pulled the leaf out and placed it on the land. This way, the ant's life was saved and she was forever indebted to the dove.

The ant and the dove became the best friends and days passed happily. However, one day, a hunter arrived in the forest. He saw the beautiful dove sitting on the tree and aimed his gun at the dove. The ant, who had been saved by the dove, saw this and bit on the heel of the hunter. He shouted from the pain and dropped the gun.The dove was alarmed by the voice of the hunter and flew away.

Moral of the story: 'A good deed never goes unrewarded'.

Forest (जंगल)	Trouble (परेशानी)	Aim (ताक लगाना, लक्ष्य साधना)
Delighted (खुश)	Indebted (एहसानमंद/अभारी)	Shouted (चिल्लाना)
Dropped (डूबना)	Scorching (झुलसानेवाली)	Nearby (पास में)

Reading-18

The Woodcutter and the Golden Axe

Once there was a woodcutter, who was working hard in the forest, for getting wood to sell for some food. As he was cutting a tree, his axe accidentally fell into the river. The river was deep and was flowing really fast, he lost his axe and could not find it again. He sat at the bank of the river and wept.

While he wept, the God of the river came and asked him what happened. The woodcutter told him what had happened. The God of the river offered to help him in getting back his axe. He disappeared into the river and retrieved a golden axe, but the woodcutter said it was not his. He disappeared again and came back with a silver axe, but the woodcutter said that was not his either. The God disappeared into the water again and came back with an iron axe. The woodcutter smiled and said it was his. The God was impressed with the woodcutter's honesty and gifted him both the golden and the silver axes.

Moral of the story: 'Honesty is the best policy'.

Neighbour (पड़ोसी)	Arise (उठना)	Retrieve (वापस पा लेना)
Bank (किनारा)	Weep (रोना)	Impressed (खुश)
Accidentally (अचानक)	Disappeared (गायब होना)	Honesty (इमानदारी)

Reading-19

The Crystal Ball

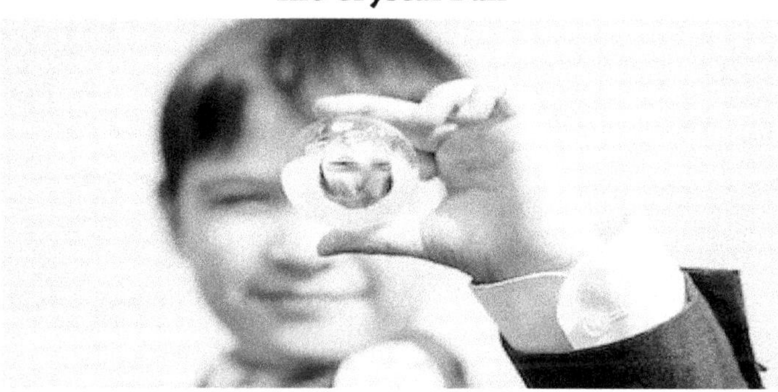

Harsh, a small boy, found a crystal ball behind the banyan tree of his garden. The tree told him that it would grant him a wish. He was very happy and he thought hard, but unfortunately, he could not come up with anything he wanted. So, he kept the crystal ball in his bag and waited until he could decide on his wish.

Days went by without him making a wish but his best friend saw him looking at the crystal ball. He stole it from Harsh and showed it to everyone in the village. They all asked for palaces, wealth and riches and lots of gold, but could not make more than one wish. In the end, everyone was angry because no one could have everything what they wanted. They became very unhappy and decided to ask Harsh for help. Harsh wished that everything would go back to how it was once before. The palaces ended, gold vanished and the villagers once again became happy and content.

Moral of the story: 'Money and wealth do not always bring happiness'.

Behind (पीछे)	Unhappy (दु:खी)	Unfortunately (दुर्भाग्य से)
Banyan tree (बरगद का वृक्ष)	Vanish (खत्म होना)	Steal (चुराना)
Grant (दान, उपहार देना)	Wish (इच्छा)	Palace (महल)

Reading-20

The Fox and the Grapes

On a hot summer day, a fox wandered across the jungle in order to get some food. He was very hungry and desperately moved from one place to another in search of food. He searched everywhere, but couldn't find anything that he could eat. His stomach was rumbling but his search continued. Soon he reached a vineyard which was laden with juicy grapes. The fox looked around to check if he was safe from the hunters. No one was around, so he decided to steal some grapes. He jumped high and high, but he couldn't reach the grapes. The grapes were too high but he refused to give up. The fox jumped high in the air to catch the grapes, but he missed. He tried once more but missed again. He tried a few more times, but couldn't reach. It was getting dark and the fox was getting angry. His legs hurt, so he gave up in the end. Walking away, he said, "I'm sure the grapes were sour anyways".

Moral of the story: 'We pretend to hate something when we can't have it'.

Wander (इधर-उधर भटकना)	Rumble (गड़गड़ना)	Give up (छोड़ना)
Sour (खट्टा)	Vineyard (अँगूर का बाग)	Laden (भरा हुआ)
Refuse (मना करना)	In order to (मकसद)	Hunters (शिकारी)

Reading-21

Friends Forever

Once upon a time, there lived a mouse and a frog, who were the best of friends. Every morning, the frog would hop out of the pond to visit the mouse, who lived inside the hole of the tree. He would spend time with the mouse and go back home. One day, the frog realised that he was making too much of an effort to visit the mouse who never came to meet him at the pond. This made him angry, and he decided to make things right by forcefully taking him to his house.

The frog tied a string to the mouse's tail and tied the other end to his own leg, and hopped away. The mouse started getting dragged with him. Then, the frog jumped into the pond to swim. However, when he looked back, he saw that the mouse had started to drown and was struggling to breathe. The frog quickly untied the string from his tail and took him to the shore. Seeing the mouse with his eyes barely open the frog was very sad, and he immediately regretted pulling him into the pond.

Moral of the story: 'We shouldn't be rigid for something'.

Realise (महसूस करना)	Untie (खोलना)	Inside (अंदर)
Hole (बिल)	String (डोरी)	Pond (तालाब)
Spend (खर्च करना)	Drag (खींचना)	Barely (कठिनाई से)

Reading-22

The Elephant and her Friends

Once upon a time, a lone elephant made her way into a strange forest. It was new to her, and she was looking around to make friends. She approached a monkey and said, "Hello, monkey" would you like to be my friend?" The monkey said", you are too big to swing like me, therefore I can't be your 'friend'. The elephant then went to a rabbit and asked the same question. The rabbit said, "you are too big to fit in my burrow", therefore I can't be your friend. The elephant also went to the frog in the pond and asked the same question. The frog replied. "You are too big to jump therefore, I can't be your friend".

The elephant was really sad because she couldn't make friends. Then, one day, when she saw all the animals running deeper in the forest, she asked a bear what the fuss was about. The bear said, "The lion was after them, hence they were running to save themselves". The elephant went up to the lion and said. "Please don't hurt these innocent people. Please leave them alone". The lion roared at the elephant and said to move aside. Then the elephant got angry and pushed the lion with all her might. All the animals came out slowly and started rejoicing after the lion's defeat. They went to the elephant and said to her, "You are just the right size to be our friend".

Moral of the story: 'Size doesn't matter, the person matters'.

Strange (अजीब)	Fuss (हंगामा, हलचल)	Leave (छोड़ना)
Approach (पहुँचना)	Hurt (नुकसान पहुँचाना)	Might (ताकत)
Swing (झूलना)	Innocent (मासूम)	Rejoice (आंनद करना)
Burrow (बिल)	Alone (अकेला)	Defeat (हार)

Reading-23

The Golden Apples of a Tree

There lived two brothers near a forest. The elder one was very mean to the younger brother. He would finish all the food and wear all the new clothes of his younger brother. One day, the elder brother decided to go to the forest to get some firewood and sell it in the market. As he went around, chopping tree after tree, he reached near a magical tree. The tree said, "Oh kind sir, please do not cut my branches. If you spare me. I will give you golden apples". He agreed, but the greedy elder brother was disappointed with the less quantity of golden apples which the tree gave him. One day the greedy elder brother came to him and threatened the tree that he would cut the tree entirely if it didn't give more apples. The magical tree showered sharp and tiny needles onto the elder brother. The elder brother fell on the ground.

The younger brother was worried. Finally he found him lying in pain near the tree. The younger brother rushed to him and removed each needle. Then the elder brother apologised to the tree. The tree saw the change in the elder brother's heart and gave them all the golden apples. Then they reached home happily.

Moral of the story: 'We should be kind and gracious'.

Wear (पहनना)	Chop (टुकड़े करना)	Spare (माफ करना)
Disappointed (उदास)	Decide (नीर्णय करना)	Threaten (धमकी)
Greedy (लालची)	Apologise (माफी मांगना)	Shower (बौछार)

Reading-24

The Greedy Lion

During a hot summer day, a lion was hungry in the forest. He went to hunt for his food when he found a hare roaming around alone. The lion thought that the hare was too small to satisfy his hunger. Therefore, the lion let the hare go. Then a beautiful deer passed by and he decided to take his chance. He ran after the deer but since he was weak, he could not catch the deer. Tired and defeated, the lion went back to look for the hare to fill his stomach for the time being, but the hare ran away from there. The lion was sad and remained hungry for a long time.

Moral of the story: 'We shouldn't be greedy'.

Hungry (भूखा)	Alone (अकेला)	Hunt (शिकार करना)
Satisfy (संतुष्ट करना)	Roaring (दहाड़ना)	Hare (खरगोश)
Run away (भागना)	Stomach (पेट)	Weak (कमज़ोर)
Struggle (सघंर्ष)	Defeat (हार)	Remain (बाकी रहना)

Reading-25

When the Difficult Time Comes

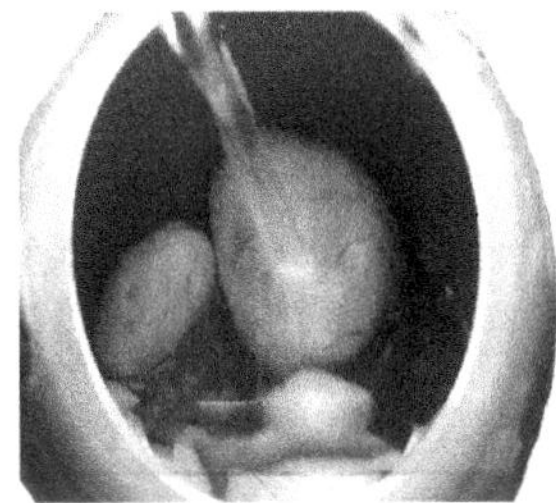

This is a motivational story, which teaches us a lesson how adversity changes people in difficult situations. There was a girl named Pooja who lived with her mother and father in a village. One day, her father gave her a simple task. He took three vessels filled with boiling water. He placed an egg in one vessel, a potato in the second vessel, and some tea leaves in the third vessel. He asked Pooja to keep an eye on the vessels for about fifteen to twenty minutes. After fifteen or twenty minutes, he asked Pooja to peel the potato and egg and strain the tea leaves. Pooja was puzzled. She didn't understand what her father was trying to explain her.

Then, her father explained, "all the three items were put in the same circumstances. See how they have responded differently, the potato turned soft, the egg turned hard, and the tea leaves changed the colour and taste of the water. He further said, "we all are like one of these items. When adversity calls, we respond exactly the way they do, now, are you a potato, an egg, or tea leaves?

Moral of the story: 'We can choose how to respond to a difficult situation'.

Explain (बतलाना)	Puzzle (हैरान)	Separate (अलग करना)
Vessel (बर्तन)	Peel (छीलना)	Boil (उबालना)
Keep an eye (नज़र रखना)	Circumstance (हालात)	Adversity (परेशानी)

Appendix (B)

List of Irregular Verbs

Forms of Verbs

There are three forms of verbs. They are closely associated with tenses. A list of some verbs given below.

Verb के तीन रूप होते हैं, जो tense व्यक्त करने के लिए प्रयोग में लाये जाते हैं।

नीची दिये गये Verbs के तीनों रूपों के देखें।

Group-I

नीचे दिए गए verbs में 3rd form एंव 2nd form एक जैसे हैं

S. No.	Words	Nature	Meaning	Verb (2)	Verb (3)
1.	Buy	Verb	खरीदना	Bought	Bought
2.	Dance	Verb	नाचना	Danced	Danced
3.	Jump	Verb	कूदना	Jumped	Jumped
4.	Leave	Verb	छोड़ देना	Left	Left
5.	Live	Verb	रहना	Lived	Lived
6.	Look	Verb	देखना	Looked	Looked
7.	Make	Verb	बनाना	Made	Made
8.	Meet	Verb	मिलना	Met	Met
9.	Open	Verb	खोलना	Opened	Opened
10.	Say	Verb	कहना	Said	Said
11.	Shine	Verb	चमकना	Shone/Shined	Shone/Shined

Group-II

नीचे दिए गए Verbs में 1st form, 2nd form एंव 3rd form तीनों अलग-अलग होती हैं।

S. No.	Words	Nature	Meaning	Verb (2)	Verb (3)
1.	Break	Verb	टुकड़े करना	Broke	Broken
2.	Do	Verb	करना	Did	Done
3.	Drink	Verb	पीना	Drank	Drunk

4.	Give	Verb	देना	Gave	Given
5.	Go	Verb	जाना	Went	Gone
6.	Grow	Verb	उगना	Grew	Grown
7.	Know	Verb	जानना	Knew	Known
8.	See	Verb	देखना	Saw	Seen
9.	Sing	Verb	गाना	Sang	Sung

Group-III

नीचे दिए गए Verbs के सभी forms एक जैसे हैं।

S. No.	Words	Nature	Meaning	Verb (2)	Verb (3)
1.	Bet	Verb	शर्त लगाना	Bet	Bet
2.	Bid	Verb	बोली लगाना	Bid	Bid
3.	Cast	Verb	फैकना/डालना	Cast	Cast
4.	Cut	Verb	काटना	Cut	Cut
5.	Hurt	Verb	पीड़ा पहुँचाना	Hurt	Hurt
6.	Read	Verb	पढ़ना	Read	Read

S. No.	Words	Nature	Meaning	Verb (2)	Verb (3)
1.	Abuse	Verb	गाली देना	Abused	Abused
2.	Act	Verb	काम करना	Acted	Acted
3.	Add	Verb	जोड़ना	Added	Added
4.	Admire	Verb	प्रशंसा करना	Admired	Admired
5.	Adopt	Verb	स्वीकार करना/गोद लेना	Adopted	Adopted
6.	Advise	Verb	उपदेश देना	Advised	Advised
7.	Aid	Verb	मदद करना	Aided	Aided
8.	Allow	Verb	अनुमति देना	Allowed	Allowed
9.	Answer	Verb	उत्तर देना	Answered	Answered
10.	Appeal	Verb	अनुरोध करना	Appealed	Appealed
11.	Appear	Verb	प्रकट करना	Appeared	Appeared
12.	Appoint	Verb	नियुक्त करना	Appointed	Appointed

13.	Apologise	Verb	क्षमा/विनती करना	Appologised	Appologised
14.	Arise	Verb	उठना	Arose	Arisen
15.	Arrest	Verb	गिरफ्तार करना	Arrested	Arrested
16.	Arrive	Verb	पहुँचना	Arrived	Arrived
17.	Ask	Verb	पूछना/कहना	Asked	Asked
18.	Assess	Verb	आंकलन/जाँचना	Assessed	Assessed
19.	Attack	Verb	आक्रमण करना	Attacked	Attacked
20.	Awake	Verb	जागना	Awoke	Awaken
21.	Bark	Verb	भौंकना	Barked	Barked
22.	Bath	Verb	स्नान करना	Bathed	Bathed
23.	Battle	Verb	लड़ाई करना	Battled	Battled
24.	Be	Verb	होना	Was/Were	Been
25.	Bear	Verb	जन्म देना	Bore	Born
26.	Bear	Verb	सहन करना	Bore	Borne
27.	Become	Verb	बनना	Became	Become
28.	Beg	Verb	भीख मांगना	Begged	Begged
29.	Begin	Verb	शुरू करना	Began	Begun
30.	Behave	Verb	व्यवहार करना	Behaved	Behaved
31.	Believe	Verb	विश्वास करना	Believed	Believed
32.	Belong	Verb	का होना	Belonged	Belonged
33.	Beseech	Verb	बिनती करना	Beseeched	Beseeched
34.	Beware	Verb	सावधान रहना	Bewared	Bewared
35.	Bid	Verb	आज्ञा देना	Bade	Bidden
36.	Bind	Verb	बाँधना	Bound	Bound
37.	Bite	Verb	दाँत से काटना	Bit	Bitten
38.	Blaze	Verb	चमकना/फैलना	Blazed	Blazed
39.	Bleed	Verb	खून बहना	Bled	Bled
40.	Bless	Verb	आशीर्वाद देना	Blessed	Blessed
41.	Boast	Verb	डींग मारना	Boasted	Boasted
42.	Boil	Verb	उबालना	Boiled	Boiled
43.	Boost	Verb	बढ़ाना	Boosted	Boosted

44.	Borrow	Verb	उधार लेना	Borrowed	Borrowed
45.	Bow	Verb	झुक जाना/प्रणाम करना	Bowed	Bowed
46.	Break	Verb	टुकड़े हो जाना	Broke	Broken
47.	Build	Verb	निर्माण करना	Built	Built
48.	Burn	Verb	जलना/जलाना	Burnt	Burnt
49.	Burst	Verb	फटना	Burst	Burst
50.	Buy	Verb	खरीदना	Bought	Bought
51.	Cajole	Verb	खुशामद करना	Cajoled	Cajoled
52.	Call	Verb	बुलाना	Called	Called
53.	Carry	Verb	ले जाना	Carried	Carried
54.	Carry on	Verb	जारी रखना	Carried on	Carried on
55.	Crazy about	Verb	दिवाना होना	Crazied about	Crazied about
56.	Catch	Verb	पकड़ना	Caught	Caught
57.	Change	Verb	बदलना	Changed	Changed
58.	Chase	Verb	पीछा करना	Chased	Chased
59.	Check	Verb	जाँच करना	Checked	Checked
60.	Chew	Verb	चबाना/जुगाली करना	Chewed	Chewed
61.	Choose	Verb	चुनना	Chose	Chosen
62.	Cite	Verb	तलब करना	Cited	Cited
63.	Claim	Verb	दावा करना	Claimed	Claimed
64.	Clap	Verb	ताली बजाना	Clapped	Clapped
65.	Clash	Verb	झगड़ा करना	Clashed	Clashed
66.	Clean	Verb	साफ करना	Cleaned	Cleaned
67.	Climb	Verb	चढ़ना	Climbed	Climbed
68.	Cling	Verb	चिपटना	Clung	Clung
69.	Close	Verb	बंद करना	Closed	Closed
70.	Collect	Verb	इकट्ठा करना	Collected	Collected
71.	Come	Verb	आना	Came	Come
72.	Complain	Verb	शिकायत करना	Complained	Complained
73.	Conflict	Verb	किसी से असहमत होना	Conflicted	Conflicted
74.	Confuse	Verb	उलझन में डाल देना	Confused	Confused

75.	Conquer	Verb	जीतना	Conquered	Conquered
76.	Consent	Verb	राज़ी होना	Consented	Consented
77.	Consider	Verb	मानना	Considered	Considered
78.	Consult	Verb	सलाह देना	Consulted	Consulted
79.	Convey	Verb	पहुँचाना/सूचित करना	Conveyed	Conveyed
80.	Cook	Verb	पकाना	Cooked	Cooked
81.	Copy	Verb	नकल करना	Copied	Copied
82.	Count	Verb	गिनना	Counted	Counted
83.	Cover	Verb	ढकना	Covered	Covered
84.	Crash	Verb	दुर्घटना	Crashed	Crashed
85.	Creep	Verb	रेंगना	Crept	Crept
86.	Criticise	Verb	अलोचना करना	Criticised	Criticised
87.	Cross	Verb	पार करना	Crossed	Crossed
88.	Cry	Verb	चिल्लाना(रोना)	Cried	Cried
89.	Cuddle	Verb	गले लगाना	Cuddled	Cuddled
90.	Dance	Verb	नाचना	Danced	Danced
91.	Dare	Verb	हिम्मत करना	Dared	Dared
92.	Deceive	Verb	धोखा देना	Deceived	Deceived
93.	Decide	Verb	निर्णय करना	Decided	Decided
94.	Decorate	Verb	सजाना	Decorated	Decorated
95.	Defeat	Verb	हारना	Defeated	Defeated
96.	Desire	Verb	इच्छा करना	Desired	Desired
97.	Detain	Verb	रोकना/ठहराना	Detained	Detained
98.	Die	Verb	मरना	Died	Died
99.	Diffuse	Verb	फैलाना	Diffused	Diffused
100.	Dig	Verb	खोदना	Dug	Dug
101.	Dip	Verb	डुबोना	Dipped	Dipped
102.	Discover	Verb	खोज करना	Discovered	Discovered
103.	Dispute	Verb	झगड़ा करना	Disputed	Disputed
104.	Dive	Verb	डुबकी	Dived	Dived
105.	Divide	Verb	बाँटना	Divided	Divided

106.	Do	Verb	करना	Did	Done
107.	Draw	Verb	खींचना	Drew	Drawn
108.	Dream	Verb	सपना देखना	Dreamed	Dreamed
109.	Drink	Verb	पीना	Drank	Drunk
110.	Drive	Verb	चलाना	Drove	Driven
111.	Drown	Verb	डूबाना	Drowned	Drowned
112.	Dry	Verb	सूखना/सुखाना	Dried	Dried
113.	Dwell	Verb	रहना	Dwelt	Dwelt
114.	Dye	Verb	रंगना	Dyed	Dyed
115.	Earn	Verb	कमाना	Earned	Earned
116.	Eat	Verb	खाना	Ate	Eaten
117.	Elaborate	Verb	विस्तार से करना	Elaborated	Elaborated
118.	Elope	Verb	भागकर शादी करना	Eloped	Eloped
119.	Emphasise	Verb	ज़ोर देना	Emphasised	Emphasised
120.	Employ	Verb	काम पर रखना	Employed	Employed
121.	Enter	Verb	प्रवेश करना	Entered	Entered
122.	Eradicate	Verb	जड़ से उखाड़ना	Eradicated	Eradicated
123.	Exasperate	Verb	भड़काना/चिढ़ाना	Exasperated	Exasperated
124.	Exile	Verb	देश से निकालना	Exiled	Exiled
125.	Exist	Verb	अस्तित्व होना	Existed	Existed
126.	Explain	Verb	समझाना	Explained	Explained
127.	Face	Verb	सामना करना	Faced	Faced
128.	Fail	Verb	असफल होना	Failed	Failed
129.	Fall	Verb	नीचे गिरना	Fell	Fallen
130.	Fame	Verb	शोहरत/प्रसिद्धि	Famed	Famed
131.	Fear	Verb	डरना	Feared	Feared
132.	Feed	Verb	खिलाना	Fed	Fed
133.	Feel	Verb	अनुभव करना	Felt	Felt
134.	Fell	Verb	गिराना	Felled	Felled
135.	Fence	Verb	बाड़ लगाना	Fenced	Fenced
136.	Fight	Verb	लड़ना	Fought	Fought

137.	Fine	Verb	जुर्माना लगाना	Fined	Fined
138.	Finish	Verb	समाप्त करना	Finished	Finished
139.	Flee	Verb	भाग जाना	Fled	Fled
140.	Fling	Verb	ताना मारना	Flung	Flung
141.	Float	Verb	तैरना (सतह पर)	Floated	Floated
142.	Fly	Verb	उड़ना	Flew	Flown
143.	Forbid	Verb	मना करना	Forbade	Forbidden
144.	Forget	Verb	भूलना	Forgot	Forgotten
145.	Fracture	Verb	हड्डी का टूटना	Fractured	Fractured
146.	Freeze	Verb	जमाना/जमना	Froze	Frozen
147.	Gainsay	Verb	विरोध करना	Gainsaid	Gainsaid
148.	Gather	Verb	इकट्ठा होना	Gathered	Gathered
149.	Give	Verb	देना	Gave	Given
150.	Glance	Verb	निगाह डालना	Glanced	Glanced
151.	Go	Verb	जाना	Went	Gone
152.	Grab	Verb	पकड़ लेना	Grabbed	Grabbed
153.	Graze	Verb	चरना	Grazed	Grazed
154.	Grind	Verb	पीसना	Ground	Ground
155.	Grow	Verb	उगना	Grew	Grown
156.	Hang	Verb	लटकाना	Hung	Hung
157.	Hang	Verb	फांसी लगाना	Hanged	Hanged
158.	Hesitate	Verb	हिचकिचाना	Hesitated	Hesitated
159.	Hatch	Verb	अंडे सेना	Hatched	Hatched
160.	Hate	Verb	घृणा करना	Hated	Hated
161.	Have	Verb	प्राप्त करना	Had	Had
162.	Hear	Verb	सुनना	Heard	Heard
163.	Help	Verb	सहायता करना	Helped	Helped
164.	Hide	Verb	छिपाना/छिपना	Hid	Hidden
165.	Hike	Verb	सफर/यात्रा करना	Hiked	Hiked
166.	Hoist	Verb	फहराना	Hoisted	Hoisted
167.	Hold	Verb	थामना	Held	Held

168.	Hunt	Verb	शिकार करना	Hunted	Hunted
169.	Imitate	Verb	नकल करना	Imitated	Imitated
170.	Improve	Verb	सुधारना/बेहतर करना	Improved	Improved
171.	Influence	Verb	असर डालना	Influenced	Influenced
172.	Invite	Verb	निमंत्रण देना	Invited	Invited
173.	Irritate	Verb	भड़काना/चिड़ाना	Irritated	Irritated
174.	Isolate	Verb	अलग करना	Isolated	Isolated
175.	Join	Verb	साथ में होना	Joined	Joined
176.	Jostle	Verb	धक्का देना	Jostled	Jostled
177.	Jump	Verb	कूदना	Jumped	Jumped
178.	Keep	Verb	रखना	Kept	Kept
179.	Keep off	Verb	दूर रहना	Kept off	Kept off
180.	Keep on	Verb	लगे रहो	Kept on	Kept on
181.	Kill	Verb	जान से मारना	Killed	Killed
182.	Kneel	Verb	घुटनों के बल झुकना	Knelt	Knelt
183.	Knit	Verb	बुनना	Knitted	Knitted
184.	Know	Verb	जानना	Knew	Known
185.	Laugh	Verb	हँसना	Laughed	Laughed
186.	Lay	Verb	अंडा देना	Laid	Laid
187.	Lead	Verb	मार्ग दिखाना	Led	Led
188.	Learn	Verb	याद करना/सीखना	Learned	Learned
189.	Leave	Verb	छोड़ देना	Left	Left
190.	Lend	Verb	उधार देना	Lent	Lent
191.	Lick	Verb	चाटना	Licked	Licked
192.	Lie	Verb	लेटना	Lay	Lain
193.	Lie	Verb	झूठ बोलना	Lied	Lied
194.	Like	Verb	चाहना	Liked	Liked
195.	Listen	Verb	सुनना (ध्यान से)	Listened	Listened
196.	Live	Verb	रहना	Lived	Lived
197.	Look	Verb	देखना	Looked	Looked
198.	Lose	Verb	खोना/हारना	Lost	Lost

199.	Love	Verb	प्रेम करना	Loved	Loved
200.	Make	Verb	बनाना	Made	Made
201.	Marry	Verb	विवाह करना	Married	Married
202.	Mean	Verb	अर्थ लगाना	Meant	Meant
203.	Measure	Verb	माप का होना	Measured	Measured
204.	Meet	Verb	मिलना	Met	Met
205.	Melt	Verb	पिघलाना	Melted	Melted
206.	Mend	Verb	सुधारना	Mended	Mended
207.	Mend	Verb	मरम्मत करना	Mended	Mended
208.	Mix	Verb	मिलाना, मिलना	Mixed	Mixed
209.	Mock	Verb	मज़ाक उड़ाना	Mocked	Mocked
210.	Move	Verb	हिलाना, हिलना	Moved	Moved
211.	Mow	Verb	घास काटना	Mowed	Mowed
212.	Name	Verb	नाम रखना	Named	Named
213.	Need	Verb	आवश्यकता होना	Needed	Needed
214.	Nip	Verb	सख्ती से कुचलना	Nipped	Nipped
215.	Obey	Verb	आज्ञा मानना	Obeyed	Obeyed
216.	Occur	Verb	होना	Occurred	Occurred
217.	Open	Verb	खोलना	Opened	Opened
218.	Oppose	Verb	विरोध करना	Opposed	Opposed
219.	Order	Verb	आदेश देना	Ordered	Ordered
220.	Outbreak	Verb	भड़क उठना	Outbroke	Outbroken
221.	Overtake	Verb	तेज़ी से आगे निकल जाना	Overtook	Overtaken
222.	Owe	Verb	देनदार होना	Owed	Owed
223.	Pacify	Verb	नाराज़ व्यक्ति को शांत करना	Pacified	Pacified
224.	Pardon	Verb	क्षमा करना	Pardoned	Pardoned
225.	Partake	Verb	भाग लेना	Partook	Partaken
226.	Partition	Verb	विभाजन/बँटवारा करना	Partitioned	Partitioned
227.	Pay	Verb	चुकाना	Paid	Paid
228.	Peep	Verb	झाँकना	Peeped	Peeped
229.	Perspire	Verb	पसीना निकलना	Perspired	Perspired

230.	Persuade	Verb	मनाना	Persuaded	Persuaded
231.	Pile	Verb	ढेर लगाना	Piled	Piled
232.	Pinch	Verb	चुटकी लेना	Pinched	Pinched
233.	Plant	Verb	पौधा लगाना	Planted	Planted
234.	Play	Verb	खेलना	Played	Played
235.	Plough	Verb	खेत जोतना	Ploughed	Ploughed
236.	Pluck	Verb	तोड़ना (जैसे फूल तोड़ते हैं)	Plucked	Plucked
237.	Poison	Verb	विष देना	Poisoned	Poisoned
238.	Praise	Verb	प्रशंसा करना	Praised	Praised
239.	Pray	Verb	प्रार्थना करना	Prayed	Prayed
240.	Preach	Verb	उपदेश करना	Preached	Preached
241.	Prepare	Verb	तैयार करना	Prepared	Prepared
242.	Pretend	Verb	बहाना बनाना	Pretended	Pretended
243.	Prevent	Verb	रोकना	Prevented	Prevented
244.	Promise	Verb	वचन देना	Promised	Promised
245.	Promote	Verb	प्रोत्साहित करना	Promoted	Promoted
246.	Protest	Verb	विरोध करना	Protested	Protested
247.	Prove	Verb	सिद्ध करना	Proved	Proved
248.	Pull	Verb	खींचना	Pulled	Pulled
249.	Punish	Verb	दण्ड देना	Punished	Punished
250.	Push	Verb	धक्का देना	Pushed	Pushed
251.	Quarrel	Verb	झगड़ना	Quarrelled	Quarrelled
252.	Quench	Verb	प्यास बुझाना	Quenched	Quenched
253.	Rain	Verb	वर्षा होना	Rained	Rained
254.	Raise	Verb	उठाना/खड़ा करना	Raised	Raised
255.	Reach	Verb	पहुँचना	Reached	Reached
256.	Read	Verb	पढ़ना	Read	Read
257.	Receive	Verb	पाना, प्राप्त करना	Received	Received
258.	Refrain	Verb	खुद को रोकना	Refrained	Refrained
259.	Refuse	Verb	इंकार करना	Refused	Refused

260.	Regain	Verb	पुनः प्राप्त	Regained	Regained
261.	Remember	Verb	याद करना	Remembered	Remembered
262.	Repair	Verb	मरम्मत करना	Repaired	Repaired
263.	Repent	Verb	पछताना	Repented	Repented
264.	Reply	Verb	जवाब देना	Replied	Replied
265.	Require	Verb	ज़रूरत होना	Required	Required
266.	Rescue	Verb	बचाना/रक्षा करना	Rescued	Rescued
267.	Resign	Verb	त्यागपत्र देना	Resigned	Resigned
268.	Resist	Verb	रोकना	Resisted	Resisted
269.	Resistance	Verb	बाधा डालना	Resistanced	Resistanced
270.	Resonate	Verb	गूंजना	Resonated	Resonated
271.	Rest	Verb	आराम करना	Rested	Rested
272.	Return	Verb	लौटाना, लौटना	Returned	Returned
273.	Revamp	Verb	सुधार	Revamped	Revamped
274.	Ride	Verb	सवारी करना	Rode	Ridden
275.	Ring	Verb	बजना/बजाना	Rang	Rung
276.	Rise	Verb	उगना/उठना	Rose	Risen
277.	Rival	Verb	विरोधी होना	Rivalled	Rivalled
278.	Roar	Verb	गरजना	Roared	Roared
279.	Rob	Verb	लूटना	Robbed	Robbed
280.	Save	Verb	बचाना	Saved	Saved
281.	Saw	Verb	आरे से चीरना	Sawed	Sawed
282.	Say	Verb	कहना	Said	Said
283.	See	Verb	देखना	Saw	Seen
284.	Seek	Verb	अपेक्षा करना/ढूँढना	Sought	Sought
285.	Segment	Verb	भाग/खंड करना	Segmented	Segmented
286.	Select	Verb	चुनना (छाँटकर)	Selected	Selected
287.	Sell	Verb	बेचना	Sold	Sold
288.	Send	Verb	भेजना	Sent	Sent
289.	Settle	Verb	बस जाना/फैसला करना	Settled	Settled
290.	Shake	Verb	हिलाना	Shook	Shaken

291.	Shine	Verb	चमकना	Shined	Shined
292.	Shock	Verb	सदमा पहुँचना	Shocked	Shocked
293.	Shoot	Verb	गोली मारना	Shot	Shot
294.	Shrink	Verb	सिकुड़ना	Shrank	Shrunk
295.	Siege	Verb	घेरा बंदी	Sieged	Sieged
296.	Sing	Verb	गाना	Sang	Sung
297.	Sit	Verb	बैठना	Sat	Sat
298.	Sleep	Verb	सोना	Slept	Slept
299.	Slip	Verb	फिसलना	Slipped	Slipped
300.	Blow	Verb	हवा का चलना	Blew	Blown
301.	Slow down	Verb	आवाज़ धीमी करना	Slowed down	Slowed down
302.	Speak	Verb	बोलना	Spoke	Spoken
303.	Spend	Verb	खर्च करना	Spent	Spent
304.	Spill	Verb	छलकना	Spilled	Spilled
305.	Spit	Verb	थूकना	Spat	Spat
306.	Squeeze	Verb	निचोड़ना	Squeezed	Squeezed
307.	Stab	Verb	छुरा मारना	Stabbed	Stabbed
308.	Stabilise	Verb	मज़बूत/दृढ़ होना	Stabilised	Stabilised
309.	Steal	Verb	चुराना	Stole	Stolen
310.	Stick	Verb	चिपकना	Stuck	Stuck
311.	Stir	Verb	हिलाना	Stirred	Stirred
312.	Stop	Verb	रोकना	Stopped	Stopped
313.	Strike	Verb	चोट मारना	Struck	Struck
314.	Stroke	Verb	सहलाना	Stroked	Stroked
315.	Study	Verb	पढ़ना	Studied	Studied
316.	Summon	Verb	बुलवाना, बटोरना	Summoned	Summoned
317.	Suspect	Verb	संदेह करना, शक करना	Suspected	Suspected
318.	Swear	Verb	शपथ लेना	Swore	Sworn
319.	Sweep	Verb	झाड़ू देना	Swept	Swept
320.	Swim	Verb	तैरना	Swam	Swum
321.	Swing	Verb	झूलना	Swung	Swung

322.	Tag	Verb	जोड़ना, मिलाना	Tagged	Tagged
323.	Take	Verb	लेना	Took	Taken
324.	Talk	Verb	बात करना	Talked	Talked
325.	Talk back	Verb	जुबान चलाना	Talked back	Talked back
326.	Tangle	Verb	उलझना	Tangled	Tangled
327.	Teach	Verb	पढ़ाना/सीखाना	Taught	Taught
328.	Tear	Verb	फाड़ना	Tore	Torn
329.	Tell	Verb	कहना	Told	Told
330.	Tempt	Verb	लुभाना	Tempted	Tempted
331.	Think	Verb	सोंचना	Thought	Thought
332.	Threaten	Verb	धमकाना, डराना	Threatened	Threatened
333.	Tie	Verb	पट्टी बाँधना	Tied	Tied
334.	Tighten	Verb	फँसना/ठसकर बांधना	Tightened	Tightened
335.	Touch	Verb	छूना	Touched	Touched
336.	Trust	Verb	विश्वास करना	Trusted	Trusted
337.	Try	Verb	प्रयत्न करना	Tried	Tried
338.	Tussle	Verb	लड़ाई	Tussled	Tussled
339.	Tweak	Verb	सुधारना	Tweaked	Tweaked
340.	Understand	Verb	समझना	Understood	Understood
341.	Untidy	Verb	मैला	Untidied	Untidied
342.	Uproot	Verb	जड़ से उखाड़ना	Uprooted	Uprooted
343.	Use	Verb	इस्तेमाल करना	Used	Used
344.	Utilise	Verb	उपयोग में लाना	Utilised	Utilised
345.	Veil	Verb	छिपाना/पर्दा करना	Veiled	Veiled
346.	Violate	Verb	कानून का उल्लंघन करना	Violated	Violated
347.	Wait	Verb	प्रतीक्षा करना	Waited	Waited
348.	Walk	Verb	चलना	Walked	Walked
349.	Wander	Verb	घूमना	Wandered	Wandered
350.	Wash	Verb	धोना	Washed	Washed
351.	Waste	Verb	नष्ट करना	Wasted	Wasted
352.	Watch	Verb	निगरानी करना	Watched	Watched

353.	Waylay	Verb	ताक में रहना	Waylaid	Waylaid
354.	Wear	Verb	पहनना	Wore	Worn
355.	Weave	Verb	बुनना	Wave	Woven
356.	Web	Verb	जाल बनाना	Webbed	Webbed
357.	Wed	Verb	विवाह करना	Wedded	Wedded
358.	Weep	Verb	रोना	Wept	Wept
359.	Win	Verb	जीतना	Won	Won
360.	Wish	Verb	चाहना	Wished	Wished
361.	Withstand	Verb	सामना	Withstood	Withstood
362.	Wobble	Verb	लड़खड़ाना	Wobbled	Wobbled
363.	Wonder	Verb	हैरान होना	Wondered	Wondered
364.	Work	Verb	काम करना	Worked	Worked
365.	Worship	Verb	पूजा करना	Worshipped	Worshipped
366.	Wound	Verb	घायल करना	Wounded	Wounded
367.	Wrap	Verb	लपेटना	Wrapped	Wrapped
368.	Wring	Verb	मरोड़	Wrung	Wrung
369.	Write	Verb	लिखना	Wrote	Written
370.	Yield	Verb	झुकना/पैदा करना	Yielded	Yielded
371.	Yoke	Verb	जोतना	Yoked	Yoked
372.	Zip up	Verb	चेन लगाना	Zipped up	Zipped up

Appendix (C)

Useful Vocabulary

Here are some important words which are very useful in our daily life.

Days	
Monday	सोमवार
Tuesday	मंगलवार
Wednesday	बुधवार
Thursday	गुरूवार
Friday	शुक्रवार
Saturday	शनिवार
Sunday	रविवार

Months			
January	जनवरी	July	जुलाई
February	फरवरी	August	अगस्त
March	मार्च	September	सितम्बर
April	अप्रैल	October	अक्टूबर
May	मई	November	नवम्बर
June	जून	December	दिसम्बर

Seasons	
Winter	सर्दी
Spring	बसंत
Rainy Season	बरसात
Summer	गर्मी
Autumn	पतझड़

Time			
Second	सेकेण्ड	Minute	मिनट
Hour	घंटा	Day	दिन
Night	रात	Week	सप्ताह
Afternoon	दोपहर	Evening	शाम
Century	सौ वर्ष	Midnight	आधी रात
Day after tomorrow	आने वाला कल	Tomorrow	कल
Fortnight	दो सप्ताह	Month	महीना
Quarter Year	तीन माह	Half Year	आधा वर्ष
Year	वर्ष	Decade	दस वर्ष
Day before Yesterday	परसो (बीता हुआ कल)	Yesterday	बिता हुआ कल

Fruits			
Apple	सेब	Mango	आम
Apricot	खुबानी	Musk-melon	खरबूजा
Banana	केला	Orange	संतरा
Berries	बेर	Pineapple	अनन्नास
Blackberry	जामुन	Papaya	पपीता
Cherry	चेरी	Peach	आड़ू
Citron	चकोतरा	Plum	बेर
Coconut	नारियल	Gooseberry	आंवला
Custard apple	शरीफा	Sapodilla	चीकू
Date	खजूर	Pear	नाशपाती
Kiwi	कीवी	Avocado	ऐवकाडो
Loquat	लोकाट	Mulberry	शहतूत
Pomegranate	अनार	Grapes	अँगूर
Raspberry	रसभरी	Strawberry	स्ट्रॉबेरी
Sweet orange	मौसमी	Wood-apple	बेल
Tamarind	इमली	Starfruit	कमरख

Vegetables			
Beans	लोबिया	Brinjal	बैंगन
Beetroot	चुकन्दर	Mushroom	मशरूम
Bitter gourd	करेला	Ridged gourd	तोरी
Carrot	गाजर	Arum	अरबी
Cauliflower	फूलगोभी	Pumpkin	कद्दू
Coriander leaf	धनिया	Capsicum	शिमला मिर्च
Garlic	लहसुन	Tomato	टमाटर
Ginger	अदरक	Potato	आलू
Gourd	लौकी	Sweet potato	शकरकंद
Green onion	हरे प्याज़	Broccoli	ब्रॉकोली
Lady finger	भिंडी	Cabbage	बंद गोभी
Mint	पोदीना	Peas	मटर
Onion	प्याज़	Cucumber	खीरा
Radish	मूली	Turnip	शलजम

Parts of Body			
Finger	उगँली	Fist	मुट्ठी
Foot	पैर	Hair	बाल
Hand	हाथ	Head	सिर
Heel	ऐड़ी	Heart	दिल
Kidney	गुर्दा	Intestines	अंतड़ी
Ankle	टखना	Nail	नाखून
Neck	गर्दन	Nose	नाक
Nerve	नस	Navel	नाभि
Nostril	नथुना	Palate	तालु
Palm	हथेली	Wrist	कलाई
Rib	पसली	Knee	घुटना
Shoulder	कंधा	Spleen	तिल्ली
Skin	चमड़ी, त्वचा	Skull	खोपड़ी

Stomach	पेट	Thigh	जांघ
Throat	गला	Thumb	अँगूठा
Tongue	जीभ	Toe	पैर का अँगूठा
Waist	कमर	Wart	मस्सा
Whiskers	लम्बी मूंछ	Mole	तिल

Colours			
Azure	आसमानी	Black	काला
White	सफेद	Blue	नीला
Yellow	पीला	Grey	सलेटी
Green	हरा	Pink	गुलाबी
Red	लाल	Maroon	गहरा सुर्ख
Orange	सतंरी	Pale	हल्का पीला
Purple	जामुनी	Brown	भूरा
Scarlet	गहरा लाल	Violet	बैंगनी

Occupations			
Architect	मकान का नक्शा बनाने वाला	Carpenter	बढ़ई
Author	लेखक	Doctor	चिकित्सक
Barber	नाई	Blacksmith	लोहार
Butcher	कसाई	Hawker	फेरी वाला
Cobbler	मोची	Dyer	रंगने वाला
Dentist	दंत चिकित्सक	Watchman	चौकीदार
Farmer	किसान	Astrologer	ज्योतिषी
Gardener	माली	Juggler	बाज़ीगर
Gate-Keeper	दरबान	Painter	चित्रकार
Grocer	परचून बेचने वाला	Fisherman	मछुवारा
Jeweller	जोहरी	Electrician	बिजली कारीगर
Milkman	दूध वाला	Mason	राज मजदूर
Oilman	तेली	Nurse	नर्स
Palmist	हाथ देखने वाला	Wrestler	पहलवान

Physician	चिकित्सक	Book-binder	जिल्दसाज़
Pilgrim	यात्री	Goldsmith	सुनार
Pleader	वकील	Sculptor	शिल्पकार
Postman	डाकिया	Maid-servant	नौकरानी
Priest	पुजारी	Potter	कुम्हार
Sweeper	सफाई कर्मचारी	Cook	रसोइया
Teacher	अध्यापक	Singer	गायक
Waiter	परोसनेवाला	Sailor	नाविक
Washerman	धोबी	Pharmacist	दवा साज़

Sounds	
Beating of drums	ढ़ोलों की गुड़गुड़ाहट
Chattering of teeth	दांतों की किटकिटाहट
Chiming of bells	घंटियों का बजना
Clanking of chains	ज़ंज़ीरों की खनखनाहट
Clatter of hoofs	खुरों की टाप
Cracking of fire	आग की घूं-घूं
Creaking of doors and shoes	जूतों या दरवाज़ों की चरमर
Hissing of snakes	साँपों का फुफ्कारना
Jingling of coins	सिक्कों की खनखनाहट
Rattle of wheels	पहियों की खड़खड़
Rustling of leaves	सूखे पत्तों की खड़-खड़
Thunder of clouds	बादलों की गरज
Tick of clock	घड़ी की टिक-टिक
Honking of horn	भौंपू की पौं-पौं
Zooming of aeroplane	वायुयान की गुर्राहट

Household Articles			
Almirah	अलमारी	Comb	कंघी
Bottle	बोतल	Table	मेज़
Bucket	बाल्टी	Oven	तंदूर
Cauldron	कड़ाही	Tin	डिब्बा
Chair	कुर्सी	Whisk	कपड़े झाड़ने का ब्रश
Cutlery	चाकू, छुरी	Bin	डिब्बा
Dustpan	कूड़े का तसला	Peeler	छीलने वाला
Fridge	फ्रिज	Knife	चाकू
Funnel	कीप	Fork	काँटा
Hanger	काँटा	Mop	पोंछा
Iron	प्रेस	Fan	पंखा
Key	चाबी	Curtain	परदा
Lid	ढकना	Tooth pick	दंत खोदनी
Mat	चटाई	Mortar	खरल-ओखली
Mixer	मिलानेवाला	Straw	पीने की नली
Nut-Cracker	सरौता	Stove	चूल्हा मिट्टी के तेल का
Pestle	मूसल	Pincer	चिमटी
Pillow	तकिया	Grate	चुल्हे की जाली
Pitcher	घड़ा मटका	Jug	जग
Quilt	रजाई	Spoon	चम्मच
Rolling board	चकला	Rolling pin	बेलन
Safety pin	कोना न चुभने वाला पिन	Ladder	सीढ़ी
Scissors	कैंची	Mirror	आईना

Sieve	छलनी	Tray	थाली
Spittoon	पीकदान	Broomstick	झाड़ू
Tongs	चिमटा	Basket	टोकरी
Tumbler	गिलास	Jar	मर्तबान

Flowers			
Jasmine	चमेली	Rose	गुलाब
Lotus	कमल	Marigold	गेंदे का फूल
Sunflower	सूरजमुखी	Periwinkle	सदाबहार
Touch-me-not	छूई-मुई	Daisy	गुलबहार
Daffodil	नरगिस	Mogra	मोगरा
Tube Rose	रजनीगंधा	Blue Water Lily	नीलकमल

Trees			
Teak	सागवान	Sheesham	शीशम
Pine	चीड़	Oak	बबूल
Neem	नीम	Fir	देवदार
Date Palm	खजूर	Betel nut tree	सुपारी का पेड़
Banyan	बरगद	Bamboo	बाँस
Ficus religiosa	पीपल	Acacia	बबूल

Animals			
Alligator	मगरमच्छ	Bull	सांड
Ape	लंगूर	Ass	गधा
Bear	भालू	Bitch	कुतिया
Buffalo	भैंस	Cock	मुर्गा

Camel	ऊँट	Cat	बिल्ली
Cow	गाय	Calf	बछड़ा
Deer	हिरण	Elephant	हाथी
Dog	कुत्ता	Donkey	गधा
Fox	लोमड़ी	Goat	बकरा
Frog	मेढक	Fish	मछली
Horse	घोड़ा	Hen	मुर्गी
Jackal	सियार	Sheep	भेड़
Monkey	बंदर	Mare	घोड़ी
Rabbit	खरगोश	Squirrel	गिलहरी
Rat	चूहा	Ox	बैल
Stag	बारहसिंघा	Tiger	चीता
Tortoise	कछुआ	Wolf	भेड़िया

Birds			
Crow	कौवा	Duck	बत्तख
Dove	फाख्ता	Eagle	बाज़
Kite	चील	Nightingale	बुलबुल
Cuckoo	कोयल	Owl	उल्लू
Parrot	तोता	Peacock	मोर
Pigeon	कबूतर	Partridge	तीतर
Quail	बटेर	Sparrow	गौरेया
Swallow	अबाबील	Swan	हंस

ANSWERS OF TESTS

Test No.-1

Ans-1: (a) Amit (b) Twenty (c) Red
(d) Cricket (e) Pizza (f) Newspaper

Ans-2: Twenty six

Ans-3: Five, a, e, i, o, u

Ans-4: (a) Lock (b) Fish (c) Mat
(d) Fan (e) Egg (f) Umbrella

Ans-5: (a) Bus (b) Sun (c) Pen
(d) Moon (e) Jar (f) Tap

Ans-6: (a) B, C, D (b) M, N, O

Ans-7: (a) Lotus Temple (b) Qutub Minar
(c) Red Fort (d) Taj Mahal

Ans-8: (a) Ant (b) Ostrich (c) Intelligence

Ans-9: (a) Teena (b) Intelligent boys
(c) The Moon (d) My friends
(e) I (f) My brothers and my sisters
(g) the Foolish boy (h) The daughter of Mr. Gupta

Ans-10: (a) Interrogative (b) Imperative (c) Interrogative
(d) Exclamatory (e) Declarative/Assertive/Affirmative

(f) Imperative (g) Imperative (h) Exclamatory
(i) Negative (j) Negative

Ans-11: (a) he became a doctor.
(b) he sang nicely.
(c) the children were playing.
(d) these are very difficult questions.

Ans-12: (a) (✓) (b) (×) (c) (×) (d) (✓)
(e) (×) (f) (✓)

Ans-13: (i) (c) (ii) (d) (iii) (e) (iv) (b) (v) (a)

Ans-14: (a) Father Broom Milk
(b) Glass Milk Table
(c) Energy Sun
(d) Mobile

Ans-15: (a) Thick (b) Listen (c) Strong

Ans-16: (a) A few (b) Many (c) Little (d) Much

Ans-17: (a) Mohan's house (b) His grandfather's stick
(c) Kartar Singh's shop (d) Students' intelligence
(e) the employees' salaries (f) Women's hostel
(g) Teachers' work (h) Mr Das' office

Ans-18: (a) (×) (b) (×) (c) (✓)
(d) (×) (e) (✓) (f) (×)

Ans-19: (a) Comparative - More beautiful
Superlative - Most beautiful
(b) Comparative - Older, elder
Superlative - Oldest, eldest
(c) Comparative - Farther, Further
Superlative - Farthest, Farthest
(d) Comparative - Less
Superlative - Least
(e) Comparative - More intelligent
Superlative - Most intelligent
(f) Comparative - Blacker
Superlative - Blackest
(g) Comparative - Later, latter
Superlative - Latest, last
(h) Comparative - Healthier/More Healthy
Superlative - Healthiest/Most Healthy.

Ans-20: (a) Books (b) Spectacles (c) Children
(d) Scissors (e) Furniture (f) Matches

Ans-21: (a) Uncle (b) Men (c) Lioness
(e) Brother (f) Nephew (g) Mare
(d) Cow (h) She

Ans-22: (a) Boxes (b) Spies (c) Women
(d) Children (e) Mice (f) Leaves
(g) Diagnoses (h) Criteria (i) News
(j) Kidneys

Ans-23: (i) (b) Mr. Rakesh Gupta (ii) (c) Mrs. Ritu Arora
(iii) (f) Miss Nisha Verma (iv) (g) Ms. Alka Kumar

Ans-24: (a) Sister (b) Madam (c) Princess
(d) Waiteress (e) Niece (f) Mother
(g) Grandmother (h) Fiancee

Ans-25: (a) Milkman (b) Pilot (c) Carpenter
(d) Nurse (e) Tailor (f) Cobbler
(g) Teacher (h) Barber (i) Postman
(j) Washerman.

Test No-2

Ans-1: (a) o (b) a (c) the (d) o
(e) an (f) a (g) a (h) a
(i) the (j) the

Ans-2: (a) an (b) a (c) a (d) a
(e) a (f) a (g) a (h) an

Ans-3: (a) o (b) a (c) the (d) o
(e) a (f) a (g) a (h) the
(i) a (j) the (k) a (l) a
(m) o (n) an (o) a (p) the
(q) the

Ans-4: (a) is (b) is (c) are (d) are

Ans-5:

	Negative	Interrogative
(a)	This isn't your book.	Is this your book?
(b)	That isn't your daughter.	Is that your daughter?
(c)	These aren't his keys.	Are these his keys?
(d)	Those aren't our bikes.	Are those our bikes?
(e)	This house isn't Mohan's.	Is this Mohan's house?

Ans-6: (a) me, him (b) him (c) him (d) he, us
(e) me (f) him, he (g) he, him (h) them

Ans-7: (a) him (b) they (c) me (d) he

Ans-8: (a) A wife is a woman who has a husband.
(b) A mechanic is a person who repairs cars.
(c) A car is a vehicle which/that has four wheels.
(d) Camel is the ship of desert that runs very fast.

Ans-9: (a) I don't like people who are unfriendly.
(b) Volvo is the bus that goes fast.
(c) I know someone that can play the DJ well.
(d) I like the children who are not rigid.
(e) Do you know the girl that lives upstairs?
(f) He likes films which have suspense.

Ans-10: (a) An elephant is an animal that/which has a long trunk.
(b) A laptop is an electronic device that/which business people use.
(c) Flowers are something that/which make environment beautiful.

(d) A suitcase is a bag that/which people take on holiday.

(e) Do you know the children who/that live in Shahdara.

(f) The man who/that works in this factory is not friendly.

Ans-11: (a) Chips are potatoes that/which are cut and fried.

(b) Cricket is a game that/which has eleven players.

(c) A wife is a person who/that does all domestic work.

(d) Coffee is a drink that/which people drink in winter.

(e) A cobbler is a person who/that makes shoes.

Ans-12: (a) I (b) She (c) He (d) It

(e) They (f) We (g) You

Ans-13: (a) Is this yours? (b) No, I think it's his.

(c) No, it isn't mine. (d) Is it yours?

(e) No, it isn't mine. (f) Perhaps, it's theirs.

(g) Have you got ours? (h) No, I have got mine.

(i) This isn't mine. (j) No, it's theirs.

Ans-14: (a) My (b) Hers (c) Their (d) My, Mine

(e) Your (f) Yours (g) Her (h) Her

Ans-15: (a) is (b)are (c) is (d) is

(e) am (f) are (g) are (h) is

(i) am (j) are

Ans-16: (a) am (b)is (c) is (d) are

(e) is (f) is (g) are

Ans-17: (a) have (b) has (c) has
(d) has (e) have

Ans-18: (a) am (b) has (c) is
(d) has (e) are (f) have

Ans-19: (a) is (b) are (c) these
(d) are (e) are (f) I'm not
(g) that

Ans-20: (a) was (b) were (c) is
(d) are

Ans-21: (a) has (b) had (c) had
(d) has (e) had

Ans-22: (a) were (b) was (c) were (d) was

Ans-23: (a) were (b) was (c) were (d) was

Ans-24: (a) It is dark.
(b) He is an honest man/person.
(c) Earth is round.
(d) India is a great country.
(e) Mohan and Sohan are not helpless.
(f) Was Pandit Jawaharlal Nehru the first Prime Minister of India?
(g) They are not businessmen.
(h) Is the future of Rohan not bright/Isn't the future of Rohan bright?

(i) Are we not honest/Aren't we honest?

(j) Are stars not in the sky/Aren't stars in the sky?

(k) Was father at home/Was there father at home?

(l) Was your school not in Laxmi Nagar/Wasn't your school in Laxmi Nagar?

(m) Was there water not on the floor/Wasn't there water on the floor?

(n) Was Kavita not with Mohan/Wasn't Kavita with Mohan?

Ans-25: (a) I will/shall be there tomorrow.

(b) He will not be busy on Sunday.

(c) Will she not be ready?

(d) We have time.

(e) She/He has a book.

(f) Mohan doesn't have an old car/Mohan has not an old car.

(g) They have not five pens/They don't have five pens.

(h) I don't have a computer/I have not a computer.

(i) I have not five computers/I don't have five computers.

(j) Doesn't Mohan have a mobile/Has Mohan not a mobile?

(k) Don't they have a house/Have they not a house?

(l) She had a car/That girl had a car.

(m) Rohan had no money/Rohan didn't have money.

(n) Had Mohan's father not three cows/Didn't Mohan's father have three cows?

(o) Didn't you have an answer/Had you not an answer?

(p) Had that man no good clothes/Didn't that man have good clothes?

(q) Will you not have four cars after one year/Won't you have four cars after one year?

(r) Will unemployed people not have employment after this year/Won't unemployed people have employment after this year?

(s) Will educated people not have jobs/Won't educated people have jobs?

(t) Will you not have time on Diwali/Won't you have time on Diwali/during Diwali/on the day of Diwali?

Test No-3

Ans-1: (a) He is 30-years-old.

(b) This book is very thick.

(c) Correct

(d) I'm not a patient, I'm a doctor.

(e) Her name's Kavita/Her name is Kavita.

Ans-2: (a) Correct (b) Correct

(c) No, I am not, I'm a doctor. (d) Correct

(e) No, I'm not.

Ans-3: (a) Is that your bag? (b) This is your car.

(c) This is my husband Mohan. (d) Who are those people?

(e) Are these your children?

Ans-4: (a) Are (b) Are (c) Is (d) Is

Ans-5: (a) There are ten thousand women in the function.

(b) There is water in the tank.

(c) In Mumbai the buses are red.

(d) There is an old woman in the street.

(e) This is my box.

(f) Are the children in the room?

(g) The fish are in the river.

(h) The sandwiches are fresh.

Ans-6: (a) Who's Ahmed's brother?

(b) Rosy, Rehana and Sohana's house.

(c) Kavita lives with her brother.

(d) Correct

(e) Your phone is better than mine.

(f) This is not yours.

(g) They know my name but I don't know theirs.

(h) My health is not fine today.

Ans-7: (a) o honesty (b) a tomato (c) o sugar

(d) an owl (e) o apple juice (f) a mobile

Ans-8: Plural forms:

(a) not possible (b) umbrellas (c) oranges

(d) not possible (e) potatoes (f) not possible

(g) not possible (h) not possible (i) rupees

(j) not possible.

Ans-9: (a) How much (b) How many

(c) How many (d) How much

Ans-10: (a) Much → There aren't many books.

(b) is → How many books are in the bag?

(c) bitting → The dog is biting me.

(d) aple → Mohan is eating an apple

(e) runing → She is running very fast.

(f) is swiming → They are swimming really well.

Ans-11: (a) on (b) on (c) on

(d) at, on (e) at (f) at

Ans-12: (a) in (b) at (c) in

(d) at (e) in the past (f) in the winter

(g) at midnight (h) at the moment

Ans-13: (a) to, from (b) out of, along, over

(c) none (d) on, off.

Ans-14: (a) was (b) were (c) were

(d) was not (e) were not (f) was not

Ans-15: (i) (a) was, (b) was (c) was (d) was (e) were

(ii) (a) were

(iii) (a) were (b) were (c) was (d) were (e) was

(f) were (g) were

Ans-16: (a) How long was lockdown during corona?

(b) Were you getting bored sitting at home?

(c) Was your friend infected from corona?

(d) Were people in the houses during lockdown?

Ans-17: (a) tall (b) sad (c) fast (d) hot

(e) noisy (f) cheap (g) exciting (h) young

(i) new (j) poor

Ans-18: (a) the safest

(b) the most dangerous

(c) the cheapest

(d) the most delicious

(e) the most boring

(f) the best

(g) the most relaxing

(h) the cleanest

Ans-19: (a) Taj Mahal is the most interesting building in Agra.

(b) Chennai is the furthest place from Delhi.

(c) This is the best book in the world.

(d) She is the oldest lady in her family.

Ans-20: (a) Were Sheetal and Rahul late?

(b) Was her anger dangerous?

(c) Is he a doctor?

(d) Are we happy?

Ans-21: (a) Was she Fatima? (b) Where will you go?

(c) How long was the film? (d) Where is his bag?

Ans-22: (a) Many (b) Much (c) Many
(d) Much (e) Many (f) Much

Ans-23: (a) T (b) F (c) T
(d) T (e) F (f) F

Ans-24: (i) (f) (ii) (c) (iii) (d)
(iv) (b) (v) (a) (vi) (e)

Ans-25: (a) isn't it? (b) is it? (c) hasn't he
(d) did they? (e) did I? (f) does she?
(g) could I? (h) were they? (i) hasn't he?
(j) aren't I (k) will you? (l) shall we?

Ans-26: (a) It's ten to ten.
(b) It's a quarter past eleven.
(c) It's a quarter to eleven.
(d) It's half past ten.

1 Alphabet

Answers

Exercise-1

A	D	F	G	I	K
P	R	T	V	Z	

Exercise-2

b	e	g	i	k	o
q	s	v	x	y	

Exercise-3

A – a	B – b	C – c	D – d	E – e
F – f	G – g	H – h	I – i	J – j
K – k	L – l	M – m	N – n	O – o
P – p	Q – q	R – r	S – s	T – t
U – u	V – v	W – w	X – x	Y – y
Z – z				

Exercise-4

(a) 26 (b) 5 (c) 21

2 Vowel Sound

Exercise-1

Sound of 'A' – 'a':-

(a) a	(b) a	(c) a	(d) a
(e) a	(f) a	(g) a	(h) a

Exercise-2

Sound of 'E' – 'e':-

(a) e	(b) e	(c) e	(d) e
(e) e	(f) e	(g) e	(h) e

Exercise-3

Sound of 'I'– 'i':-

(a) i	(b) i	(c) i	(d) i
(e) i	(f) i	(g) i	(h) i

Exercise-4

Sound of 'O'– 'o':-

(a) o	(b) o	(c) o	(d) o
(e) o	(f) o	(g) o	(h) o

Exercise-5

Sound of 'U'– 'u':-

(a) u	(b) u	(c) u	(d) u
(e) u	(f) u	(g) u	(h) u

3 Sentences

Exercise-1

(a)	1. ✓	2. ×	3. ✓	4. ✓	5. ×	6. ×
(b)	1. has	2. am	3. reads	4. runs	5. plays	
(c)	1. d	2 e	3. a	4. b	5. c	

Exercise-2

1. He became a doctor.
2. She sang beautifully.
3. The children were reading.
4. These are very difficult questions.
5. Father has sold his bike.
6. He told me an interesting story.
7. The baby is crying.
8. We asked him to go.

Exercise-3

(a)
1. Interrogative
2. Imperative
3. Affirmative
4. Imperative
5. Imperative
6. Exclamatory
7. Negative
8. Affirmative
9. Interrogative
10. Interrogative
11. Imperative
12. Exclamatory
13. Exclamatory

(b)
1. Interrogative
2. Declarative
3. Interrogative
4. Negative
5. Interrogative
6. Declarative
7. Declarative
8. Exclamatory
9. Imperative
10. Exclamatory
11. Imperative
12. Negative

4 Subject and Predicate

Exercise-1

(a) 1. Shambu wrote a letter.

2. Students are in the school.

3. They will come tomorrow.

4. Mohan is teaching well.

5. Children are playing in the park.

(b) 1. (d) 2. (c) 3. (e) 4. (a) 5. (b)

Exercise-2

(a) Subject		Predicate
1.	The boy	Stood on the wall.
2.	Sight	What a horrible was?
3.	Mohan	Has been watering the plants?
4.	You	Get out of the room.
5.	It	How shocking is?
6.	We	Shall go to park tomorrow?
7.	The child	Was weeping.

8.	I	May help you?
9.	Rahul	Has been doing her work.
10.	The children	Are swimming in the pond.

(b)

1. The path of glory
2. The days of our youth
3. All the five boys
4. Some very beautiful girls
5. Karan my neighbour
6. Those who live in glass houses
7. The boy with the blue trousers
8. The rumour that he has passed
9. The man who wrote this book
10. Some boys and girls

5 Naming Words or Nouns

Exercise-1

1. Book	2. Tub	3. Sun	4. Apple
5. Flower	6. Tin	7. Bus	8. Star

Exercise-2

1. (h)	2. (g)	3. (d)	4. (a)
5. (e)	6. (b)	7. (f)	8. (c)

Exercise-3

Places	**Animals**	**Persons**	**Things**
America	Lion	Woman	Truck
Red Fort	Ox	Child	Computer
School	Ant	Boy	Air
Garden	Elephant	Pilot	Book

Exercise-4

(a) No answer (b) No answer (c) No answer (d) No answer

Exercise-5

(a)
1. Dog common noun
2. Pooja proper noun, hospital common noun
3. Mohan proper noun, boy common noun
4. Rajasthan proper noun
5. Pen common noun

(b)
1. The police, collective noun
2. Rice, material noun
3. Gold, material noun
4. Class, collective noun
5. Plastic, material noun

(c)
1. Strike
2. Boldness
3. Freshness
4. Health, wealth
5. Bravery

6 Singular and Plural

Exercise-1

1. Stools 2. Sites 3. Buckets 4. Moons
5. Trees

Exercise-2

1. (b) Books (✓) 2. (a) Cup (✓) 3. (b) Plates (✓)
4. (a) Dog (✓) 5. (b) Boys (✓) 6. (b) Brushes (✓)

Exercise-3

1. Boxes 2. Tomatoes 3. Watches
4. Brushes 5. Glasses

Exercise-4

(a) 1. Ladies 2. Candies 3. Cherries
4. Butterflies 5. Babies 6. Berries

(b) 1. Toys 2. Rays 3. Boys
4. Days 5. Donkeys 6. Keys

Exercise-5

1. Lives 2. Knives 3. Wolves
4. Wives 5. Leaves 6. Thieves

Exercise-6

1. Photos 2. Children 3. Roofs
4. Oxen 5. Mice 6. Families
7. Shelves 8. Calves 9. Teeth
10. Wishes 11. Sheep 12. Deer

7 Gender

Exercise-1

(a) **Male:** 1. Groom 2. Brother 3. Son 4. Horse 5. Uncle

Female: 6. Bride 7. Sister 8. Daughter 9. Aunt 10. Mare

(b)

1.	Father	Mother
2.	Daughter	Son
3.	Bull	Cow
4.	Fox	Vixen
5.	Peacock	Peahen

(c)

	Masculine	**Feminine**
1.	King	Queen
2.	Bachelor	Spinster
3.	Man	Woman
4.	Monk	Nun
5.	Sir	Madam
6.	Lord	Lady

(d)

Masculine : Hero, Lion, Drone, Stag, Bull

Feminine : Lioness, Queen, Waitress, Stewardess, Fox

Neuter : Mobile, Carrot, Truck, Car, Table

Common : Teacher, Person, Parent, Banker, Bird

8 Apostrophe's

Exercise-1

1. Mohan's house
2. Rita's heater
3. Peter's car
4. The dog's tail
5. Vishvas' pen

Exercise-2

(a) 1. Mohan's 2. Sunita's 3. Women's 4. Vikas' 5. Persons'

(b) 1. ' 2. ' 3. ' 4. ' 5. 's

Exercise-3

1. Farmers' problems/The problem of farmers.
2. The history of India.
3. The plants of flowers.
4. The Red Fort of Delhi.
5. Mohan's mobiles/The mobiles of Mohan.
6. The cost of this book is one hundred fifty rupees.
7. These are the horses of Sunil/These are Sunil's horses.
8. The water of that glass was dirty.
9. My father's brother is a doctor/The brother of my father is a doctor.

10. The height of Qutub Minar is eighty feet.
11. The people of China are laborious.
12. The water of this well is sweet.
13. This is not Jag Mohan's cow/This is not the cow of Jag Mohan.
14. The boys of this street are not educated.
15. The cost of this book is not 100 rupees.
16. Is Delhi not the capital of India?
17. Is the wall of his house broken?
18. The members of my family are not lazy.
19. Was that girl's name not Kalawati/Was the name of that girl not Kalawati.
20. Will his grandmother's health not be good/will the health of his grandmother not be good.
21. This is a girls' college/This is the college of girls.
22. Those are Raja's friends/Those are the friends of Raja.

Use of Surnames (Mr., Mrs., Ms. and Miss [Titles]

- No answers
- As per students.

10 Adjectives

Exercise-1

1. Big 2. Small 3. Blind 4. Two 5. Old

Exercise-2

Naming words	Describing words
<u>Mother</u>	Angry
Mohan	Two
Giraffe	Tall
Tea	Hot

Exercise-3

1. **<u>My</u>**, possessive adjective.
2. **<u>Red</u>**, adjective of quality.
3. **<u>Two</u>**, adjective of numbers.
4. **<u>These</u>**, demonstrative adjective.
5. **<u>Each,</u>** distributive adjective.
6. **<u>Some</u>**, adjective of quantity.
7. **<u>How much,</u>** interrogative adjective.

Exercise-4

1. (c) 2. (g) 3. (f) 4. (e) 5. (b) 6. (d) 7. (a)

Exercise-5

(a) Cold (b) Warm (c) Hot (d) Interesting (e) Big
(f) Three (g) Sweet

Exercise-6

(a) Naught Ripe Yellow Sad Good

(b) (a) Big (b) Red (c) Four (d) Four (e) Two

Exercise-7

1. A few 2. A little 3. Few 4. The little 5. Little

Short Notes

- A few : कुछ दिन (countable noun)
- A little : Knowledge है लेकिन कम
- Few : न के बराबर लोग
- The little : है लेकिन जो थोड़ा पानी आप के लिए रखा था वह definite है।
- Little : न के बराबर

Exercise-8

1. Bigger 2. Thicker 3. More beautiful 4. Heavier

Exercise-9

1. Easier 2. Taller 3. Bigger 4. More risky/Riskier

Exercise-10

1. Bigger 2. Taller 3. Stronger

Exercise-11

1. Faster 2. Fastest 3. Most beautiful

11 Articles

Exercise-1

(a)	1. a	2. a	3. an	4. an	5. an	6. a
(b)	1. a	2. an	3. a	4. a	5. an	
	6. a	7. an	8. an	9. an	10. a	

Exercise-2

1. Mukesh is a doctor.
2. Mohan is a very good boy.
3. This is a fox.
4. This is an old N.G.O.
5. This is water.
6. This is Ashok.
7. These are children.
8. He is not an ordinary man.
9. My father is not a dishonest man.
10. This is not a historical event.
11. That is not rice.
12. That will not be water.
13. Is this a school?
14. Did he meet with an M.L.A.?
15. Is Mohan an honest man?
16. Is butter useful?

17. Was Madhubala a famous actress?
18. Is butter not useful?
19. Is Kavita not an intelligent girl?
20. Were you not a responsible person?
21. Was that not a tree?
22. Was that not an umbrella?
23. Was that not oil?
24. Was that not a one-eyed man?
25. Obama was an American president.
26. This is a national game.
27. I shall (will) be an I.A.S.
28. Mohan is not an ideal citizen.
29. Is this an M.L.A?
30. Will Mohan be an intelligent student?
31. Will/shall I not have a job?
32. Is your father not an N.C.C. officer?

Exercise-3

(a) 1. a 2. an 3. the 4. the 5. a

(b) (i) 1. a 2. a 3. the 4. a

(ii) 1. a 2. the

(iii) 1. an 2. a 3. the 4. the

(iv) 1. an 2. the

(v) 1. a 2. the

Exercise-4

1. The horse is useful.
2. The Quran is a religious book.
3. The 15th of August is a memorable day.
4. Monkeys are not lazy.
5. The Hindus are not orthodox.
6. The world is so/very beautiful.
7. Is the Times of India an English newspaper?
8. Is Taj Mahal crown of India?
9. Are the farmers of Punjab rich?
10. Is the Punjab mail not a good train?
11. Is water not cold in the winter season?
12. Are the Indians not brave?
13. Are cats vegetarian?
14. Is water fresh?
15. Is the water of that jar fresh?

12 Pronouns

Exercise-1

(a)	(a) It	(b) He	(c) She	(d) He
(b)	(a) She	(b) He	(c) They	(d) We
(c)	1. I	2. She	3. He	4. You
(d)	1. We	2. They	3. You	
(e)	1. We	2. They	3. You	4. You, You

Exercise-2

(a) 1. I 2. Me 3. I 4. Me
5. Me 6. Me

(b) 1. a 2. b 3. a

Exercise-3

(a) 1. Us 2. We 3. Us 4. We
5. Us

(b) 1. a 2. b 3. a

Exercise-4

(a) 1. They 2. Them 3. Them 4. They

(b) 1. b 2. b 3. a

Exercise-5

(a) 1. He 2. Him 3. She 4. Her

(b) 1. b 2. a 3. b

Exercise-6

(a)	(a) Mine	(b) Theirs	(c) Ours	(d) Hers	(e) His
(b)	1. Mine	2. Yours	3. Ours	4. Theirs	5. Hers
	6. His				

Exercise-7

(a)	(a) My	(b) Their	(c) Our	(d) Her	(e) Its
(b)	1. His	2. My	3. Our	4. Its	5. Your
	6. Her	7. Their			

Exercise-8

1. This is my house.
2. This is your mistake.
3. This is their responsibilty.
4. This is our street.
5. This is her cycle.
6. This is his mobile.
7. We are doctors and this is our hospital.
8. This is a chair and its one leg is broken.
9. These are his/her mistakes.
10. These are our trees.
11. Mohan is my son.
12. Mr. Raj Kumar is our neighbour.
13. I shall (will) become their leader.
14. The enemy of Pakistan is our friend.
15. His/Her friends are lazy.
16. Mohan, Pooja and their friends are in the field.
17. His/Her friend is not my friend.
18. I shall (will) become your good partner.
19. I am in my country.
20. We are in our class.
21. The thieves are in their house.

22. Kavita is in her village.
23. Children are in their houses.
24. People are in their cars.
25. This is my own mistake.
26. This is our own book.
27. Their friends were not thieves.
28. Was that his/her own decision?
29. Are your minds not sharp?
30. This cow is mine.
31. This country is ours.
32. These mobiles are theirs.
33. This mistake is yours.
34. Is this pen yours and that book theirs?
35. Was his/her book in the hand and ours in the bag?

Exercise-9

1. The car which is red in colour is mine.
2. The house which is across the river is beautiful.
3. The book which you are looking for in the house I have.
4. The pen which is lying on the table is mine.
5. The purse which I found yesterday is hers.
6. The dog which he bought has died.
7. Can I see the mobile which you bought yesterday?
8. I have found/got my mobile which I had lost.
9. The knife which is in the kitchen is sharp.
10. The house which you bought is very old.

Exercise-10

1. These are the books which I purchased last year from the book fair.
2. This is the letter which I wrote.
3. One who sleeps, loses/The man who sleeps he loses.
4. The man who knows English gets respect.

5. The books which are cheap sell well.
6. The boy who fell was my brother.
7. This is the book which my father gave me on Sunday.
8. This is the cow which gives much milk.
9. The teachers who teach attentively get respect.
10. The students who wander on the road weep during examinations.
11. The potatoes which are in the field nowadays are tasty.
12. One who is the student of today will be the citizen of tomorrow.
13. The boy who doesn't work hard, remains unsuccessful in life.
14. The mobile which he gave me lost/had lost.
15. The students who are sharp/intelligent, score high.

Exercise-11

1. There is nothing here that can attract the audience's attention.
2. There is nothing that can stop me to go there.
3. Is this the same house that you were telling?
4. I knew what he wanted to give her.
5. What cannot be said must not be said.
6. What cannot be cured must be endured.
7. What he says about you is right/true.
8. The disease that cannot be cured must be endured.
9. What he says is good.
10. This is the same car that got an accident yesterday.
11. This is the same book that we needed.
12. All that you think yours is not yours.
13. This is the only book that I haven't read yet.
14. This is the same book that I like the most.
15. What is said once cannot be unsaid.
16. What he wants, I will give instantly/immediately.
17. Those who pull rickshaws are very strong.
18. The house in which she lives is old.
19. What is good for you may be bad for me.
20. The boys whose houses are far from school come by bus.

13 Use of 'This', 'That', 'These', 'Those'

Exercise-1

(a) 1. यह एक बिल्ली है? 2. यह एक अंडा है?
3. यह एक पलंग है? 4. यह एक कुत्ता है?

(b) 1. This is a chair. 2. This is a tin.
3. This is a bus. 4. This is a glass.

Exercise-2

(a) 1. वह एक गाय है। 2. वह एक खिड़की है।
3. वह एक पेड़ है। 4. वह एक नक्शा है।

(b) 1. That is a sun. 2. That is a tree.
1. That is a hen. 4. That is a spoon.

Exercise-3

(a) 1. ये अंडे हैं? 2. ये बकरियाँ हैं?
3. ये बिल्लियाँ हैं? 4. ये पलंग हैं?

(b) 1. These are chairs. 2. These are cows.
3. These are books. 4. These are computers.

Exercise-4

(a) 1. वे तारें हैं? 2. वे पेड़ हैं?
3. वे झाड़ियाँ हैं? 4. वे मेज़ हैं?

(b) 1. Those are books. 2. Those are stars.
3. Those are horses. 4. Those are cows.

Exercise-5

1. That house was dirty.
2. These fruits are sweet.
3. That boy will be an I.A.S.
4. This girl is intelligent.
5. That room will be empty.
6. Those houses are weak.
7. These chairs are not old.
8. Is this water dirty?
9. Were those boys not honest?
10. Will those bread/chapaties not be stale?

14 Use of To Be (Am/Is/Are)

Exercise-1

(a) 1. am 2. is 3. is 4. are

(b) 1. am 2. is 3. is 4. are 5. are

Exercise-2

1. is 2. are 3. is 4. am 5. are 6. are

Exercise-3

1. I am a man of my words.
2. This house is 'To let'/This house is empty for "To let".
3. Mother is at home.
4. It is too much sunshine today.
5. They are laborious/they are hard workers.
6. I am punctual.
7. I am ill.
8. My brother is kind.
9. We are students.
10. It is an umbrella.

Exercise-4

1. Pooja is not my sister.
2. Mohan is not your enemy.
3. You are not a faithful servant.
4. Sugar is not in the tin/box.

5. I am not ready.
6. Anil and Sunil are not friends.
7. It is not in order.
8. They are not in the school.
9. His/Her mother is not ill.
10. Water is not in the tank.

Exercise-5

1. Is phone upside down?
2. Am I with you?
3. Is Ravi father of Anil?/Is Ravi Anil's father?
4. Are they thieves?
5. Is that right?
6. Are children in the street?
7. Are clothes in the almirah?
8. Are you at home?
9. Are we responsible of this mistake?
10. Am I guilty?

Exercise-6

1. Am I not an intelligent student/Aren't I an intelligent student?
2. Am I not your friend/Aren't I your friend?
3. Is father not in anger/Is father not angry/Isn't father angry?
4. Is it not red colour/Isn't it red colour?
5. Are they not at home/Aren't they at home?
6. Are we not with you/Aren't we with you?

7. Is it not wrong/Isn't it wrong?
8. Is that boy not married/Isn't that boy married?
9. Are you not right/Aren't you right?
10. Is sugar not in the tea/Isn't sugar in the tea?

Was/Were

Exercise-7

1. was 2. were 3. were 4. was

Exercise-8

1. was 2. was 3. were 4. was 5. was

Exercise-9

1. Mohan was a big liar.
2. Father was very sad/unhappy.
3. I was ready.
4. Poor were homeless.
5. Farmers were poor in Punjab.
6. Abhijeet and Ravi were friends.
7. My uncle was doctor.
8. Children were happy.
9. Pooja was absent yesterday.
10. His/Her sister was rich.

Exercise-10

1. Class was not dirty.
2. It was not the red colour.
3. I was not ready.

4. Building was not small.
5. Book was not upside down.
6. I was not enemy of anyone.
7. His/her childhood was not difficult.
8. Children were not at home.
9. People were not there.
10. It was not right.

Exercise-11

1. Was Santosh a lawyer?
2. Were you in Delhi?
3. Was book good?
4. Were we right?
5. Was school empty?
6. Was that something on your saree?
7. Were clothes wet?
8. Were children intelligent?
9. Were bananas sweet?
10. Was somebody at the door?

Exercise-12

1. Were people not educated in ancient times/Weren't people educated in ancient times?
2. Were women not fit/healthy/Weren't women fit/healthy?
3. Was that king not cruel/Wasn't that king cruel?
4. Were old movies not good/Weren't old movies good?
5. Was I not with you/Wasn't I with you?

6. Was phone not upside down/Wasn't phone upside down?
7. Were clothes not wet/Weren't clothes wet?
8. Were we not right/Weren't we right?
9. Were fifty pages not in the book/Weren't fifty pages in the book?
10. Was cover not over the book/Wasn't cover over the book?

Shall be/Will be

Exercise-13

1. This child will be something.
2. They both will be happy after marriage.
3. I will be there at 1 : 00.
4. It will be right.

Exercise-14

1. We shall not be sad.
2. It will not be right.
3. I will not be at home tomorrow.
4. They will not be busy.

Exercise-15

1. Shall you be with me?
2. Will they be doctors?
3. Will school be open tomorrow?
4. Will tea become hot within 1 minute?

Exercise-16

1. Will that boy not be a doctor/Won't that boy be a doctor?
2. Will you not be at home tomorrow/Won't you be at home tomorrow?
3. Shall we not be ready/Shan't we be ready?
4. Will he not be sad at all/Won't he be sad at all?

15 Use of To Have (Use of Has, Have and Had)

Exercise-1

(a) 1. have 2. has 3. have 4. has
5. has 6. have 7. have 8. have

(b) 1. has 2. has 3. have 4. have 5. have 6. has

(c) 1. have 2. have 3. have 4. has

(d) 1. I have a computer.
2. You have a book.
3. He/She has two servants.
4. He/She has a big house.
5. Goat has two horns.
6. He/She has a parrot.
7. Mohan has a cow.
8. You all have many work.
9. Everyone has books.
10. Children have many toys.

Exercise-2

(a) 1. do not have 2. has no 3. do not have
4. have not 5. does not have 6. have not
7. has no 8. have no

(b) Tick (✓) the correct word:

1. do not have 2. have no 3. has not
4. have no 5. do not have 6. do not have
7. has not 8. have no 9. has no
10. has not

(c) 1. You do not have a bag of rice/You have not a bag of rice.
2. Mohan does not have old key/ Mohan has not an old key.
3. They do not have an old car/They have not an old car.
4. He/She does not have water/He/She has no water.
5. I do not have time/I have no time.
6. Anil does not have much wealth/Anil has not much wealth.

7. It does not have any solution/It has not any solution.
8. Children do not have even a single toy/Children have not even a single toy.
9. We do not have self-confidence/We have no self-confidence.
10. Farmers do not have many resources/Farmers have not many resources.

Exercise-3

1. Do you have backache/Have you backache?
2. Does she/he have a house/Has she/he a house?
3. Do you have a pen/Have you a pen?
4. Do servants have freedom/Have servants freedom?
5. Do we have time/Have we time?
6. Do they have a bag of rice/Have they a bag of rice?
7. Do children have sweets/Have children sweets?
8. Do poor have food/Have poor food?
9. Does Bimla have a broom/Has Bimla a broom?
10. Does his/her father have a scooter/Has his/her father a scooter?

Exercise-4

1. Do you not have time/Have you no time?
2. Do they not have a bag/Have they not a bag?
3. Do the asses not have horns/Have the asses no horns?
4. Do they not have much honey/Have they not much honey?
5. Do we not have a computer/Have we not a computer?
6. Does father not have a key/Has father not a key?
7. Does Shivam not have tea leaves/Has Shivam no tea leaves?
8. Do you not have invitation/Have you no invitation?
9. Does that man not have a blanket/Has that man not a blanket?
10. Does that boy not have a heart/Has that boy not a heart?

Note: 1. Don't you have time? 2. Don't they have a bag?
3. Doesn't that boy have a heart?

Had

Exercise-5

(a) 1. has 2. have 3. has 4. have 5. had 6. has
7. had 8. had 9. had 10. have

(b) 1. had 2. has 3. had 4. had 5. has
6. had 7. has 8. had

(c) 1. They had hope. 2. I had confidence.
3. We had a book. 4. He/She had enough time.
5. Ram and Manohar had a bicycle.

Exercise-6

1. I had no water/I did not have water.
2. He/She had not a copy/He/She did not have a copy.
3. Mohan had not a bottle/Mohan did not have a bottle.
4. We had no peace/We did not have peace.
5. You had no manners./ You did not have manners.
6. They had not many books/They did not have many books.

Exercise-7

1. Had they perfume/Did they have perfume?
2. Had Manohar a new car/ Did Manohar have a new car?
3. Had farmers own lands/Did farmers have own lands?
4. Had she a dressing table before marriage/
   Did she have a dressing table before marriage?
5. Had his/her father a property/Did his/her father have a property?
6. Had I a chance that time/Did I have a chance that time?
7. Had you a mosquito net/Did you have a mosquito net?

8. Had we self-control/ Did we have self-control?
9. Had Pooja a new frock/Did Pooja have a new frock?
10. Had mother two leaves/Did mother have two leaves?

Exercise-8

1. Had mother not a dupatta/Did mother have not a dupatta/Did mother have no dupatta?
2. Had father no turban on his head/Did father have no turban on his head?
3. Had we no self-confidence/Did we have no self-confidence?
4. Had you no ability/Did you have no ability?
5. Had Bhutan no facility/Did Bhutan have no facility?
6. Had you no need/Did you have no need?
7. Had they no debt/Did they have no debt?
8. Had Indians no quilts after 1947/Did Indians have no quilts after 1947?
9. Had Seema no sandal/Did Seema have no sandal?
10. Had you no knowledge/Did you have no knowledge?

Note:

1. Didn't mother have a dupatta?
2. Didn't father have a turban on his head?

Shall have/Will have

Exercise-9

1. I shall have a new computer in the next week.
2. We shall have freedom.
3. Girls will have government jobs.
4. Unemployed will have employments.
5. I shall have a good chance.

Exercise-10

1. Mohan will not have any facility this month.
2. We shall not have employment.
3. Farmers will not have government aids.
4. I shall not have medicines.
5. It will not have enough competition in the market.

Exercise-11

1. Will you have a book tomorrow?
2. Shall I have success in my life?
3. Will it have bad elements?
4. Shall we have peace?
5. Will she/he have a new house?

Exercise-12

1. Shall I not have salary/Shan't I have salary?
2. Shall we not have a vote of right/Shan't we have a vote of right?
3. Will he/she not have a job/Won't he/she have a job?
4. Will they not have a computer/Won't they have a computer?
5. Will orphan children not have education/Won't orphan children have education?

16 Introductory

Exercise-1

1. It is a window.
2. It is a book.
3. It is a dog.
4. It is 4 o'clock.
5. It is snowing.
6. It was a eunuch at the door.
7. It is Saturday today.
8. It was a cute child.

Exercise-2

1. It is foolish to talk to him.
2. It is necessary to educate farmers.
3. It is so difficult to get rid of this girl.
4. It is good to feed the poor.
5. It is easy to learn English.
6. It is a matter of shame.
7. It is possible.
8. It doesn't matter.
9. It matters.
10. It will take two minutes.
11. It takes two minutes.
12. It has been two days to me meeting.
13. It has been many years to me having seen mother.
14. It has been five years to us having eaten good food.
15. It has been two years to me reading this book.
16. It has been ten days.
17. It had been many years.

18. It has been ten years having seen Mohan.
19. It has been evening.
20. It has been many days going out in this lockdown/during lockdown.
21. It was I who poked you.
22. Is it the girl who gave a marriage proposal to your brother?
23. Is it not he who hit our car?
24. It is not only I who went there.
25. It is not only we who ate rice.
26. It is not he who purchased this mobile.
27. Is it he who has read this book?
28. Is it not you who have seen this film?
29. Is it the girl who has complained?
30. It is a female who has killed this man.
31. Was it not father who helped us?
32. Who is it that/who has solved this problem?

Exercise-3

(a) 1. There is 2. There are 3. There is
4. There were, There is 5. There were, There are

(b) 1. are 2. are 3. is 4. is 5. is
6. are

Exercise-4

1. There shall be peace in the evening today.
2. There is a problem in it.
3. There is a mosque in front of the temple.
4. There will be a library in my village.
5. There was a boy here.
6. There were two boys in the street.

Exercise-5

1. There is no water in the glass.
2. There was no student in the class/There was not a student in the class.
3. There were no stars in the sky.
4. There were not two books in my hand.
5. There will not be anyone at home tomorrow/There will be no one at home tomorrow.

Exercise-6

(a) 1. is there 2. are there 3. is there 4. were there 5. was there

(b) 1. are 2. is 3. are 4. are 5. is

(c)
1. Is there T.V. in your house?
2. Were there no rice in the bag?
3. Was there water in that pot?
4. Was there moon in the sky?
5. Were there sixty students in the school?
6. Will there be election in the next month?
7. Were there not five calls in mobile?
8. Are there not four rooms in that house?

Exercise-7

1. They will let me do work.
2. Mohan lets his brother watch T.V.
3. In village, mother let father cook food.
4. My family members were letting me sleep late during vacations.
5. Police let the thieves go.
6. Now, they are letting us live peacefully.
7. Now, Hira Lal lets his daughter study.

Exercise-8

1. Mohan did not let his sister marry to that boy.
2. Villagers were not letting the farmers burn crops.
3. Our bad deeds will not let us live peacefully.
4. Kavita does not let any boy sit near her.
5. Parents were not letting their children talk on phones.
6. I will not let you purchase this house.
7. Mohan did not let anyone sleep yesterday night.

Exercise-9

1. Does Mohan not let his wife do a job?
2. Do the rich not let the poor stand in front of them?
3. Will you not let me attend your marriage?
4. Do police let thieves rob/steal?
5. Is government letting farmers produce sugarcanes?
6. Was Kavita not letting you work?
7. Will your father not let us dance?
8. Did their bad habits not let them live?
9. Does the brother of the girl let Mohan meet with her?
10. Will you not let me know one thing?

Exercise-10

1. Let Mohan go.
2. Let your sister study.
3. Let me speak.
4. Let Sunita complete her talk first.

5. Let that boy drink water.
6. Don't let latecomers enter the class.
7. Don't let trees die.
8. Don't let Rohit inject the injection into his body.
9. Don't let that boy plug off the charger.
10. Let me know one thing.

Exercise-11

(a)
1. Let's play cricket.
2. Let's dance.
3. Let's enjoy outside in the rain.
4. Let's watch T.V.
5. Let's celebrate a party.

(b) 1. (d) 2. (e) 3. (a) 4. (b) 5. (c)

17 Short Forms

Exercise-1

(a) 1. e 2. a 3. f 4. b 5. c
6. g 7. d

(b) 1. Was not 2. Are not 3. They are
4. I am 5. Is not 6. He will
7. Will not 8. You are 9. It is
10. She is not 11. I was not 12. I will not
13. She was not 14. We will 15. She will not
16. You were not

Exercise-2

(a) 1. Do not 2. Does not 3. Did not
4. Has not 5. Have not 6. Had not

(b) 1. I've 2. She's 3. It's
4. I'd 5. He'd 6. It'd
7. I haven't 8. She hasn't 9. It hasn't
10. You haven't 11. They've 12. They'd
13. We've 14. We hadn't

18 Telling the time

Exercise-1

1. 7 : 00 AM   2. 1 : 30 PM   3. 2 :15 PM
4. 2 : 45 PM   5. 3 : 20 PM   6. 5 : 50 PM

Exercise-2

1. (iii)   2. (v)   3. (vi)   4. (vii)
5. (i)   6. (ii)   7. (iv)

Exercise-3

1.  8 : 50

2.  12 : 05

3. 10 : 55

4.  7 : 00

5.  9 : 10

6.  1 : 15

7.  1 : 40

8.  3 : 45

9.  11 : 30

10. 9 : 50

11.  12 : 00

12. 2 : 35

Exercise-4

1. 1 : 35 2. 10 : 30 3. 11 : 50 4. 1 : 00
5. 4 : 45 6. 5 : 05 7. 6 : 45

Exercise-5

(a) 1. c 2. b 3. a 4. b 5. b 6. b

(b)
1. Quarter past twelve
2. Twenty five to eight
3. Quarter to nine
4. Twelve o'clock
5. Five past four
6. Ten to ten
7. Quarter past eleven
8. Twenty past eleven

Exercise-6

1. It is 7 o'clock.
2. It is half past seven.
3. It is a quarter past seven.
4. It is a quarter to eight.
5. It is ten past five.
6. It is five minutes to eight.
7. It is not 5 o' clock.
8. Is it 5 o'clock?
9. Is it not 5 o'clock?
10. It is a quarter to four.
11. It is a quarter past five.

19 Interrogative Sentences

Exercise-1 (What)

1. What happend?
2. What do you want?
3. What did he tell you?
4. What should I do for you?
5. What is your brother?
6. What is the problem?
7. What are we doing?

Exercise-2 (When)

1. When does Mohan get up/wake up?
2. When do you go to school?
3. When does he eat?
4. When is your birthday?
5. When will they understand?
6. When will you do your work?
7. When did we go there?

Exercise-3 (Who)

1. Who is she/he?
2. Who is the Prime Minister of India?
3. Who is with you?
4. Who invented the television?

5. Who will be the chief guest/Who will become the chief guest?
6. Who will bring milk?
7. Who broke my pen/Who had broken my pen?

Exercise-4 (Where)

1. Where is your house?
2. Where is Mohan?
3. Where is Pooja from/Where does Pooja come from?
4. Where is your father from/Where does your father belong to?
5. Where is the Taj Mahal?
6. Where is Laxmi Nagar?
7. Where do they live?

Exercise-5 (Whom)

1. For whom are you looking?
2. With whom does he want to meet?
3. To whom is Suresh talking?
4. To whom will you give this gift?
5. For whom is your mother cooking food?
6. With whom will I go?
7. Whom are we scaring?

Exercise-6 (Which)

1. Which team won the tournament?
2. Which mobile is mine?
3. Which city do they live in?
4. Which fruit juice does your wife like the most?

5. Which of those boys will win?
6. Which newspaper do we read?
7. Which film did he/she watch last?

Exercise-7 (Whose)

1. Whose tea is that?
2. Whose chair is that?
3. Whose house are you buying/purchasing?
4. Whose house is that?
5. Whose father was sick/ill?
6. Whose car were they driving?
7. Whose son is he/that boy?

Exercise-8 (Why)

1. Why did you come there?
2. Why does he tell a lie/lie?
3. Why are children so angry today?
4. Why do they want to do a government job?
5. Why are you angry?
6. Why did our father educate us?
7. Why are you here?

Exercise-9 (How)

1. How have I come here or How did I come here?
2. How is everthing going on?
3. How did he become a criminal?
4. How does he live there?

5. How did you do it/that?
6. How is weather there?
7. How is your father?

Exercise-10 (How much)

1. How much water was there in that pot?
2. How much time do you study?
3. How much milk do they drink/take?
4. How much time will we take to finish it?
5. How much fee did he take/charge?
6. How much ghee will be in this tin?
7. How much water is there in this bucket?

Exercise-11 (How many)

1. How many windows and kitchens are there in this house?
2. How many cars does Manohar have?
3. How many trees are there in this garden?
4. How many languages do they speak?
5. How many students are there in our class?
6. How many brothers and sisters does he/she have?
7. How many seats are there in that bus?

Exercise-12 (How far)

1. How far is Red Fort from here?
2. How far do you cover in a day?
3. How far did Mohan throw a stone?
4. How far is their thought right/correct?

5. How far do we walk?
6. How far is market from his/her house?
7. How far does she drive in a whole day?

Exercise-13 (How long)

1. How long will you stay in Delhi?
2. How long have they been living here?
3. How long has he known you?
4. How long will Mohan live there/stay there?
5. How long has she been getting ill/sick?
6. How long will we take to reach there?
7. How long did students stay in the class?

Exercise-14 (How often/How many times)

1. How often | How many times do you change your mobile in a year?
2. How often | How many times does Mohan go to school in a month?
3. How often | How many times do we blink our eyes in a minute?
4. How often | How many times has she/he seen this movie?

Exercise-15 (What kind of/what sort of/ what type of)

1. What sort of computer will she buy?
2. What kind of clothes does Mohan wear?
3. What type of language should we learn?
4. What kind of business are you doing?

Exercise-16

1. aren't you?
2. is he?
3. does he?
4. weren't they?
5. wasn't she?
6. isn't he?
7. aren't I?
8. isn't he?
9. are you?
10. is he?
11. was she?
12. were they?
13. have you?
14. will you?
15. did he?
16. is she?
17. isn't she?
18. did he?
19. weren't they?
20. aren't they?
21. aren't I?
22. do you?
23. did they?
24. won't you?

Exercise-17

1. don't you?
2. didn't she?
3. didn't he?
4. doesn't she?
5. doesn't he?
6. doesn't she?
7. don't you?
8. don't they?
9. didn't I?
10. didn't they?

Exercise-18

1. wouldn't you?
2. would you?
3. mustn't she?
4. shouldn't they?

20 Prepositions

Exercise-1

1.	(at) Taj Hotel	2.	(into) AC room	3.	(against) Wall
4.	(at) Home	5.	(in) Zoo		

Exercise-2

(a) 1. in 2. on 3. under

(b) 1. on 2. under 3. in 4. in

(c) 1. in 2. on 3. over 4. on 5. in 6. near

(d) 1. in 2. over 3. between 4. to 5. on 6. near 7. In front of 8. with 9. from 10. for

Exercise-3

1. in 2. in 3. in 4. in 5. on
6. at 7. in 8. on 9. in 10. at, in

Exercise-4

1. above 2. under 3. in front of 4. over
5. under 6. above 7. behind 8. among
9. underneath 10. between

Exercise-5

1. on 2. in 3. on 4. on 5. on 6. at, at
7. at 8. at

Exercise-6

1. for 2. by 3. at 4. between 5. within
6. until

Exercise-7

1. on 2. across 3. off 4. into 5. into
6. out of 7. from, to 8. along 9. out of 10. through

Exercise-8

(a) 1. to 2. behind 3. between 4. with
5. in front of

(b) 1. to 2. in 3. with 4. of 5. under
6. on 7. after 8. for

(c) 1. on 2. near 3. on 4. in front of
5. to

Exercise-9

(a) 1. on 2. at 3. in 4. at 5. at
6. in 7. on

(b) 1. behind 2. in front of 3. near 4. behind

(c) 1. among 2. between 3. between 4. among

(d) 1. for 2. from 3. to 4. from
5. to 6. to 7. from 8. to
9. for 10. from

(e) 1. into 2. out of 3. in 4. in
5. into

How We Can Bring Grammar On Our Tongue.

We can learn English by practice. There are many people who try to learn English but they are not able to learn it, because they do not follow the natural way of learning language. We can learn it through Ears + Mind + Tongue.

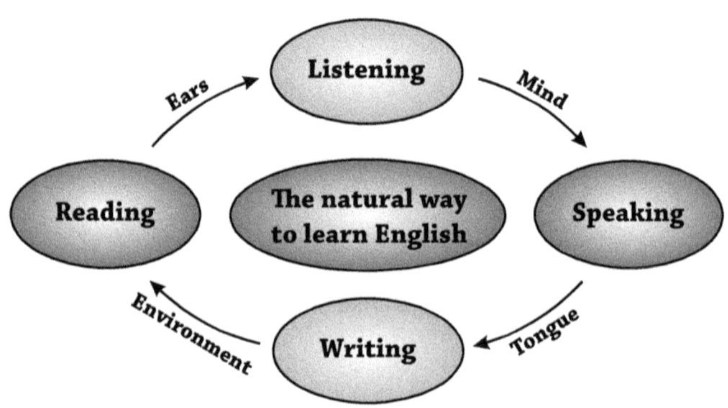

Grammar सिर्फ़ सीखने से **English** नहीं आती बल्कि

Grammar के इस्तेमाल से

English बोलना सीख सकते हैं।

जब तक हमारी ज़बान नहीं चलेगी, **English** ज़बान बोलनी नहीं आएगी।

No Environment No English.

www.ingramcontent.com/pod-product-compliance
Ingram Content Group UK Ltd.
Pitfield, Milton Keynes, MK11 3LW, UK
UKHW022002190726
13853UKWH00004B/1677